*The path of the righteous is like the morning sun,
shining ever brighter till the full light of day.
Give careful thought to the paths of your feet and be
steadfast in all your ways. Do not turn to the right
or the left; keep your foot from evil.
Proverbs 4:18,26-27*

*****

The Journey
Discovering the Invisible Path
The Pathway to Authentic Christianity

By Kenneth L. Birks

Published by Straight Arrow Ministries
Fourth Edition, Updated 2024

Cover Design by Hans Bennewitz

straitarrow.net
Copyright © 2016

Unless otherwise indicated, all Scripture quotations are taken from The Holy Bible, New King James Version.
© 1982 by Thomas Nelson, Inc.

Acknowledgments

I want to acknowledge the special people who have invested in this book through their life-changing contribution by being an integral part of my life. They are as follows:

My beautiful wife and best friend, Lydia Pro Birks, for being a constant source of encouragement to me throughout our married life and in the writing of this book.

My father and mother, Chester and Elizabeth Birks, not only prayed me into the Kingdom but were excellent examples of what it means to be a godly Christian.

My first pastor from my hometown, Norm Stueckle, prayed with me at the altar on that eventful morning in March 1974.

My spiritual father, Dick Benjamin, who provided me with the spiritual covering and foundation in the Word of God that helped launch me into the ministry and continues to sustain and inspire me, even now. He also wrote an excellent review in the back of the book.

My Bible Teachers at the Charismatic Bible College of Anchorage Dick Strutz and Jim Feeney.

My spiritual heritage is Abbott Loop Community Chapel in Anchorage, Alaska, where I received a firm foundation in the Lord.

Bob Mumford, whose books and tapes have been a valuable resource to me through the years.

Francis Anfuso, my pastor at The Rock of Roseville, has been a shining example of what it means to represent Jesus well and who reminds us that our best days are still ahead.

Foreword

For many people, a journey into the Bible is like flying into the Bermuda Triangle, tackling an unsolved mystery, or hopelessly laboring over a puzzling paradox. They throw up their hands in futility, believing the massive book is too big, too old, and too complex to be understood.

But the reality is far less scary.

The Bible is not just the most published book of all time; it is the clearest path to understanding the riddle of life. I remember the days before smartphones when I'd be driving around a city trying to find a person to ask directions, with my hope of getting to the desired location resting on the perceptions of a stranger. I'm so grateful for GPS Global Positioning Systems. I'd probably be lost every day of my life without its guidance. But with this simple tool, I now drive with confidence and even enjoy the ride.

I believe *The Journey* by Ken Birks is your GPS for the Bible. The problem is solved. The riddle is deciphered. Like a trusted guide, Ken makes complex concepts simple and masterfully unpacks the Bible's greatest mysteries. He provides a sure foundation upon which to build a lifetime of insight.

Ken has been a trusted friend and leader in our church for nearly two decades, and beyond our relationship, he has been a pastor and gifted Bible teacher for over 30 years. When I need a scripture explained, I often ask Ken for his wisdom; frankly, I have never been disappointed.

If I were building a house, I'd hire a master builder. If I didn't understand the Bible and wanted a solid foundation for my Christian life, I'd study this book, *The Journey*, and let a master teacher like Ken Birks guide me down the path of life.

—Francis Anfuso, Founding Pastor, the Rock of Roseville —

The Journey
Discovering the Invisible Path

By Kenneth L. Birks

Table of Contents

	Acknowledgments	Page i
	Foreword by Francis Anfuso	Page iii
Intro	Introduction	Page 1
Chapter 1	Exploring the Beauty and Majesty of God	Page 7
Chapter 2	A New Beginning — The Journey Begins	Page 21
Chapter 3	Path Less Traveled — Repentance & Conversion	Page 29
Chapter 4	Getting an Identity Makeover	Page 39
Chapter 5	Navigational Tools — Word and Spirit	Page 47
Chapter 6	Seven Essentials Needed for the Journey	Page 69
Chapter 7	Into the Wilderness — Finding Purpose in Trials	Page 87
Chapter 8	Breaking Free from Your Past	Page 95
Chapter 9	Immersed Into the Body of Christ	Page 107
Chapter 10	Spiritual Gifts and the Body of Christ	Page 119
Chapter 11	Discipleship and Ministry	Page 135
Chapter 12	The Need for Guardrails	Page 145
Chapter 13	Destiny & Purpose — Your Future	Page 157
Chapter 14	Staying the Course	Page 167
Chapter 15	New Jerusalem Awaits Our Arrival	Page 173

Bible Study or Small Group Questions	Page 179
About the Author: Kenneth L Birks	Page 213
Devotional Books by Kenneth L Birks	Page 214
Books and Workbooks by Kenneth L Birks	Page 215
Reviews and References	Page 217
Connect with Ken Birks Online	Page 219

The Journey
Discovering the Invisible Path

Introduction

We live in a world created in the beauty and wonder of what was initially intended to give us glimpses into the eternal treasures God has stored up for all those who have come to believe in His Son, Jesus Christ.

Just as each of us has been born of a natural birth that brought us into this world, there is a spiritual birth God desires for us, a birth that is designed to get us into the unseen beauty and wonder of the eternal realm where God resides—the kingdom of heaven.

Once we are spiritually born or born again, the Holy Spirit comes to live within us to reveal to our natural senses the great mystery of the eternal Godhead in all the glory of the Father. We are given the mind of Christ, or God's divine nature, to see into this invisible realm, and thus, our journey into the unforeseen begins.[1]

John 3:3 Jesus answered and said to him, "Most assuredly, I say to you, unless one is born again, he cannot see the kingdom of God."

Luke 17:20-21 Now, when He was asked by the Pharisees when the kingdom of God would come, He answered them and said, "The kingdom of God does not come with observation; [21] nor will they say, 'See here!' or 'See there! For indeed, the kingdom of God is within you."

As Christians, our calling is that of a pilgrimage or journey. Peter, one of Jesus' disciples, refers to us as pilgrims in his first epistle.[2] God called us to be like our father Abraham, who traveled through this world by faith, not knowing where he was going. He was a pilgrim looking for a city unknown to his natural eyes—a city whose builder and maker was God, which he could only see through his spiritual eyes.[3]

Psalm 85:5 Blessed is the man whose strength is in You, whose heart is set on pilgrimage.

---

[1] 1 Corinthians 2:16, 2Peter 1:4
[2] 1 Peter 1:1, 2:11
[3] Hebrews 11:8-10

If we are to be like Abraham, we, too, must focus on those things that are above and not seen. We become faithful sojourners or pilgrims by concentrating on what is above—the invisible realm of God's kingdom.
2 Corinthians 4:18 while we do not look at the things which are seen, but at the things which are not seen. For the things which are seen are temporary, but the things which are not seen are eternal.

The Christian life is a journey into this invisible kingdom realm that has the potential of either being the most exciting and adventurous journey you will ever experience or the most tedious and miserable experience. Unfortunately, many have defaulted to the latter—not because they wanted or desired to. They lacked the faith and vision to enter an invisible path to their natural eyes.

Jesus said, *"Narrow is the gate, and difficult is the way that leads to life, and few find it."*[4]

When we default to the latter experience, we do not gain a clear and compelling understanding of authentic Christianity.

Ask yourself, "Which path has my journey taken me on?"

You may conclude that you have been pushing the default button rather than walking in true faith. If so, don't lose heart because God is with you and delights in revealing authentic faith!
2 Corinthians 5:7 For we walk by faith, not by sight.

Ignoring what the natural man sees and hears is a constant battle because it comes naturally to us. We are human beings made up of carnal (natural) desires and dreams. It requires faith to see beyond the natural into the kingdom realm that has the potential of leading us into a life filled with adventure and the abundant life Jesus promised—a life filled with righteousness, joy, and peace in the Holy Spirit.[5]

As Adam and Eve were initially destined to live as eternal beings and not experience death, so are we. When we're born again, the Holy Spirit, who is immortal, comes to live with us, and death loses its sting.[6] It is in this eternal realm that God has intended us to live. He has put eternity in the hearts of humanity.[7] The problem is that we have an enemy who does whatever it takes to keep us from experiencing all God has intended for our lives.[8] He knows once we break past the barrier of unbelief, there is no stopping us from fulfilling the purpose for which we were created. We become a threat to him and his domain.

---

[4] Matthew 7:13-14
[5] Romans 14:17
[6] 1 Corinthians 15:55-56
[7] Ecclesiastes 3:11
[8] James 4:7

Introduction

One of the significant challenges of our faith is the ability to see into this invisible kingdom realm. Our ability to see into the invisible gives us the capacity to be led by the Spirit with the eyes of our understanding opened to the heavenly realm as His Spirit reveals all that God has prepared for us.[9]

1 Corinthians 2:9-10 But as it is written: "Eye has not seen, nor ear heard, nor have entered into the heart of man the things which God has prepared for those who love Him." [10] But God has revealed them to us through His Spirit. For the Spirit searches all things, yes, the deep things of God.

We must be courageous and ask ourselves honestly, "Are our steps ordered by the heavenly realm or our natural understanding?"

As we set our affections on that which is above (the kingdom realm), the Lord orders our steps.[10] So the question is, are our affections set on the heavenly or natural, temporal realms?"

We must continually resist the devil and his influences while submitting our souls to God if we are to be kingdom-minded people who live and reign on this invisible path. Because God yearns jealously towards us, He gives us more grace or the supernatural ability for the journey when we humble ourselves by submitting to Him.[11]

The story of God's purpose for humanity has been unfolding throughout eternity. The story begins with the world's creation, with Adam and Eve placed in the Garden God created for them to dwell in. Then, with the fall of Adam and Eve, the story continued through the annals of time. So many patriarchs, prophets, kings, shepherds, fishermen, tax collectors, and ordinary people like you and me have all had and are having our roles defined by our creator.

We were all created to play a particular role uniquely designed according to our personality, gifting, innate abilities and talents, and the many experiences we've picked up, whether good or bad. As we willingly enter into the role God has designed for us, we can enter into the discovery of all He has created us to be. Furthermore, when we willingly embrace this role, we experience the abundant life He promised us.[12]

Everything God creates is with a purpose. So when He created you, He had a definite purpose related to His purposes on the earth, as we see in the following Scripture.

Jeremiah 1:5 "Before I formed you in the womb I knew you; before you were born, I sanctified you; I ordained you a prophet to the nations."

---

[9] Ephesians 1:17-21
[10] Colossians 3:2
[11] James 4:5-7
[12] John 10:10

We may not be called prophets to the nations, but just as God knew Jeremiah before He formed him in the womb, He also knew you and me. He had a role already ordained for Jeremiah, just as He does for you and me. The question is, are we living the role God designed for us in particular, or are we lost and wandering souls still looking and searching for what life is all about and coming up empty?

You may have caught glimpses of His purpose for your life at times, but you have never been able to capture them before they slip away. If so, it's time to seize God's purpose for your life. We have many defining *(or kairos)* moments during our lifetime designed to help us discover our destiny and purpose.[13] The key is to learn how to interpret these moments and see them as signposts that point toward what God has in store for us.

As a Christian, this book aims to give you a glimpse into the path God has proposed for your life to aid you in seizing your destiny and purpose. In doing so, you can live the role created for you. Whether you are just starting your journey, are in the middle, or have become detoured and lost your way, this book will help you. It will help shine the light on the invisible path that leads to God's goodness and experiencing His kingdom within to give you the most incredible adventure of your life. Is this something you desire for your life, or are you content to live in the ruts of life?

If you genuinely desire an incredible adventure in faith, you can say at the end of your life, just as the apostle Paul said, *"I have fought the good fight, I have finished the race, and I have kept the faith,"* this book is for you.

Are you ready to enter the unseen path with your carnal eyes on the excitement? If so, fasten your seatbelt, for you are about to be launched into the ride of your life on a path that will lead you into great adventures of faith—a course filled with joy and anticipation of what God will do next.

Remember that God's thoughts towards you are beautiful, wonderful, and peaceful as you travel toward your destiny. He desires to give you a future that is full of hope.

Jeremiah 29:11 For I know the thoughts that I think toward you, says the Lord, thoughts of peace and not of evil, to give you a future and a hope.

---

[13] Definitions of Kairos and Defining Moments: Kairos is an ancient Greek word meaning the right or opportune moment (the supreme moment). A defining moment is a point in your life when you made a very important decision or had an experience that changed you forever—an event that typifies or determines all subsequent related occurrences. (Sources: Wikipedia and Oxford Dictionary)

Introduction

Psalm 16:11 You will show me the path of life; in Your presence is the fullness of joy; at Your right hand are pleasures forevermore.

My prayer for you is *that the God of our Lord Jesus Christ, the Father of glory, may give you the spirit of wisdom and revelation in the knowledge of Him, the eyes of your understanding enlightened; that you may know what is the hope of His calling, what are the riches of the glory of His inheritance in the saints, and what is the exceeding greatness of His power toward us who believe, according to the working of His mighty power which He worked in Christ when He raised Him from the dead and seated Him at His right hand in the heavenly places, far above all principality and power and might and dominion, and every name that is named, not only in this age but also in that which is to come.*[14]

---

[14] Ephesians 1:17-21

Exploring the Beauty and Majesty of God

Chapter One

Great is the LORD! He is most worthy of praise! His greatness is beyond discovery—Psalm 145:3 (NLT)

One of life's greatest pursuits is discovering God in all His glory and majesty. This discovery enables you to come to a deeper understanding and revelation of who God is. It allows you to experience His beautiful attributes coming alive in your heart, resulting in greater intimacy with Him. You will be able to see with the eyes of your understanding the wonders He has prepared for you as you partake of all He has for you on this incredible journey.

Genuine and False Perceptions of Who God Is

Many of us have grown up with misconceptions about who God is. As a result, we have been afraid of getting too close to Him. In addition, many of our false perceptions of God were based on how we may have viewed authority figures, including our fathers or mothers. As a result, we tend to project onto God the unloving characteristics of people who have influenced our lives to some degree.

For example, if we viewed our fathers or other authority figures as mean and cruel, we would most likely see God similarly. If we viewed them as being distant, uncaring, and uninvolved, that's how we would view God. You may have had a pushy father who was inconsiderate or who may have violated you in some way. Or maybe your father was like a drill sergeant who made unreasonable demands from you without any expression of satisfaction. You would likely feel that God wouldn't accept you unless you measured up to His perfection. Maybe your father or other authority figures were overly critical and didn't believe in you or your capabilities. The list goes on.

We must also consider that our world is under the sway and influence of the enemy of our faith—Satan.[15] His goal is to give us an immensely distorted view of who God is so that we won't have affection or desire toward Him. No wonder so many people have a distaste for God.

How you perceive God will affect how you relate to Him. Therefore, it is of the utmost importance that we have a correct Biblical view of who God is. It is essential to see and perceive God in the way He has revealed Himself through His Word because every aspect of His Word is pure and equips us to be complete in Him.[16] A correct Biblical view allows us to see and perceive God as someone who likes and loves us no matter what we have done. The following Scripture reveals the bottom line of how God genuinely thinks about us as individuals.

Jeremiah 29:11 For I know the thoughts that I think toward you, says the LORD, thoughts of peace and not of evil, to give you a future and a hope.

When we begin to perceive God in the same way He perceives us, there is an agreement in the Spirit that brings us to a deeper level of intimacy and understanding with Him. This new level of intimacy causes us to seek Him with a heart of assurance, coming boldly into His presence rather than shrinking back in fear and intimidation. The following two verses from Jeremiah reveal this:

Jeremiah 29:12-13 Then you will call upon Me and go and pray to Me, and I will listen to You. [13] And you will seek Me and find Me when you search for Me with all your heart.

A true revelation of God in His transcendent and personal attributes will help us appreciate and place a more excellent value on our new relationship with our Father in heaven. It will enable us to willingly embrace Christ's mind and attitudes—God's divine nature.

We ultimately become a reflection of who we believe God to be. Many Christians misrepresent God because they lack a true revelation and understanding of who He is. Jesus perfectly represents the Father because He knew Him in all His transcendent and personal attributes. He came to reveal the true heart of the Father.[17]

The world does not understand who the Father is because they only see what the enemy of our faith is showing them—a false perception. We are to be a city set on a hill that allows the world to see the reflection of the Father as He shines through our lives.

As we come to know the Father in all His wonderful attributes, we discover He desires to share His attributes with us by allowing us to be

---

[15] 1 John 5:19
[16] Psalm 119:140, Proverbs 30:5, 2 Timothy 3:16
[17] Hebrews 1:3

partakers of His divine nature. He encourages us to do so by giving us the many promises in His Word, as seen in the following Scripture. As a result, we reflect His glory just as Jesus did.

2 Peter 1:4 "By which have been given to us exceedingly great and precious promises, that through these you may be partakers of the divine nature..."

As we begin to embrace and walk in the wonderful promises God has given to us through His Word, His divine nature begins to take root, with His characteristics showing forth as new fruit. As we continue our pilgrimage, He changes us into His image from glory to glory.[18]

The kingdom life we experience has the power to transform our lives. A whole new level of freedom and deliverance comes from each paradigm shift.[19] Not only do we receive the motivation to change, but we also gain the power to change. We realize we are no longer enslaved to sin but renewed by the kingdom's influence within.[20]

Ephesians 1:19 "...and what is the exceeding greatness of His power toward us who believe, according to the working of His mighty power."

The Transcendent Attributes of God

With this in mind, let's look at God's transcendent attributes—meaning God is above all and distinct from all He has made. God has revealed all of His transcendent attributes through His Word. God's transcendent and personal characteristics help us see the reality of who He is and His ability to transform our lives from our mundane carnal limitations to who He has created us to be in Christ.[21]

Getting started will be difficult without God's transcendent and personal attributes taking root in our lives. Seeing the beauty and wonder of the path before us will be challenging. We will lack the motivation, wisdom, and understanding to tackle some of the more difficult aspects of this journey. It will be a dull and mundane existence on a path that only leads to being saved so as by fire.[22] Frankly, I'm unsure what that means, but I'm confident I don't want to find out.

The Holy Spirit of God, the third person of the Godhead, lives and resides within us. It is He who enables us to have the mind of Christ or the divine nature of God. He continually searches out the heart of the Father to reveal the deep things of the Father.

As we take a few moments to focus on what God's transcendent and personal attributes are, we will see how they affect us. As we meditate

---

[18] 2 Corinthians 3:17-18
[19] 2 Corinthians 3:17
[20] Romans 6:19-20
[21] This section was adapted from "The Knowledge of the Holy" by A.W. Tozer
[22] 1Corinthians 3:14-16

on the beauty of who God is, our misconceptions of Him begin to fade away.

Psalm 27:4 One thing I have desired of the Lord, that will I seek: that I may dwell in the house of the Lord all the days of my life, to behold the beauty of the Lord, and to inquire in His temple.

God is Self-Existent. What does this mean, and how does it affect our lives? In reality, it means God has life in Himself.[23] God is not a created being. He has no beginning or end. God's self-existence can be hard to grasp, as our lives have both a beginning and an end as far as life here on earth is concerned. As created beings, we have life because God created us, but God solely exists because of Himself. We draw our energy from God and owe our lives to Him, but He has infinite power from Himself and owes His life to no one.

Psalm 90:2 Before the mountains were brought forth, or ever You had formed the earth and the world, even from everlasting to everlasting, You are God.

The fact that God has endless energy in Himself separates Him from His creation. He is the Supreme Being and the source of all other beings. Because of this, He is the only one we are to worship.

To live life to its fullest, we must depend upon His power and self-existence, for it is in Him that we live and move. Just as God breathed breath into Adam, and he became a living being, we have our life. Without God, we wouldn't exist.

Acts. 17:28 "For in him we live, and move, and have our being, as also some of your own poets have said, 'For we are also His offspring.'

Our lives are affected by God's self-existence to a greater degree when we willingly acknowledge and make Him our sufficiency. As a result, we enter into all that He has provided and prepared for us as we journey forward. He will continually supply the necessary grace as we navigate life's mysteries. God, our Father, will abundantly pour into our lives as we faithfully adhere to the path before us.

2 Corinthians 5:8 And God is able to make all grace abound toward you, that you, always having all sufficiency in all things, may have an abundance for every good work.

God is Spirit. God exists on a different plane from us and is not subject to the limitations of a physical body in the way we are. Because God is Spirit, He is not physical or material but is intensely personal and can be worshiped only at an individual level—from our spirit to His.

John 4:24 God is Spirit, and those who worship Him must worship in spirit and truth.

---

[23] John 5:26

As we worship God in spirit and truth, He pours into our spirits and souls through the Holy Spirit. We then receive all that He has prepared for us. As we journey forward, we will come to many places where we need His provision and divine enablement to make it from one phase to another. As we open our hearts and minds to Him through worship, He freely pours into us what is needed.

When we fail to worship God and acknowledge His greatness in our lives, we begin to walk in our sufficiency and get stuck on the path to the degree that it disappears before us. We wander without direction and become somewhat disengaged and lost. Finally, we wonder, "Why am I not being loaded with His benefits daily and going without rather than enjoying the abundant life He promised?" [24]

The beautiful thing about God is that once we recognize we have lost our way, repent, and turn to Him, He will get us faced in the right direction. So then, as we allow His sufficiency to rule us, He is gracious and merciful as He guides us along the path of righteousness.

God is One. What does this mean, and how does God being One affect our lives? There is only One God; however, He exists in three different persons: the Father, the Son, and the Holy Spirit.

1 John 5:7 For there are three that bear witness in heaven: the Father, the Word, and the Holy Spirit; and these three are one.

The Father, the Son, and the Holy Spirit are not three separate Gods but three manifestations of the same God. They are equally important. For example, in our relationship with God, we need all three personalities of the Godhead to complete us. Our access to God the Father is through Jesus Christ, the Son, by the Holy Spirit.[25] When Jesus went to heaven, He sent the Holy Spirit to live within us. Therefore, the Father, the Son, and the Holy Spirit work together purposefully.

The Godhead is evidenced by references to all three persons, such as in Matthew 28:19, where it says we are to be baptized in the name of the Father, Son, and Holy Spirit. God also refers to Himself as plural in Genesis 1:26, which says, *"Let Us make man in Our image."*[26]

The Hebrew word for "One" in relationship to "One God" is *"Echad."* It is a compound word meaning *united, altogether, together*, such as one body with many members. The Godhead has one will, with the Father, the Son, and the Holy Spirit working together in complete oneness, harmony, and unity. Though aspects of God's work are often

---

[24] Psalm 68:19
[25] Ephesians 2:18
[26] Note: I have chosen to use the word "Godhead" instead of Trinity because the word "Trinity" even though a good word in describing the Godhead, is not in the Bible.

attributed more to one than the other, in every case, the Father, the Son, and the Holy Spirit are working in agreement, whether in creation, redemption, or regeneration.

The Tri-Unity of God or the Godhead is clearly seen through His creation, as the apostle Paul expresses in the first chapter of Romans. We see the sun, moon, and stars as representatives of the Godhead.[27]

Romans 1:20 For since the creation of the world His invisible attributes are clearly seen, being understood by the things that are made, even His eternal power and Godhead, so that they are without excuse.

How is the Godhead seen in creation? Let's think about this for a moment. What is it about the sun that so clearly represents Father God? Like all light and energy emanating from the Father, it is with the sun. We have already seen that God has life in Himself and draws His unlimited power from Himself. We also know from the book of Revelation that there will be no need for the sun in Heaven as all light will emanate from God, the Father.[28] What about the moon? How does the moon represent Jesus, the Son of God? Just as the moon reflects the sun's glory, so Jesus demonstrates the glory of the Father. He is the radiance of God's glory and the exact representation of His being.[29] What is it about the stars that represent the Holy Spirit? It's the Holy Spirit who expresses the omnipresence of God. Just as the stars of heaven are everywhere, the Holy Spirit is everywhere.[30]

When we connect with Jesus Christ, the Son, we connect to the fullness of the Godhead bodily. As a result, we receive all that God has made available to us through His Son.

Colossians 2:9-10 For in Him dwells all the fullness of the Godhead bodily, and you are complete in Him who is the head of all principality and power.

God is Eternal. God revealed Himself to humanity in His infinite wisdom as an eternal God. He is a being without beginning or ending, an uncreated, infinite Creator. He has also set eternity in our hearts.

Psalm 90:2 Before the mountains were brought forth, or ever You had formed the earth and world, even from everlasting to everlasting, You are God.

Ecclesiastes 3:11 (NIV) He has made everything beautiful in its time. He has also set eternity in the human heart, yet no once can fathom what God has done from beginning to end.

It's challenging to grasp the concept of God being eternal at times because we have a beginning and an ending on earth. God sees everything from His eternal perspective. As He imparts His divine nature

---

[27] For more information on the godhead see http://kenbirks.com/godhead.html
[28] Revelation 21:23
[29] Hebrews 1:1-4 (NIV), John 14:9
[30] Psalm 139:7-10

into our spirits, we catch glimpses of His eternal life and the destiny He has for us. As we adjust our thoughts to God's, who are much higher and loftier than anything we can imagine, the mind of Christ allows us to see our lives from the eternal perspective. The Holy Spirit continually searches the heart of the Father to reveal this eternal perspective into our spirits.

Eternity is a part of God's character and who He is rather than a state of being. The Biblical concept of "eternal life" is more than immortality and involves the soul and the body. From creation, humanity was made for never-ending life, not for death.

Isaiah 57:15 For thus says the High and Lofty One Who inhabits eternity, whose name is Holy: "I dwell in the high and holy place, with him who has a contrite and humble spirit, to revive the spirit of the humble, and to revive the heart of the contrite ones.

A heart of humility will bring spiritual awakening and revival to those in a relationship with the God of eternity. He will continually revive our hearts as the above Scripture says. With it comes the proper ordering of our lives during our pilgrimage. As we move forward, an appropriate perspective of God takes root in our lives. As we embrace new kingdom perspectives, our spiritual beings are transformed from the kingdom of darkness into the realm of His Son in every aspect of our lives.[31]

God is eternal and not bound by time. Having always existed, He sees the past and the future as clearly as the present. With this perspective, God better understands what is best for our lives. Knowing this, we should willingly trust Him because He knows every aspect of our journey. Even though the path may seem mysterious and unseen to us, God always sees it clearly and guides us through every twist and turn as we navigate through the dangers and pitfalls that come our way.

God is Immutable, meaning He is unchangeable in nature, meaning we can fully trust Him. He is totally reliable. Think about someone you can depend on who is entirely reliable as a person. Knowing they will always be there for you gives you peace and security. Magnify this by an infinite number, and you will begin to understand what God's Immutability means to you in your relationship with Him.

Malachi 3:6 "For I am the Lord, I do not change; therefore you are not consumed, O sons of Jacob.

As members of the human race, we all have good and bad moments, but this is not true with God. He continually remains the same. He doesn't go through times of being stronger or weaker but consistently

---

[31] Colossians 1:9-13

remains constant, never losing or gaining power. His character is unchanging, with His truth and plans to stay consistent.

Psalm 33:11 The counsel of the LORD stands forever, the plans of His heart to all generations.

Psalms 89:34 My covenant I will not break, nor alter the word that has gone out of My lips.

God has established His ways through His perfect character and His unchangeable purposes. What God does in time is already settled in eternity based upon the counsel of His wisdom and will. Therefore, we can take absolute security in the fact that God has stated in His Word concerning the end of the age and other futuristic events that will come to pass just as He proclaimed it. It doesn't matter what kind of plans the world nations come up with; they are all under the immutability of a God who cannot lie nor alter the word that has gone forth from His lips.[32]

Hebrews 6:17-18 Thus God, determining to show more abundantly to the heirs of promise the immutability of His counsel, confirmed it by an oath, [18]that by two immutable things, in which God can't lie, we might have strong consolation, who have fled for refuge to lay hold of the hope that is set before us.

Even more than this, His immutability should bring peace and security to our hearts as we realize God never differs from Himself. How often have you wanted to share something important with a loved one or a friend but shirked back because you weren't sure of their mood? We don't need to wonder whether God will be in a good mood. His attitude never changes. He is always receptive to whatever we are going through, whether it's misery or need. He's always there, full of love, patience, and mercy toward us, because His attitude never changes. He gives us the freedom and liberty to come boldly into His presence. No matter what caused us to think we may have offended Him somehow, His thoughts toward us remain constant. King David is an excellent example of someone who would often come to God pouring out his complaints, knowing God was unchangeable in His attitude.[33]

God's attitude towards us as sinners has never changed since the fall of Adam and Eve. Just as the blood of goats and lambs was used to make atonement for sins in the Old Testament, Jesus became the sacrificial Lamb for our souls by covering our sins.[34] Jesus, the Lamb of God, had to shed His blood for the atonement of our souls. And now, He continually stretches forth His hands and cries, "*Come to Me, all who are weary and heavy-laden, and I will give you rest.*"[35]

---

[32] Psalm 89:34
[33] Psalm 55:2, 142:2
[34] Psalm 55:2, 142:2
[35] Matthew 11:28

Sometimes, in our journey, we fall hard and even injure ourselves through our sin and stubbornness. As a result, we often wonder if we have the strength to get up and continue the journey. Many go astray and fall away because they feel condemned and ashamed because of the false concepts they have of God. However, we keep our feet firmly through our understanding of the beauty and wonder of who God is. We can run boldly toward Him rather than succumb to condemnation, guilt, and shame.[36]

We continually discover Jesus is there with His arms held wide open to us, saying, *"Come to Me, and I will give you rest."*

God is Omnipotent, which means He is all-powerful. Although God limits His power to give us free will, He possesses what no person or creation has. He alone is incomprehensible and inexhaustible in power. Therefore, there is absolutely nothing too difficult for Him.

Revelation 19:6 And I heard, as it were, the voice of a great multitude, as the sound of many waters and as the sound of mighty thunderings, saying, "Alleluia! For the Lord God Omnipotent reigns!

The above declaration of unlimited power is proclaimed by those standing before God in eternity with a clear view of His magnitude, majesty, and glory. They have seen and experienced God in all His glory and power. They are now proclaiming it unto us so that we are also convinced.

Jeremiah 32:17 Ah, Lord GOD! Behold, You have made the heavens and the earth by Your great power and outstretched arm. There is nothing too hard for You.

Knowing and understanding God's omnipotence gives us faith to believe in the miraculous. Nothing is too complicated for God to perform on our behalf or through us, as we believe in His omnipotence.

As Revivalist Winkie Pratney says, *"Make things hard on God and easy on you."* In other words, don't be afraid to ask God to do hard things while making it easy for you to follow through with His desires.

Ephesians 1:19-20 and what is the exceeding greatness of His power toward us who believe, according to the working of His mighty power [20]*which He worked in Christ when He raised Him from the dead and seated Him at His right hand in the heavenly places.*

Satan underestimated God's power and authority, which resulted in his loss of position and influence after God cast him to the earth like lightning.[37] Let us not underestimate our power and influence through our relationship with God. The journey ahead demands that His power and authority are active in us. There is nothing too complicated for God.

---

[36] Romans 8:1
[37] Luke 10:18

Because we are His sons and daughters, we are linked with His ability and omnipotence and can draw from it as needed.

God is Omnipresent, which means He's unlimited by space and time. He's always everywhere and is available to believers and non-believers when they call upon the Lord.

Psalm 139:7-10 Where can I go from Your Spirit? Or where can I flee from Your presence? ⁸ If I ascend into heaven, You are there; If I make my bed in hell, behold, You are there. ⁹ If I take the wings of the morning and dwell in the uttermost parts of the sea, ¹⁰ even there Your hand shall lead me, and Your right hand shall hold me.

The Holy Spirit has been eternally present with the Father and the Son throughout eternity. When we are born again, the Holy Spirit resides within us. As a result, we encounter His presence at particular times to minister in various gifts and carry out specific God-ordained tasks. The Holy Spirit is everywhere as He brings God's presence to every part of creation. Escaping God's presence is impossible. When you need Him, He's already with you.

God is Omniscient, which means He knows all things, past, present, and future, and delights in imparting His knowledge unto His people.

Years ago, I was sharing with one of my Bible teachers that I wasn't sure what God was calling me to do or be. He responded, "It's not in God's best interest to keep things a secret from you." This simple statement changed how I viewed God and His ability to reveal things to me.

Remember that God delights in opening our eyes to His understanding so we can perceive how He wants to work on our behalf. Because of His omniscience, He will show us everything, including future things. The Holy Spirit within us is constantly searching the heart of the Father to reveal these things to us.[38]

God knows the past, present, and future. God saw Adam's fall through foreknowledge, resulting in humanity's reconciliation through Jesus, the Lamb of God. The crucifixion and resurrection were predestinated events set in motion by God's foreknowledge or omniscience.

1 Peter 1:18-20 knowing that you were not redeemed with corruptible things, like silver or gold, from your aimless conduct received by tradition from your fathers, ¹⁹ but with the precious blood of Christ, as of a lamb without blemish and without spot. ²⁰ He indeed was <u>foreordained</u> before the foundation of the world but was manifest in these last times for you.

Just as God had a plan for humanity, He also sets things in motion for us based on His ability to see our lives as we move forward in Him. We

---

[38] Ephesians 1:17, 1Corinthians 2:9-10, Hebrews 4:13

simply need to open our eyes to the wonder and mystery of how He is working in our lives. He is Omniscient and knows all things.

The Personal Attributes of God

God is Love. We must be rooted and grounded in God's love, understanding the width, length, depth, and height of His great love for us.[39] That's a lot to grasp, but the rewards are worth what we will experience.

1 John 3:1 Behold what manner of love the Father has bestowed on us, that we should be called children of God! Therefore, the world does not know us because it does not know Him.

God bases His love on the fact that He loved us in our most unlovable condition–when we were still rebelling against Him. He sought us out while we did everything possible to hide from Him.

Romans 5:8 But God demonstrates His love toward us, in that while we were still sinners, Christ died for us.

Luke 19:10 for the Son of Man has come to seek and to save that which was lost.

Knowing God's great love should cause us to have an overwhelming sense of love and gratitude toward Him by loving Him with all of our hearts, souls, and minds.[40] He who is forgiven much loves much.[41]

God is Holy with a perfection of purity that fills us with awe. He reveals His holiness because when Adam and Eve sinned, He expelled them from the Garden and cursed them to live outside it. They now had to work and toil. Even though God could not tolerate sin, He provided atonement for their sin by shedding the blood of an animal and covering them with its skin. Thus began the story of redemption and atonement through spilled blood. God's holiness has always provided a way for His children to come to Him despite their sinful disobedience.

Leviticus 17:11 For the life of the flesh is in the blood, and I have given it to you upon the altar to make atonement for your souls; for it is the blood that makes atonement for the soul.

Without the beauty of God's grace accomplished through Jesus Christ, we would not be able to approach God. In His mercy, He made a way for us to approach Him without shame or guilt.

Hebrews 4:16 Let us, therefore, come boldly to the throne of grace, that we may obtain mercy and find grace to help in time of need.

The blood shed by Jesus due to His crucifixion on the cross presents us before the Father as righteous and perfect in that He has perfected

---

[39] Ephesians 3:17-19
[40] Matthew 22:37 (God's love is dealt with in greater detail in Chapter six)
[41] Luke 7:47

those who are being sanctified forever.[42] Because of this, we can stand in His presence with imputed righteousness and holiness we could never have accomplished on our own.

2 Corinthians 5:21 For He made Him who knew no sin to be sin for us, that we might become the righteousness of God in Him.

We will never be any more holy and righteous than we are in God's eyes right now. As a result, you don't have to stay on a performance treadmill to please God. You're already perfect because of His imputed righteousness towards you. Therefore, performance is nothing more than your righteousness trying to please God.

God is merciful and full of grace. Jesus came to reveal the glory of the Father in grace, truth, and mercy. Through His mercy, we obtain mercy.[43]

A great example of God's mercy is the story of Jesus and the woman caught in adultery.[44] Rather than condemn her, He reached out in perfect love, compassion, and mercy, which allowed the goodness of God to lead her to repentance.

No matter what we have done, we can always come boldly to the Throne of Grace to receive mercy from God, who sympathizes with our weaknesses.[45] He leads us to repentance in whatever area we are struggling with when we allow His goodness to fill our hearts. He is full of love, mercy, and grace flowing from His goodness. God is tenderhearted and sympathetic in the very fiber of His being and delights in pouring blessings into our lives.[46]

God takes great pleasure in your happiness and well-being. The invisible path becomes visible as you dwell on His goodness and mercy. Doubt and unbelief no longer cloud your vision. Instead, you can see the life He has planned for you. You can now step out in faith, knowing that God is for you and nothing is against you.[47]

There is nothing about our lives that surprises Him. He has seen our lives from beginning to end and still demonstrates His great love toward us.

Romans 5:8 But God demonstrates His own love toward us, in that while we were still sinners, Christ died for us.

---

[42] Hebrews 10:14
[43] Romans 11:31
[44] John 8:10-11
[45] Hebrews 4:14-16
[46] Psalm 68:19
[47] Romans 8:31

This act of love from God gives us the confidence to stay on the path that leads to fulfilling our destiny and purpose in Him. When we fully grasp the significance of how much God loves and likes us, even in our most darkened and corrupt states, we receive the confidence and assurance to find forgiveness and move forward in His grace and mercy with lightness in our steps.

Francis Anfuso writes in his book, "Perfectly Positioned:"[48] *How can we who are not only guilty but morally filthy possibly be holy in the sight of God, Who knows our every motive and thought as well as our words and actions? The answer is that because of our union with Christ, God sees His holiness as our holiness. Therefore, when God the Father looks at us, He doesn't see our miserable performance. Instead, He sees Jesus' perfect performance. And because of the perfect holiness of Jesus, He sees us as holy and without blemish."*

God is Wisdom. A.W. Tozer writes, *"God realizes the best designs by the best possible means. He cannot make a mistake. He is all-wise."* He then defines wisdom as *"the ability to devise perfect ends and to achieve those ends by the most perfect means."*

Psalm 104:24 *O LORD, how manifold are Your works! In wisdom, You have made them all. The earth is full of Your possessions;*

Another quote from A.W. Tozer says, *"All of God's acts are done in wisdom because of the integration of these attributes of His being. He is not tainted by sin or selfishness; His actions are motivated by the awareness of ultimate good; He sees and knows all that can be seen and known. Because His understanding is infinite, His wisdom is boundless."*

In conclusion, everything seen in the heart of the Father is revealed to us through the life and ministry of Jesus Christ. He came to reveal the heart of the Father. Jesus manifested all of these characteristics through the ministry of the Holy Spirit in His life. He was given the Holy Spirit without measure.

When asked to show us the Father, Jesus said to one of His disciples, *"You've been with me all this time, Philip, and you still don't understand? To see Me is to see the Father. So how can you ask, 'Where is the Father?' Don't you believe that I am in the Father, and the Father is in Me?"*[49]

As created beings, we were created in God's image, allowing us to experience His divine attributes as well. All that the Father reveals has to pass through our unperfected state of being, giving us glimpses into

---

[48] francisanfuso.com
[49] John 14:8-10 MSG

the unfathomable depths of God. His Word working with the Spirit of God allows us to see Him as He is.

Ask the Father to reveal His heart to you as you search the Scriptures to discover His greatness and divine nature. As we find out who God is through the Scriptures, we come to know Him as He has revealed Himself to us.

As we have seen, God's greatness is beyond discovery. He desires for us to discover His creative beauty in our lives, which helps to point us toward our destiny and keeps us on track as we journey along the path that holds the keys to our future. May the Lord's beauty and fascination be with us as we journey toward our destiny in Him![50]

---

[50] Psalm 90:17

A New Beginning
The Journey Begins

Chapter Two

Therefore, if anyone is in Christ, he is a new creation; old things have passed away; behold, all things have become new—2Corinthians 5:17

The Christian journey begins when we are genuinely born again and translated from the kingdom of darkness into the kingdom of the Son. As a result, a great opportunity lies before us. We are given the keys to the kingdom and receive access to the wonders of God's grace that lead us onto the invisible and mysterious path that lies before us.

You are on a journey in which you will experience the fullness God intended for your life as your spiritual eyes are enlightened to this new paradigm of thinking God has purposed for you.[51]

The Bible refers to our common salvation experience as a great salvation that Old Testament prophets, righteous men, and even angels desired to look into but could not experience.[52] We now have the privilege of experiencing something these great heroes of our faith could never experience. Paul writes to the Ephesians church, *"We are now partakers of the mystery of Christ, which was not made known to people in other generations as it has now revealed by the Spirit of God's holy apostles and prophets."*[53] Our heavenly Father draws us into His heart in a way they could never experience.

Having the Eyes of Our Understanding Opened

As we allow the Holy Spirit to open our eyes to the wonders we find on God's path, we can appreciate all He has given us. We now have all things that pertain to life and godliness.[54] All we will ever need in life is

---

[51] Ephesians 1:17-18
[52] Matthew 13:16, 2Peter 1:12
[53] Paraphrased form Ephesians 3:4-5
[54] 2 Peter 1:3

available on this path that leads to the unforeseen purposes of God. As we are bold enough to take the steps that lead into this invisible kingdom realm, we experience all that God has intended for us.

Are you ready for such a journey? If so, may God bless you mightily as you allow the Holy Spirit to open the eyes of your understanding so that you can move forward in faith toward an unknown destiny.

Before salvation, our minds were trained to respond according to our carnality and logical reasoning. Now that we have been born again and made new, God desires us to learn how to live and function according to faith and be spiritually minded. As spiritual beings, we can no longer lean on our understanding.[55] As we purpose to see with the eyes of our understanding, the Holy Spirit is within us to illuminate the path and direct our steps more correctly unto Him.

As we see and hear through our spirit, our lives are shaped by what is invisible rather than visible. When we see and hear through our spirit, we connect with the power and victory that allows us to find our way through the world's maze. We can see the invisible forces of God and His kingdom at work, giving us the confidence to accept whatever comes our way.

Getting Started

Getting started on the path of life begins with a salvation experience from a God who is rich in mercy. He fills us with faith, hope, and love while loading us with benefits daily.[56] Having heard the joyful sound from the Throne of Grace, we begin to walk with great joy and enthusiasm as we embrace the new nature God is pouring into us. As a result, our old nature and ways begin to dissipate. We enter into a new sense of invincibility, which gives us the courage to start the journey wherein lies our destiny that is yet to unfold before our eyes.

Our salvation experience is a result of our belief in Jesus Christ.[57] We must believe He is much more than a great prophet or teacher. He is the Son of God, manifested in the flesh, who came to give His life as a ransom for our sins.[58] He did this by dying on the cross, rising from the dead, and ascending into Heaven from where He came.

As the Scriptures clearly say, *"He is the only way to the Father, and there is no other name under heaven given among men by which we experience salvation."*[59]

---

[55] Proverbs 3:5
[56] Psalm 68:19
[57] Romans 10:9-10
[58] John 1:1,14, 3:16
[59] John 14:6, Acts 4:12

1 Timothy 2:5-6 For there is one God and one Mediator between God and men, the Man Christ Jesus, ⁶ who gave Himself a ransom for all, to be testified in due time,

One of the most astonishing facts concerning Christ and the atonement He made for our sins is that He became sin for us. Jesus, who was without sin, was filled with sin as He hung on the cross and cried to the Father in agony, *"Why have You forsaken Me?"*

Because Jesus was full of the sins of the world, His Father could no longer look upon Him. The close intimacy He continually experienced with Him during His time on earth was no longer there. As a result, He died a sinner's death and became our righteousness. Because Jesus died for our sins, we are now totally righteous in Him. Those who are being sanctified, He has perfected forever in one act.[60]

2 Corinthians 5:21 For He made Him who knew no sin to be sin for us, that we might become the righteousness of God in Him.

Many years ago, I came across a tract explaining the punishment Christ bore on our behalf. Here it is. It's called "Justice." The author is unknown.

Justice

At the end of time, millions of people were scattered on a great plain before God's throne. Some of the group near the front talked heatedly – not with cringing shame but with belligerence. "How can God judge us? How can He know about suffering?" snapped a joking brunette. She jerked back a sleeve to reveal a tattooed number from a Nazi concentration camp. "We endured terror, beatings, torture, and death!"

In another group, a black man lowered his collar. "What about this?" he demanded, showing an ugly rope burn. Lynched for no other crime but being black! "We suffocated in slave ships, were wrenched from loved ones, and toiled until only death gave release."

Far out across the plain were hundreds of such groups. Each had a complaint against God for the evil and suffering He had permitted in His world. How lucky God was to live in heaven where all was sweetness and light, where there was no weeping, no fear, no hunger, and no hatred. Indeed, what did God know about what man had been forced to endure in this world? And after all, God leads a pretty sheltered life, they said.

So, each group sent out a chosen leader who had suffered the most. There was a Jew, a Black, an untouchable from India, an illegitimate, a person from Hiroshima, and one from a Siberian slave camp. In the center of the plain, they consulted each other. At last, they were ready to

---

[60] Hebrews 10:14

present their case. It was rather simple: He must endure what they endured before God could be their judge. They decided that God should be sentenced to live on earth—as a man!

But, because He was God, they set certain safeguards to be sure He could not use His divine powers to help Himself. Let Him be born to a hated minority. Let the legitimacy of His birth be doubted so that no one will know who His father is. Let Him champion a cause so just but so radical that it brings down upon Him the hate, the condemnation, and eliminating efforts of every major traditional and established religious authority. Let His dearest friends betray him. Let Him be indicted on false charges, tried before a prejudiced jury, and convicted by a cowardly judge. Let Him see what it is to be terribly alone and entirely abandoned by every living thing. Let Him be tortured and let Him die the most humiliating death—with common thieves.

As each leader announced their portion of the sentence, loud murmurs of approval went up from the great crowd of people. There was a long silence when the last had finished pronouncing the verdict. No one uttered another word. No one moved. For suddenly, all knew: God already had served His sentence.

God served His sentence in the person of His Son, Jesus Christ. But, unfortunately, Jesus got a bad deal. The Bible says He took your sin and my sin on Himself and offered back His righteousness. He died so that we might have life. The wages or price of sin are misery, guilt, lack of peace of mind, death, and hell. But Jesus died on the cross to save us from that sin so that we might have real peace, abundant life, and eternal life.

We despised Him and rejected Him—a man of sorrows, acquainted with the bitterest grief. We turned our backs on Him and looked the other way when He went by. He was despised, and we didn't care. It was our grief He bore, our sorrows that weighed Him down. And we thought His troubles were a punishment from God for His sins! But He was wounded and bruised for our sins. He was chastised that we might have peace; He was lashed—and we were healed! [61]

~

The Father Deals with us as Individuals.

For all of us who have come to know Christ, we have our stories to tell. The Father deals with each of us as individuals He has created. He,

---

[61] Isaiah 53:3-10 Living Bible

A New Beginning—The Journey Begins

our Creator, has fearfully and wonderfully created us, and He knows every aspect of our lives.

Psalm 139:13-16 For You formed my inward parts; You covered me in my mother's womb. [14] I will praise You, for I am fearfully and wonderfully made; marvelous are Your works, and that my soul knows very well. [15] My frame was not hidden from You when I was made in secret and skillfully wrought in the lowest parts of the earth. [16] Your eyes saw my substance, being yet unformed. And in Your book, they all were written, the days fashioned for me, when as yet there were none of them.

When the Father draws us unto Christ, we must choose to accept or reject Him. We must either acknowledge Him as the Lord of our lives or harden our hearts to the truth He desires to impart. The beautiful thing about God is that He never gives up on us but is long-suffering towards us and continually woos us into His presence.

Psalms 86:15 But You, O Lord, are a God full of compassion, and gracious, longsuffering and abundant in mercy and truth.

Thankfully, God was very patient with me. I was stubborn, continually resisting His wooing until I was broken and worn out. Finally, his long-suffering overcame my resistance as I surrendered to His Lordship. Thus, my journey with Christ began.

I have often likened my journey to a fisherman trying to land a big fish. When it first bites at the bait and gets the hook into its mouth, the fisherman jerks the line and sets the hook. He then lets the fish run with the line before slowly reeling it in. He may repeat this process several times until the poor fish is worn out from the fight and succumbs to the net that lands him on shore or in the boat.

With me, it took three long years after getting the hook in my mouth. I was in Vietnam and had been heavily involved in drugs when, one day, I experienced violent convulsions from getting a shot of penicillin. The penicillin must have reacted to all the drugs I was taking during that season in my life. Later that evening, I received a vision of my life flashing before me. It became one of the most decisive defining moments I would ever experience.

Even though I was raised in a healthy Christian environment and made several false starts at trying to be a Christian as a child, I never fully surrendered to the Lord. As a result, during my teenage years and early 20s, I rebelled strongly against my upbringing. I allowed the world and drugs to get a death grip on my soul and became a very deceived, lost, and wandering soul. I tried to fill my life with everything except what God wanted. I have written about this period of my life in another book titled, *"The Adventures of Space and Hobo."*[62]

---

[62] spaceandhobo.booksbyken.com

I came to understand the long-suffering of God. He never gave up on me even though I rebelled against Him. He continually reminded me that He was there watching over me and protecting me from myself. He would reel me in occasionally to remind me He was still watching over me, only to let go again, but never completely releasing me. He is a gracious and compassionate God who loves us even in our most disgusting states.

Romans 5:8 But God demonstrates His own love toward us, in that while we were still sinners, Christ died for us.

At the end of this season, I was on the verge of losing it. I was a broken and tattered vessel that had lost all sense of reality. I was a burned-out hippie freak with no sense of purpose. I had become lost in isolation.

In my memoir, I wrote, *"Despite my heart being somewhat disengaged, the seed was still there, and I didn't want to lose it. However, I also didn't feel I was ready to become a wholehearted follower of Jesus at this point in my life. It was interesting, though, how the Lord would bring me in touch from time to time with what was happening in the Jesus people culture."*

"In some unique and mysterious way, I sensed God was leading me despite my stubbornness and refusal to submit to Him. Sensing God was still with me gave me peace, knowing He was long-suffering with me and hadn't given up on me. But the question was, how long would He continue to allow me to have my way?"

I eventually came to a place where I sensed the time had come when God would reel me in for the final catch, or I would break the line of communication, and He would give me over to the hardness of my heart. During this season, I discovered how God leads us to repentance through His goodness and mercy.

Romans 2:4 or do you despise the riches of His goodness, forbearance, and longsuffering, not knowing that the goodness of God leads you to repentance?

Over the next three months, I experienced the goodness of God, leading me to genuine repentance. It culminated one Sunday morning when my family invited me to attend my niece's baby dedication. I kneeled at the altar in the church I had grown up in and fully surrendered to Jesus.

God is no respecter of persons. His call goes out to everyone. It went out to me—a poor, lost, and wandering soul who had rebelled against Him and continually goes out to everyone regardless of their state of mind. Salvation through Jesus Christ is an all-inclusive gift, meaning He died for everyone, not just a chosen few.

A New Beginning—The Journey Begins

John 3:16 For God so loved the world that He gave His only begotten Son, that whoever believes in Him should not perish but have everlasting life.

When the Bible says, *"Whoever believes in Him has eternal life,"* it means God is no respecter of persons. He died for everyone so we can all claim salvation in Christ for ourselves. Our part is to believe in Him.

Hebrews 2:9 But we see Jesus, who was made a little lower than the angels, for the suffering of death crowned with glory and honor, that He, by the grace of God, might taste death for everyone.

Romans 5:18 Therefore, as through one man's offense judgment came to all men, resulting in condemnation, even so through one Man's righteous act the free gift came to all men, resulting in justification of life.

Since all humanity came under judgment in Adam, all humanity must come, at least, into the possibility of eternal life in Jesus Christ. So then, when we come to a place of brokenness and humility, the Father can draw our hearts unto His Son, the Lord Jesus Christ.

Psalm 138:6 Though the LORD is on high, yet He regards the lowly, but the proud He knows from afar.

Psalm 34:18 The LORD is near to those who have a broken heart and saves such as have a contrite spirit.

During this season, I was on the verge of losing it. I was a burned-out hippie freak now being drawn into the heart of Jesus by God our Father.[63] As a result, I came to a place of complete belief and trust in the reality of who Jesus is.

When we come to this place of sincerely believing that God raised Jesus from the dead and repent of our sins, we are born again, and our journey into this beautiful, invisible, and spiritual path begins.

Romans 10:9-10 (NASB) that if you confess with your mouth Jesus as Lord and believe in your heart that God raised Him from the dead, you will be saved; ¹⁰ for with the heart a person believes, resulting in righteousness, and with the mouth he confesses, resulting in salvation.

The key is that we must believe with our hearts. The word "believe" is an action word. Our hearts must be involved. Heartfelt belief is much more than just intellectual knowledge. The Bible says even the demons in hell believe.[64] Genuine faith is when your whole life aligns with what you think. You adhere to it.

Jesus is the Mediator between Man and God

Every one of us begins our life with a natural birth. Jesus referred to this birth as being "born of water"—the natural birth resulting from a woman's water breaking during childbirth.[65] Unfortunately, through

---

[63] John 6:44
[64] James 2:19-20
[65] John 3:1-9

Adam, sin entered this world. Because of his sin, all humanity is separated from God and needs a Savior. Jesus is the Savior of humanity and the only mediator between man and God, which is why He is the only way to man's salvation.

Salvation is a gift from God, and there is no amount of good works we can do to earn it.[66] It's Free! Salvation has nothing to do with whether we deserve it or not. God bestows His unmerited favor upon us despite ourselves—a result of our belief in the person of Jesus Christ and who we believe Him to be.

Once we accept Jesus Christ for who He is by coming to Him with repentant hearts, we are born again of the Spirit. His Holy Spirit then comes to abide within us.

Receiving the born-again experience is inspiring because all things become new. God entirely forgives us when we ask forgiveness for our sins and past transgressions. As far as the East is from the West, our past is entirely wiped clean. He removes the weight of sin from our lives.[67]

2 Corinthians 5:17 Therefore, if anyone is in Christ, he is a new creation; old things have passed away; behold, all things have become new

Becoming a new creation sets us up to begin the most incredible journey anyone could ever ask for—a journey into the mysterious and invisible realms where God exists.

Revelation 3:20 Behold, I stand at the door and knock. If anyone hears My voice and opens the door, I will come into him and dine with him, and he with Me.

Have you ever heard His voice? Has He been knocking at your door? If so, open your heart to Him and allow Him into your life, and you'll be ready for the greatest adventure of your life—a life designed for the person God created you to be.

---

[66] Ephesians 2:6-8
[67] 1 John 1:9, Psalm 103:12, Hebrews 10:17

The Path Less Traveled
Repentance & Conversion

Chapter Three

At that time, the disciples came to Jesus, saying, "Who then is greatest in the kingdom of heaven?" Then Jesus called a little child to Him, set him in the midst of them, and said, "Assuredly, I say to you, unless you are converted and become as little children, you will by no means enter the kingdom of heaven.
Matthew 18:1-3

As wonderful and adventurous as this path may be, many will never find it. It is a hidden path that can only be found or seen by those whose eyes are enlightened. At the entrance is the cross, which we must now pick up. As we do, we're enlightened to all that exists on the path.

Jesus said, *"He who does not take up his cross and follow after Me is not worthy of Me. He who finds his life will lose it, and he who loses his life for my sake will find it.*[68]*"*

Avoiding the Deceptive Voices of Our Culture

There are many paths to spirituality, but only one path leads to eternity in heaven with our Heavenly Father. It is the path less traveled. The only way to discover it is through Jesus Christ and adhering to the words that came from Him as He began His ministry in Galilee. He came preaching, *"Repent, for the kingdom of heaven, is at hand."*[69]

Matthew 7:13-14 *Enter by the narrow gate; for wide is the gate and broad is the way that leads to destruction, and there are many who go in by it. 14 Because narrow is the gate and difficult is the way that leads to life, and few find it.*

John 14:6 *Jesus said to him, "I am the way, the truth, and the life. No one comes to the Father except through Me."*

Will you be one of the few who discover this path, or will you be among those who spend their lives listening to the myriad voices in our

---

[68] Matthew 10:38-39
[69] Matthew 4:17

culture and world screaming for your attention? We must reject these voices if we are to discover His way.

The voices of our culture and even some within the Church are caught in deceit and ignorance. They're unaware of the destruction that awaits them at the end of their path because pleasures and sensuality have numbed them. *Their god is their belly, and their glory is their shame; they have set their minds on earthly things rather than heavenly things.*[70] Those who listen and adhere to voices representing pleasure, sensuality, and spiritual deception will travel down a broad path that leads to destruction and offers nothing but an illusion of what they hoped to find.

Is this the path you desire for your life, or would you rather discover the invisible and spiritual path that leads to pleasures for evermore, the fullness of joy, and a life of fulfillment in the purposes of God? [71]

Even though we have come to believe in Jesus Christ, we make choices daily as we partake of the blessings on the path.

The apostle Paul said, *"I die daily."*[72] So, likewise, taking up the cross of Christ is an everyday thing that causes us to lose our lives for the gospel's sake.

Those who are Converted Experience Kingdom Life

Sadly, many who come to believe in Jesus never become fully converted because of an unwillingness to die to themselves and lose their life for the sake of the gospel.

Jesus says, *"Assuredly, I say to you, unless you are converted and become like children, you will by no means enter the kingdom of heaven."*[73]

God is looking for a lifestyle of repentance and humility because this is what it takes to keep us firmly adhering to His ways as we travel along a path that includes all things that pertain to life and godliness.

Sadly, it took me four long years to fully convert after tasting the incredible gift Jesus offered me. I was in Vietnam at the time when Jesus first got His hooks into me. I had a near-death experience and partially committed my life to Him. It took four long years before I finally surrendered to the cross. During those years, I became a lost and wandering soul trying to fill my life with adventure and drugs, only to discover what I was looking for was staring me in the face the whole time. Thankfully, because of God's long-suffering and mercy towards

---

[70] Philippians 3:18-19
[71] Psalm 16:11
[72] 1 Corinthians 15:31
[73] Matthew 18:3

me, I finally came to the end of myself and fully surrendered to what God wanted to do in my life. My life has been an exciting adventure in Christ ever since.

Many Are Being Seduced and Missing the Path

In much of Christianity, there is a lack of genuine conversion and transformation in those attempting to follow Christ. Instead, many are getting seduced by a Hollywood version of Christianity—a watered-down version that doesn't challenge people to put off the old nature by being crucified to the world.

The big question is, "Have we embraced the cross of Christ, or have we fallen into the false teachings of the hour?"

Jesus said there would be many false teachers and prophets at the end of the age before His return. Paul warned us that many would not endure sound doctrine but turn to false teachers with itching ears.[74] So, likewise, we must realize that Satan is out to seduce us with lies and just enough truth to get us to bite into the deception.

There is so much mixture in today's Christianity that it's sometimes hard to discern the truth. We are to rightly divide the word of truth as Paul encouraged us to do.[75] We must know it and own it for ourselves. Otherwise, we will fall into the false teachings of the hour. You may wake up one morning and realize you are on the wrong path. Thankfully, once you fully submit your heart to the Word of God and the Holy Spirit, you will again be led back to the path of life.

Much of Christianity is amid what the nation of Israel was involved in when Jeremiah prophesied the following:

Jeremiah 5:30-31 An astonishing and horrible thing has been committed in the land: The prophets prophesy falsely, and the priests rule by their own power, and My people love to have it so, but what will you do in the end?

Much of the church in today's Christianity has compromised the authority of God's Word in the area of repentance to draw large crowds, and the people love it so. It's a significant problem. There's too much secular philosophy mixed in with the kingdom message of true repentance.

---

[74] Matthew 24:4-5,24, 2Timothy 4:3-4
[75] 2 Timothy 2:15

What is True Repentance?

Let's take a few moments to ponder what true repentance is. As we have seen, Jesus came on the scene preaching, *"Repent, for the kingdom of heaven is at hand."* He commands all of us to lay down our lives and raise the white flag of surrender to enter the kingdom of God. In other words, we must change our minds about God, sin, and the Bible and yield to His authority as innocent children.[76] Jesus has become the author of eternal salvation to all who obey Him.[77]

True repentance is taking up the cross and following Jesus, which involves a denial of self and embracing the pain and suffering it represents. We are to look unto Jesus, the author and finisher of our faith, who endured the cross for the joy set before Him, despising its shame. We are to consider Him who endured such hostility from sinners against Himself, lest we become weary and discouraged.[78] Jesus told His disciples, *"If anyone would come after me, he must deny himself, take up his cross, and follow me."*[79] Is this true in your life?

True Repentance is to Change the Way We Think

In the Old Testament, we find two Hebrew words describing repentance. They are *nacham* and *shub*. *Nacham* means "to be sorry or come to regret something." *Shub* means "to turn." In the New Testament, three Greek words express repentance. They are the verbs *metanoeo*, *metamelomia*, and the noun *metanoia*, which means "a change of mind that leads to a change of behavior."

Repentance is to change the way we think about everything. When we adjust our thoughts to God's thinking, it will produce a change in the way we act. Just as Philip the Evangelist told the Ethiopian eunuch about believing wholeheartedly, the same applies to us.[80] True repentance causes us to turn towards God wholeheartedly. God is not interested in just a piece of our hearts. He wants the whole thing. When we turn to God with our entire hearts, it will change the way we think. We must never forget that God's thoughts and ways are much higher than ours.[81]

Years ago, when I fully surrendered to God's authority, I had many strange ideas about God and who He was. When I came out of the hippie culture, I was immersed in many ideas and thoughts about God that were popular during that generation. They included reincarnation, being one

---

[76] Matthew 18:3
[77] Hebrews 5:9
[78] Hebrews 12:2-3
[79] Matthew 16:24
[80] Acts 8:37, Romans 10:9
[81] Isaiah 55:8-9

with the God consciousness, and other things such as meditation and visits from the spirit, Mescalito.

Being raised in a Bible-believing family, I knew many ideas I had come in contact with during my lost years were not Biblically sound. Even though I didn't quit believing in some of the things I had picked up along the way, I consciously decided to place everything on a shelf. I didn't want what I was learning to go through the filter of my recent past and the philosophical ideas I had picked up. In shelving my old thoughts, I came to Christ as an innocent child prepared to learn and fully convert. We see this in the writings of the apostle Paul.

Colossians 2:9 Beware lest anyone cheat you through philosophy and empty deceit, according to the tradition of men, according to the basic principles of the world, and not according to Christ.

One of the reasons many are pressing the default button instead of opting for a life filled with adventure in the Holy Spirit is a lack of faith and understanding when it comes to repentance. Hosea, the Prophet, reminds us that God's people get destroyed for lack of knowledge.[82] Many are rejecting knowledge by not adhering to the Word of God. As a result, they end up with too much mixture and are not converted as little children. They get deceived by the watered-down message of repentance coming from the pulpits of the modern Church. We must all be aware of how easy it is to be cheated through subtle and ear-tickling messages, the many voices clamoring for our attention in this critical hour of the church's destiny. Otherwise, what will we do in the end?

Repentance—A Long Obedience in the Same Direction.

Eugene Peterson says: *"Repentance is not an emotion. It is not feeling sorry for your sins. It is a decision. It is deciding that you have been wrong in supposing that you could manage your own life and be your own god; it is deciding that you were wrong in thinking that you had, or could get, the strength, education, and training to make it on your own; it is deciding that you have been told a pack of lies about yourself and your neighbors and your world. And it is deciding that God in Jesus Christ is telling you the truth. Repentance is a realization that what God wants from you and what you want from God are not going to be achieved by doing the same old things or thinking the same old thoughts. Repentance is a decision to follow Jesus Christ and become his pilgrim in the path of peace."*[83]

Repentance Includes Separation From all that is Ungodly

---

[82] Hosea 4:6
[83] By Eugene Petersen from his book, "A Long Obedience in the Same Direction."

A significant part of repentance is separating from all that is ungodly, even if it means leaving your old friends behind. Remember, repentance is agreeing with God and His Word so that our minds can conform to His thinking. We've been encouraged not to be unequally yoked together with unbelievers by coming out from among them.

2 Corinthians 6:17 *"Come out from among them and be separate, says the Lord. Do not touch what is unclean, and I will receive you."* [18] *"I will be a Father to you, and you shall be My sons and daughters, says the Lord Almighty."*

As a young believer, I knew by hanging out with my old friends, I would be back in my sin with one failure after another, so I consciously decided to separate from my pot-smoking buddies to get grounded in the faith. The reality of this thinking hit home one morning, shortly after surrendering my life to Christ. On my way to a college class one morning, I picked up one of my former buddies, who was hitchhiking and happened to be toking on a joint. The next thing I knew, I was toking right along with him. I knew then that I wasn't ready to be around my former friends. My faith wasn't strong enough. Shortly after, some of my buddies came to see me and questioned why I wasn't hanging with them. I told them I had turned my life over to Christ and was no longer interested in hanging out and smoking pot with them. After that, they no longer came around.

Bob Dylan once wrote a line in a song, *"Gonna change my way of thinking and stop being influenced by fools."*[84] So, are we being influenced by fools, or are we influencing the way they think?

Repentance Causes Us to be Salt and Light

Is there ever a time to be around our former friends? Absolutely! We are to be salt and light in their lives.[85] The question is: are you an influencer or an influencee when you are with them? In my case, I was still an influencee and had no business being around them. I was hiding my light, and my salt was useless. There would come a time later on when I could be the influencer rather than the influencee, but not then.

When we fail to break from our former friends, we get pulled in two directions—the kingdom and the world. As a result, we end up with a lot of mixtures. As a pastor, I have observed people I've had continued contact with over the years. Some are stuck in the same sins they were dealing with when I first met them. The common denominator is that they never gave up their worldly friends. They didn't come out from among them to be separated as the Word commands.

---

[84] From the album "Slow Train Coming" by Bob Dylan
[85] Matthew 5:13-16

Friendship with the World is Enmity with God

James, the Lord's brother, says clearly, *"Adulterers and adulteresses! Do you not know that friendship with the world is enmity with God? Whoever, therefore, wants to be a friend of the world makes himself an enemy of God. Or do you think the Scripture says in vain, "The Spirit who dwells in us yearns jealously"?*[86]

Jesus spent a lot of time in the presence of sinners and was perfectly at peace with them. He knew full well who He was and His mission and purpose—to seek and save those who are lost. Jesus did not need to compromise His testimony. Sinners were drawn to the light that emanated from Him. He was the ultimate influencer, setting at liberty the lives of those who were bound up in sin to a life of freedom and victory as they responded to the kingdom's message of repentance coming forth from His life.

The beautiful thing is that as we embrace a lifestyle of repentance, we become fully converted and have transformed lives. Because we are now aligned with the kingdom of the Son, we take on the same characteristics found in the life of Jesus that caused Him to have such a powerful influence.

Repentance Includes a lifestyle of Practicing Righteousness.

A person who has genuinely repented and experienced conversion will have a lifestyle of practicing righteousness even though they may trip and stumble at times. They may fall several times, but each time, they will immediately get back up and run into the loving arms of their faithful High Priest, who understands and sympathizes with their weaknesses.[87] So likewise, the person who is genuinely born again and practicing righteousness falls into their Savior's loving arms, who is ready to brush them off and send them on their way without condemnation. Or guilt.[88]

1 John 3:7 Little children, let no one deceive you. He who practices righteousness is righteous, just as He is righteous.

A person not practicing righteousness does not know God or understand true salvation. They have missed the path that leads to eternal life. They must examine whether they are in the faith and have become disqualified.[89]

---

[86] James 4:4-6
[87] Proverbs 24:16 For a righteous man may fall seven times and rise again, but the wicked shall fall by calamity, Hebrews 4:14-16
[88] Romans 8:1
[89] 2 Corinthians 13:5

1 John 3:10 In this, the children of God and the children of the devil are manifest: Whoever does not practice righteousness is not of God, nor is he who does not love his brother.

John 7:21-23 "Not everyone who says to me, 'Lord, Lord,' shall enter the kingdom of heaven, but he who does the will of My Father in heaven. ²² "Many will say to Me in that day, 'Lord, Lord, have we not prophesied in Your name, cast out demons in Your Name, and done many wonders in Your name?' ²³ "And then I will declare to them, 'I never knew you; depart from Me, you who practice lawlessness!'

It is the person who practices lawlessness, not the person practicing righteousness, who occasionally stumbles to whom Jesus speaks. The promise of Romans 8:1 says, *"There is therefore now no condemnation to those who are in Christ Jesus,"* is for those who are not practicing walking according to the flesh. What is the overall testimony of your lifestyle? Is it practicing righteousness or unrighteousness? If you are still practicing immorality or any form of sinfulness, then conversion has not occurred. You are still lost in your sins.

Repentance Includes Sorrowing for our Sin

If we have come to appreciate all that Jesus went through on behalf of our sins, we will feel godly sorrow and regret for it. Our sins crucified Him, even though He was handed over to the Romans by the Jews for crucifixion.[90]

As a young Christian, I had a poster on my wall of Jesus hanging on the cross with His face wrenched with pain and agony. It constantly reminded me of what He had to endure on my behalf. It helped me appreciate the forgiveness I was experiencing during a vulnerable time when I was often tempted to fall back into my old lifestyle. It also helped produce a godly sorrow for my sinning against Him.

The apostle Paul writes, *"For godly sorrow produces repentance leading to salvation, not to be regretted; but the sorrow of the world produces death."*[91]

Godly sorrow doesn't mean we continue to wallow in our past by reminding ourselves of our sins. However, there needs to be a time when we think soberly about how our sins put Jesus on the cross and sincerely ask Him for forgiveness. I have found that when I name my sins before God, there is more of a soberness about them that doesn't come when I say cavalierly, "Forgive me for my sins."

Once I have thoroughly confessed my sins before God, I leave them and forget them, as the following Scriptures lead me to believe.

---

[90] Romans 5:8-10, 2 Corinthians 5:21
[91] 2 Corinthians 7:10

The Path Less Traveled – Repentance and Conversion

1 John 1:9 If we confess our sins, He is faithful and just to forgive us our sins and to cleanse us from all unrighteousness.

Psalm 103:12 As far as the east is from the west, so far Has He removed our transgressions from us.

Hebrews 10:17 Their sins and their lawless deeds I will remember no more.

If God has no remembrance of my sins, I won't remember them either. So, instead, I will forget the past and lay hold of all the good things He has in store for me.

As I conclude this chapter, I realize I have made some adamant statements concerning our salvation experience. Nevertheless, I have chosen not to gloss over some of the more difficult passages of Scripture. We all are responsible for rightly dividing the word of truth, especially regarding our salvation experience. Therefore, I pray that you would take to heart and seriously consider what the Holy Spirit may be speaking to you concerning your salvation experience.

Psalm 23:3 He restores my soul; He leads me in the paths of righteousness for His name's sake.

Proverbs 4:18 But the path of the is like the shining sun, that shines ever brighter unto the perfect day.

True repentance with godly sorrow will continually open the eyes of your understanding to this adventurous path that is hidden to so many. May God bless you as you journey forward and discover the wonders and blessings He has prepared for you.

Getting an Identity Makeover

Chapter Four

He who finds his life will lose it, and he who loses his life for My sake will find it.
Matthew 10:39.

If you've made it this far in the book, you've most likely decided to commit yourself to the journey ahead or, at least, discover what's ahead for you. If so, it's time to shed your old identity because the path forward requires a complete identity makeover. We must be willing to lose ourselves in Christ by dying to our old identity developed in the domain of darkness.

One of the keys to the kingdom is receiving a new identity.[92] When we come to the place where we are willing to lose our old identity, we begin the wonderful process of discovery that brings us into a complete and new identity born out of the beauty and the glory of heaven rather than the depravity of hell.[93]

A new identity in Christ is required before we can unlock the benefits and mysteries Christ has in store for us. Our old identity does not match the lock. Our new identity is the key that opens the invisible gate and unlocks the mysteries unique to each of us as we journey along the path He has chosen for us.

To succeed, we must embrace our new identity wholeheartedly as we discover God only relates to us according to our new nature. As far as God is concerned, our old nature and identity were crucified with Him. Therefore, God can't relate to something that's dead, including our old thinking paradigm. God is the God of the living, not the dead.[94] In

---

[92] Matthew 16:19
[93] Matthew 16:25-27
[94] Matthew 22:32

coming to Christ, we made a significant paradigm shift, which requires a complete identity makeover formed by the mind of Christ we now possess. It should be emerging in our lives as we become more and more consecrated to Christ.

Our old identity was shaped by thoughts and attitudes that were part of the domain of darkness. The essence of who we are is an accumulation of our thought life as it says in Proverbs—*"For as he thinks in his heart, so is he."*[95] Soreen Kierkegaard says, *"Our life always expresses the result of our dominant thoughts."*

As children growing up in a world under the influence and the sway of the enemy, we received a steady stream of information, experiences, half-truths, and lies that continually shaped our childhood perceptions.[96] These ideas and attitudes shaped and formed our identity during our formative years.[97] As painful as it is, we must let go and allow God to crucify our old paradigm of thinking.[98]

The problem is we became very attached to the identity of our youth during our formative years. It's hard to let go of something that has been part of who we are. Nevertheless, we must let go if we are to experience all that God has provided for us on this magnificent journey. As we are willing to let go and lose our lives, we will find the new life He has intended because we are now hidden with Christ in God.[99]

When we stubbornly cling to our old identity, there is no deliverance from the sinful habits and addictions that were part of it. True deliverance only comes as we embrace our new nature. The anointing that comes with the new nature breaks the yoke of sinful addictions.[100] As we purpose to walk in the Spirit, we do not fulfill the lusts of the flesh.[101]

Much of our identity in the past was a result of copying worldly influences around us. Think about how we so readily follow the trends and fashions around us. The following Scripture reveals how we are challenged not to copy the behavior and customs of the world.

Romans 12:2 (NLT) Don't copy the behavior and customs of this world, but let God transform you into a new person by changing the way you think. (by the renewing of your mind – NKJV) Then you will know what God wants you to do, and you will know how good and pleasing and perfect his will really is.

I'm continually amazed at how many Christians are caught up in copying the world's behavior and customs rather than following the

---

[95] Proverbs 23: 7
[96] 1 John 5:19
[97] Thoughts taken from the book "The Three Battlegrounds" by Francis Frangipane
[98] Galatians 6:14
[99] Colossians 3:3
[100] Isaiah 10:27
[101] Galatians 5:16

appeal of the Scriptures. Many who call themselves Christians live together in a sexual union rather than waiting until marriage. Homosexuality is accepted more and more as appropriate behavior. Cursing and swearing are accepted as the norm. The Bible still describes living together in sexual union as fornication and sinful, homosexuality as a sin, and swearing as filthy language.[102] Paul encourages us to put these things to death.

Colossians 3:5-10 Therefore put to death your members which are on the earth: fornication, uncleanness, passion, evil desire and covetousness, which is idolatry. ⁶ Because of these things the wrath of God is coming upon the sons of disobedience, ⁷in which you yourselves once walked when you lived in them. ⁸ But now you yourselves are to put off all these: anger, wrath, malice, blasphemy, filthy language out of your mouth. ⁹ Do not lie to one another, since you have put off the old man with his deeds, ¹⁰ and have put on the new man who is renewed in knowledge according to the image of Him, who created him.

Just because our culture has accepted many of these things as normal behavior doesn't mean they are right. To live godly lives, we must adjust to the standard we see emerging from the Bible. We are not to copy the behavior and customs of the world. Our new identity is born in the image of Christ, not according to worldly standards.

Our parents, educators, friends, the media, and myriads of others all had their part in the parade of sources that came forth in our formative years. These sources shaped many of our thoughts, opinions, and identities. But, as good as they may have been, if their views were not God's, then they were wrong.

Francis Frangipane writes, *"Many of our opinions about life are ours only because we know of no other way to think. Yet we protect and defend our ideas and justify our opinions as though they were born in the wombs of our own creativity."*[103]

Water Baptism Prepares Us for Our New Identity

A big part of our new identity comes from water baptism, which should be our first act of obedience following our decision to follow Christ. Christ commands it and prepares us to take on a new identity and die to the old.[104] In baptism, we identify with Jesus Christ and all He has accomplished for us.

An example or a type of how baptism brings us into our new identity can be seen when the nation of Israel journeyed from the land of Egypt

---

[102] 1 Corinthians 7:9, 1Corinthians 6:9-11
[103] "The Three Battlegrounds" by Francis Frangipane
[104] Matthew 28:18-20

to the Promised Land. In Egypt, their identity was tied up as enslaved people.

When they left Egypt, they were told to apply the lamb's blood to the doorposts of their homes.[105] As a result, they were saved from the wrath of God as the death angel went through the land and destroyed the firstborn of every creature and person. Their example is a type of our salvation and what the blood of the perfect Lamb without blemish—Jesus Christ—will do for us, which explains why Jesus is called our *Passover Lamb*.[106]

As the children of Israel left Egypt, they came up against the Red Sea—a type of water baptism. As they passed over on dry land, the Egyptians tried to follow and were drowned in the process. When the children of Israel came up on the other side, they were no longer in bondage to the Egyptians. God had wholly delivered and set them free from their past. In water baptism, God desires to do the same for us—to destroy our old nature and put us at liberty by delivering us from the slavery of our sins and the past.[107] As a result, we no longer identify with the past but with the new nature emerging from our crucifixion to the world.

Do you have faith to believe this? Faith is agreeing with God's Word.[108] When we agree with God's Word, He can work in our lives in extraordinary ways.[109] His power is mighty towards us who believe. Nothing is too difficult for Him![110] As we begin to identify with the new nature, God releases us from the bondages of the past. We are no longer slaves to sin. We are totally set free.

Water Baptism Breaks the Bondage of Sin in Our Lives

Our old identity was bound in bondage to our past, just as Israel was in bondage to the Egyptians. We see this very clearly as Peter begins to preach on the Day of Pentecost. He talks about how baptism is for the remission of sins.

Acts 2:38 Then Peter said to them, "Repent, and let everyone of you be baptized in the name of Jesus Christ for the remission of sins, and you shall receive the gift of the Holy Spirit.

The word *"remission"* here is a strong word that encompasses more than forgiveness. It means deliverance as well. The Greek word for

---

[105] Exodus 12:7
[106] 1 Corinthians 5:7
[107] Romans 6:6
[108] Romans 10:17
[109] Matthew 18:19-20
[110] Ephesians 1:19

remission is *"aphesis,"* which means freedom; to be pardoned or delivered, as well as being forgiven and set at liberty.

Jesus used this word when He said He came to proclaim liberty *(aphesis)* to the captives.[111] So, as we submit to God's plan in water baptism, He sets us free to take advantage of all that the new path represents. Otherwise, we are hindered from fully engaging in the race that is before us, as it says in the book of Hebrews.[112]

In Baptism, We Identify With Christ

Romans 6:3 Or do you not know that as many of us as were baptized into Christ Jesus were baptized into His death?

As we began to see, one of the most important things we must do is to change our identity. We can no longer identify with the world and all of its lusts and pride. Instead, we must identify with Christ and all He desires to do. As Romans chapter six shows, this process begins by identifying with Him in His death, resulting from baptism.

Our Old Nature Is Crucified With Him

Romans 6:4a,6 Therefore we were buried with Him through baptism into death, ⁶knowing this, that our old man was crucified with Him, that the body of sin might be done away with, that we should no longer be slaves of sin.

Romans 6:11 Likewise you also, reckon yourselves to be dead indeed to sin, but alive to God in Christ Jesus our Lord.

Notice that it says here, *"We are to reckon ourselves to be dead."* Our part is to agree with God's Word. We must believe that our old nature is dead. Keep in mind that the word *"believe"* is a verb or an action word. To believe involves adhering, trusting, and relying upon God's word to fully agree with what He desires to do in and through us.

Galatians 2:20 "I have been crucified with Christ; it is no longer I who live, but Christ lives in me; and the life which I now live in the flesh I live by faith in the Son of God, who loved me and gave Himself for me.

In Water Baptism, Our New Nature Comes Forth

As Christ rose from the dead and took on a new identity, so must we. Our new identity is now born in the image of Christ Himself. God's will and desire for us to embrace this beautiful new identity reflects all His wonderful attributes in Christ.

As it says in the book Philippians, *"Let this mind (or this attitude) be in you which was also in Christ Jesus."*[113]

---

[111] Luke 4:18 ...sent Me to heal the broken hearted, to proclaim **liberty** (aphesis) to the captives.
[112] Hebrews 12:1
[113] Philippians 2:5

Romans 6:4b says that just as Christ was raised from the dead by the glory of the Father, even so, we should also walk in newness of life.

Romans 6:5 For if we have been united together in the likeness of His death, certainly we also shall be in the likeness of His resurrection,

It has been said, *"When we are baptized into the name of the Father, it gives us the place of a child and all the privileges of a child, all the inheritance, and wealth of the child. We are baptized into the protection, care, and fellowship of the God of the universe as our Father. We take on all of what that union means. We have the standing of a son, the privilege of a son, and the responsibilities of a son. By that baptism, we become a joint heir with Jesus and an heir of God. When we are baptized into the name of the Holy Spirit, we are baptized into the name, wealth, power, wisdom, and glory of God's representative on earth. All that the Spirit has we are baptized into."*[114]

Everything mentioned in the above quote is part of our new identity in Christ as we purpose to put on the Lord Jesus Christ and make no provision for the flesh.[115]

Characteristics of our New Nature and Identity

Our new nature and identity are born out of the Holy Spirit's presence in our lives, which results in conformity to the image of Christ from glory to glory. The more we yield to His presence, the more we transform into His likeness. However, just because we have His presence doesn't automatically mean we experience transformation. We will always be able to quench His presence through our stubbornness and disobedience.[116] Paul said, *"I must die daily,"* which means our will is part of the process.[117]

Are we quenching His presence by not yielding to the transformation process that changes our identity? Only as we yield our vessels to the Holy Spirit's work can we experience the transformation process with our new identity taking over.

2 Corinthians 3:17-18 Now the Lord is the Spirit; and where the Spirit of the Lord is, there is liberty. 18 But we all, with unveiled face, beholding as in a mirror the glory of the Lord, are being transformed into the same image from glory to glory, just as by the Spirit of the Lord.

Humility is the Primary Element

Humility is the primary element in our walk that allows us to experience conformity to the image of Christ with the identity God intended for us to walk in. The problem is we all have unyielding egos

---

[114] Quote by E.W. Kenyon from his book, "In His Presence"
[115] Romans 13:14
[116] 1 Thessalonians 5:19
[117] 1 Corinthians 15:31

that work against what God has intended for us. Therefore, to fully take on the new nature and identity we are to have in Christ, we must first be willing to lose ourselves in Christ and die to our pride and ego.

The journey ahead demands we walk in a teachable spirit. Without a teachable spirit, we cannot see into invisible realms where God desires to take us. Instead, the path becomes blurred, putting us on a path of self-will, leading us around in circles just as the Israelites did for 40 years in the wilderness.

Every time we yield to Christ's desires, we are dying more to our old self and identity. We must be like Jesus, who gave up His reputation and emptied Himself by experiencing the cross's pain and humiliation. It takes a certain amount of pain and humiliation to die to our reputation, which is made up of self, ego, and the pride of life, which explains why Jesus said, *"If you want to follow me, you must take up your cross."*[118]

Paul reminds us in the book of Philippians that when we follow Christ, we are clothing ourselves with His attitudes.

Philippians 2:5-8 Let this mind (attitude – NASB) be in you which was also in Christ Jesus, ⁶ who, being in the form of God, did not consider it robbery to be equal with God, ⁷ but made Himself of no reputation, (but emptied Himself – NASB) taking the form of a bondservant, and coming in the likeness of men. ⁸ And being found in appearance as a man, He humbled Himself and became obedient to the point of death, even the death of the cross.

When we look at the beatitudes found in Matthew's gospel, we see humility is the foundation of all the attitudes and characteristics that are to be a part of our new nature and identity.[119] Being poor in spirit with an attitude of mourning over our sin is an attitude of humility. With humility in place, we can put on the nature and character of Christ.

As we become renewed in the spirit of our minds, we put on the new nature that is according to God in true righteousness and holiness. As a result, we put on tender mercies, kindness, meekness, long-suffering, and the other fruits of the Spirit with an attitude of forgiveness towards one another as the peace of God rules our hearts.[120]

Peter prayed that grace would multiply in our lives.[121] Unfortunately, many Christians fail to experience many aspects of God's grace. They're still trying to unlock the gate with the old key that no longer fits. As a result, they frustrate the grace of God and do not inherit the blessings that go along with it.

---

[118] Matthew 16:24
[119] Matthew 5:3-5
[120] Ephesians 4:24-32, Colossians 3:10-15
[121] 2 Peter 1:2

The multiplicity of God's grace comes through humility, the seedbed of our new identity. As we humble ourselves before God and others, we experience abundant grace for all God wants to do in and through us.[122]

Our old identity was based on our un-crucified abilities and confidence, while our new identity resulted from God's supernatural ability in our lives. Our natural God-given innate abilities are now dedicated to Christ and His purpose. We also have new spiritual skills from the supernatural seed imparted to us through the Holy Spirit and God's Word.

Our new identity includes God's divine nature as a natural outflow in our lives. This means we are enabled through God's grace to cope with whatever adversity, trial, or dilemma we may face in a godly manner and receive supernatural abilities to accomplish all that comes our way. As we are faithful to yield to God in the little things coming our way, He increases what He desires to pour into our lives.

Luke 16:10 He who is faithful in what is least is faithful also in much, and he who is unjust in what is least is unjust also in much.

God wants to open the path before us uniquely—a way that demands more and more grace poured into us for the challenges ahead. There is no limit to what He can do as we continually yield to the purposes He puts before us. Transformation into His likeness awaits us at each interval.

As you go about your day, expect God to work on your behalf in all you set your hands to do with an expectation of grace multiplied in you! Whether in the marketplace, a student, an employee at your workplace, or at your home raising children, expect God to pour His divine abilities into you.

You now have a new identity in Christ as a part of everything you do. Let it get ingrained in your heart, mind, and soul. You are a supernatural being with divine abilities. You can now do all things through Christ, who strengthens and equips you in every aspect of your journey.

2 Corinthians 5:17 Therefore, if anyone is in Christ, he is a new creation; old things have passed away; behold, all things have become new.

---

[122] Philippians 2:13

Navigational Resources Word and Spirit

Chapter Five

A false balance is an abomination to the LORD, but a just weight is His delight.
Proverbs 11:1 (KJV)

Try to imagine what it would be like to journey to an unfamiliar country without having some navigational resources as you travel. You would need maps, a compass, and a GPS device and want to know about the culture and people. You would need to know many things because most countries have differing laws, values, and customs. What works for you in your familiar surroundings may not work for you in unfamiliar surroundings.

As Christians, we were translated from the kingdom of darkness into the kingdom of the Son. We now travel as pilgrims in this world, but not of it. We are strangers.[123] Most of us spent a lot of time wandering around in Satan's domain—some succeeding by falling into his trickery and deceptive ways, while others got beat to a pulp because of their innocence and not knowing how to play by his rules. Nevertheless, we were shaped by his domain of darkness. Coming into God's kingdom, the smell of darkness and the wounds we incurred were still on us, which must now be dealt with as the light dispels the darkness within.

1 John 5:19 We know that we are of God, and the whole world lies under the sway of the wicked one.

In his commentary on this verse, Adam Clark refers to the world as being embraced in the arms of the devil, where it lies fast asleep and carnally secure, deriving its heat and power from that which Satan nourishes. He goes on to say the actions, tempers, propensities, opinions, and maxims of all worldly men prove and illustrate this. He then quotes John Wesley as saying, *"The horrible state of the world is painted in the liveliest colors; a comment on which we have in the actions,*

---

[123] Colossians 1:13

conversations, contracts, quarrels, and friendships of worldly men." He then concludes by saying, *"Their actions are opposed to the law of God in their deceit while their friendships are hollow, insincere, capricious, and fickle. As a result, they become instinct with Satan's own spirit because they are of their father the devil and therefore, his lusts they will do."*[124]

In the world, our senses are overloaded in every conceivable way. We are experiencing sensory overload! Satan is a master of his domain and knows how to entice us in every imaginable way. He bombards us daily through media, friends, conversations, and actions opposing the law of God.

How do we navigate this maze of propensities, opinions, and maxims that flow out of a world under Satan's sway?

As you can see, we need a guide to keep us on the straight and narrow as we attempt to follow the path that is ever before us.[125] We are warned in the Book of Romans to resist the squeeze of the world and not to conform to it—a challenge to us as we deal with sensory overload.[126]

You're now in the kingdom realm under the sway of the Lord Jesus Christ and must learn to get along and succeed in His domain. Thankfully, God gave us some valuable resources to help us find our way. We have the Holy Spirit and the Word of God as guides to help us. The beautiful thing about these two guides is they work together and are never in disagreement. Can you imagine going on an African Safari with two guides who constantly argue about the directions? Not so with God!

Try to imagine going on a safari without a guide. You would never make it. Along the way, there are too many dangers and pitfalls. Our world is a jungle in many ways as well. There are all kinds of dangers and pitfalls. Christians often get trapped, rendering them useless as they try to find their way. We have an enemy walking about as a roaring lion seeking whom he may devour.[127] Many lose their way before the journey barely begins because they are on a safari without availing themselves to the guides made available to them.

We serve a God who understands who we are and what is needed as we journey toward a city whose builder and maker is God.[128] Thankfully, God has given us resources to keep us from getting lost and to assure us of protection from the unforeseen dangers lurking about. The

---

[124] Adam Clarke's Commentary on 1 John 5:19 paraphrased.
[125] Matthew 7:13-14
[126] Romans 12:2
[127] 1Peter 5:8
[128] Hebrews 11:10

navigational tools needed for the journey are found in God's word and by having a relationship with the Holy Spirit.

Let's look at these directional resources God has made available to us through His Word and Spirit and how to use them. As we see in the following passages, God's word or the Bible is like a lamp unto our feet and a light unto our path.

Psalm 119:105 Your word is a lamp to my feet and a light to my path.

Psalm 119:133 Direct my steps by Your word and let no iniquity have dominion over me.

As the preceding Scriptures show, God desires to direct our steps according to His Word. We also discover in John's Gospel that the Holy Spirit is also our guide.

John 16:12-13 I still have many things to say to you, but you cannot bear them now. ¹³ However, when He, the Spirit of truth, has come, He will guide you into all truth; for He will not speak on His own authority, but whatever He hears He will speak; and He will tell you things to come.

We have excellent security with God because our two guides—the Word and the Spirit—are designed to work together. However, because God never imposes His will upon us and chooses to give us free will, we must ensure they are partnering.

When the Spirit's revelation enters our spirit, it is first pure and unadulterated. It then must pass through the doorways of our mind and be submitted to God's Word to remain pure. Without the purity of God's Word, His revelation is distilled through our un-sanctified thoughts and emotions and loses its purity. As a result, He cannot guide us as He would like to.

One of the most beautiful illustrations of the Word of God and the Holy Spirit partnering together to bring about God's purpose and direction was when the Day of Pentecost fully came, as recorded in Acts chapter two.

Pentecost Reveals How the Word and Spirit Partner Together

Pentecost was the day Jesus had told His disciples about before His ascension into the heavens. Jesus told them to wait in Jerusalem until they received the power of the Holy Spirit. As they waited with expectation, the Holy Spirit came like a mighty rushing wind with tongues of fire. They were all baptized or immersed in the Holy Spirit, just as Jesus prophesied.[129]

---

[129] Acts 10:44-46, 11:15-16

As they were experiencing this incredible outpouring of the Holy Spirit, they were all perplexed. People around them who saw and heard this happening thought they were drunk and began mocking them.

Acts 2:1-13 When the Day of Pentecost had fully come, they were all with one accord in one place. ² And suddenly there came a sound from heaven, as of a rushing mighty wind, and it filled the whole house where they were sitting. ³ Then there appeared to them divided tongues, as of fire, and one sat upon each of them. ⁴ And they were all filled with the Holy Spirit and began to speak with other tongues, as the Spirit gave them utterance. ⁵ And there were dwelling in Jerusalem Jews, devout men, from every nation under heaven. ⁶ And when this sound occurred, the multitude came together and were confused, because everyone heard them speak in his own language. ⁷ Then they were all amazed and marveled, saying to one another, "Look, are not all these who speak Galileans? ⁸ And how is it that we hear, each in our own language in which we were born? ⁹Parthians and Medes and Elamites, those dwelling in Mesopotamia, Judea and Cappadocia, Pontus and Asia, ¹⁰Phrygia and Pamphylia, Egypt and the parts of Libya adjoining Cyrene, visitors from Rome, both Jews, and proselytes, ¹¹Cretans, and Arabs—we hear them speaking in our tongues the wonderful works of God." ¹² So they were all amazed and perplexed, saying to one another, "Whatever could this mean?" ¹³ Other mocking said, "They are full of new wine."

The Scenario of What Took Place on This Historic Day:
- People from all nations were present and heard them speaking in their own languages – *Verse 5.*
- They were all confused – (mass confusion) – *Verse 6.*
- They were all amazed and marveled – *Verse 6.*
- They were perplexed – *Verse 12.*
- Others mocked – *Verse 13.*

At this juncture, the Word of God had not yet entered the context of what was happening. The disciples were all naturally excited and amazed at what happened but confused, bewildered, and unsure of what to do with it. Peter then begins to preach and quote Scripture from the Book of Joel. He used the Word of God to bring definition and purpose to what was happening. Now filled with the Holy Spirit and the Word of God, Peter allows the Word and Spirit to partner together to bring forth God's purpose in this situation.

Acts 2:14-16 But Peter, standing up with the eleven, raised his voice and said to them, "Men of Judea and all who dwell in Jerusalem, let this be known to you, and heed my words. ¹⁵ For these are not drunk, as you suppose since it is only the third hour of the day. ¹⁶But this is what was spoken by the prophet Joel:

As Peter speaks with confidence and assurance, he begins to discern the prophetic purpose concerning this situation from the Word of God.

Acts 2:29-33 "Men and brethren, let me speak freely to you of the patriarch David, that he is both dead and buried, and his tomb is with us to this day. ³⁰Therefore, being a prophet, and knowing that God had sworn with an oath to him that of the fruit of his body, according to the flesh, He would raise up the Christ to sit on his throne, ³¹he, foreseeing this, spoke concerning the resurrection of the Christ, that His soul was not left in Hades, nor did His flesh see corruption. ³² This Jesus God has raised up, of which we are all witnesses. ³³ Therefore being exalted to the right hand of God, and having received from the Father the promise of the Holy Spirit, He poured out this which you now see and hear.

The Results of the Word Partnering with the Spirit

The results of Peter introducing the Word of God into the scenario are seen in the following verses.

- The conviction of the Holy Spirit was released – *Vs.37.*
- Repentance, deliverance, and the call and promise for everyone to be a partaker came forth – *Vs. 38-39.*
- A harvest of over 3000 souls was added to the Church – *Vs. 41.*
- They all continued steadfastly in the apostles' doctrine and fellowship – *Vs. 42.*
- They entered into an atmosphere of community with a commitment to body life in Christ – *Vs. 44.*
- Total Commitment – They sold out to the Lord – *Vs. 45.*
- They continued in one accord, praising God and having favor with the people – *Vss. 46-47.*
- The Church was launched into its destiny, as were the individual members.

Imagine what would've occurred had God's word not been introduced. The purpose of God wouldn't have come forth. It would have been a spiritual playground. This unusual experience in the Holy Spirit would have produced nothing but confusion, fear, bewilderment, and mocking. It would've been a broken cistern that couldn't contain the outpouring of the Spirit—something God considers evil.[130] Instead, it took the Spirit and Word to partner to produce God's glory.

Unfortunately, this is happening in many quarters of Charismatic Christianity today, as various movements of the Spirit move across the

---

[130] Jeremiah 2:13

Christian landscape. As a result, the Lord is not glorified because the Word is not brought forth as a balancing factor. As a result, many get left in the wake of confusion and misunderstanding about God's intended purpose.

The Word of God is living, powerful, and able to discern God's intended purpose, just as it did on the Day of Pentecost.

Hebrews 4:12 For the word of God is living and powerful, and sharper than any two-edged sword, piercing even to the division of soul and spirit, and of joints and marrow, and is a discerner of the thoughts and intents of the heart.

On the other hand, what would have taken place if it had been only the Word without the experience of the Holy Spirit? They would have been locked into a dry, empty experience void of life and vitality, which also happens to God's people in today's Christianity. Remember what Jesus said, *"God is a Spirit: and **they that worship Him must worship Him in spirit and truth**."*[131]

The following passage correctly describes what happens when the Word and Spirit are not partnering together and what the result is when they do.

Proverbs 11:1 (KJV) A false balance is an abomination to the LORD: but a just weight is his delight.

The Word of God—A Lamp unto Our Feet

Let's look at how the Word of God is a lamp unto our feet and how God's Word is to affect our lives. First, it's important to understand that God's Word always precedes the Spirit's input into our lives. Our experience with the Holy Spirit is subjective in that whatever we receive from Him must be distilled through our imperfect minds, wills, and emotions.

Peter, James, and John had an enlightening experience with Jesus on the Mount. Moses and Elijah appeared, and they heard God speak from Heaven. Peter writes about this experience in one of his epistles and says, as marvelous an experience as it was, the Word of God is a more sure word of prophecy. Experiences fade over time, but God's Word never fades.

*2 Peter 1:18-19 (KJV) And this voice which came from heaven we heard, when we were with him in the holy mount. [19] **We also have a more sure word of prophecy**; whereunto ye do well that ye take heed, as unto a light that shineth in a dark place, until the day dawn, and the day dawn, and the day star arise in your hearts.*

---

[131] John 4:24

The following Scriptures show the purity of God's Word:

Psalm 119:140 Your word is very pure; therefore Your servant loves it.
Psalm 12:6 The words of the Lord are pure words, like silver, tried in a furnace of earth, purified seven times.
Proverbs 30:5 Every word of God is pure; He is a shield to those who put their trust in Him.
2 Timothy 3:16-17 All Scripture is given by inspiration of God, and is profitable for doctrine, for reproof, for correction, for instruction in righteousness, ^{17} that the man of God may be complete, thoroughly equipped for every good work.
Ephesians 5:26 that He might sanctify and cleanse her with the washing of water by the word,

Unfortunately, many Christians are Bible illiterate and have not discovered what the Bible says concerning their lives. They may hear sermons regularly, but that's not enough. Their journey is based more on subjective experiences with the Holy Spirit rather than the purity of God's Word that continually washes over them and gives them the added direction they need. Spiritual experiences without the aid of the Word of God partnering together with the Holy Spirit will only lead to deception and wandering in the wilderness and vice versa.

As we have seen, God's word is a lamp unto our feet and a light unto our path. How should this happen as a believer in Christ trying to find your way through the maze of ungodliness and deceit the enemy of your faith continually throws at you?

How is God's Word a Lamp unto our Path?

What does it take for God's Word to become a lamp unto us in such a way that it begins to direct our paths more adequately unto Him so we move in the direction that He has for our lives?

First, we must read His Word and get acquainted with it daily. We need to have a hunger and thirst for it.

As a young Christian, I would spend hours reading and studying God's Word. I was mesmerized by it. I had just come from the hippie culture, burned out from all the drugs I had been using during those years. I had lost touch with reality. Jesus and His Word became my new reality, and I immersed myself in them. As a result, I fell in love with God's word. One of the first prophecies I received as a young Christian was that my love for God's Word would bring me into intimacy with Him. To this day, my passion for His Word leads me to intimacy and sets my spirit on fire.

To get to know Jesus, you must know the Word of God. If you desire to love Jesus, you must love His Word. The first chapter of John's gospel says it very clearly. Jesus and the Word are the same: *"The Word became flesh."*

John 1:1 In the beginning was the Word, and the Word was with God, and the Word was God.

John 1:14 And the Word became flesh and dwelt among us, and we beheld His glory, the glory as the only begotten of the Father, full of grace and truth.

Jesus was a living epistle because He had spent so much time understanding who He was and His purpose through reading the Scriptures.

When Jesus came to earth, born of a virgin, He gave up His right to act as God even though He never ceased being God. He made Himself of no reputation by taking the form of a bondservant and coming in the likeness of man.[132] When Jesus walked on earth, He was not all-knowing with all wisdom. He depended upon the Holy Spirit to reveal the wisdom and knowledge of God just as we must. At the age of twelve, He was still growing in wisdom.[133] All who heard Him were astonished at His understanding.[134] Through God's Word, He began to discover who He was at a very early age. The Word of God was a lamp unto His feet, just as it must be for us.

Jesus immersed Himself in the Scriptures and was very familiar with them. We must do the same if we want the Word of God to be a lamp unto our feet and give us the direction and guidance we need.

Where Do We Start?—Reading & Meditating

Many reading plans are available to us in today's Christianity, which are beneficial. However, an excellent place to begin is with the Gospels and getting to know who Jesus is, especially the Gospel of John. If you do not understand the Bible, it's better to spend time in the New Testament, Psalms, and Proverbs before tackling the Old Testament.

To immerse ourselves in God's Word, we must read and meditate on it. Again, we see this in Joshua's life. When he was getting ready to lead the children of Israel into the Promised Land, Moses charged him to meditate on God's Word. By immersing himself in meditation, he would prosper and succeed.[135]

King David said something very similar. He said those who meditate on the Word would continually bear fruit and prosper.[136]

---

[132] Philippians 2:5-8
[133] Luke 2:52
[134] Luke 2:42-52
[135] Joshua 1:8
[136] Psalm 1:1-3

How is meditating in God's Word different than reading it? To meditate involves inviting the Holy Spirit to speak as we ponder what we are learning and how it affects our lives. By pondering, we fellowship with the Word and Spirit at the same time. By inviting the Holy Spirit to speak as we read, we allow them to partner in bringing us into the Promised Land for our lives. When we ponder the path of our feet, we will succeed in whatever we are doing.[137]

There may be times during your regular devotional time when a particular Scripture jumps out at you. When this happens, it's a divine Selah—a time to pause and reflect—to ask the Holy Spirit what He's trying to show you. Take the time to focus and meditate on the Scripture and what the Lord reveals to you. Then, once He shows you, note it so you won't forget. If you habitually do this—entering it into your journal—you will most likely see a thought pattern of where the Holy Spirit is leading you. Making this a habit allows the Word and Spirit to partner as they lead you into truth and God's path.

Bible Study

Bible study is another way to understand God and His Word better. As a Bible-believing Christian, you must know why you believe what you believe. It is imperative. It gives you an authority in God's Word. It's not enough to believe something because you heard it in a sermon or shared by someone you respected. We all have a responsibility to search the Scriptures for ourselves.

I tell my students: "Don't believe it just because I said it. Study it for yourselves so that you own the truth." It's essential to own the truth. The apostle Paul affirmed this principle when he said the Bereans were more fair-minded than the Thessalonians because they searched the Scriptures daily to determine whether his words were true.[138] He also exhorted us to study to divide the truth rightly.

2 Timothy 2:15 Be diligent to present yourself approved to God, a worker who does not need to be ashamed, rightly dividing the word of truth.

When we have a firm grasp of God's Word, especially in the foundational truths and principles, our senses are exercised to discern good and evil. The writer of the Book of Hebrews refers to those who are unskilled in the Word as babes in Christ who are still in need of solid food.

Hebrews 5:12-14 For though by this time you ought to be teachers, you need someone to teach you again the first principles of the oracles of God; and you have come to need milk and not solid food. [13] For everyone who partakes only of milk is

---

[137] Proverbs 4:26
[138] Acts 17:10-11

unskilled in the word of righteousness, for he is a babe. ¹⁴ But solid food belongs to those who are of full age, that is, those who by reason of use have their senses exercised to discern both good and evil.

If it's true that today's Christians are often Bible illiterate, as I suspect, we have a problem. That's why we have churches full of babes in Christ lost in spiritual playgrounds that are nothing more than spiritual nurseries in which they can participate. A good Bible-believing church should preach and teach the whole counsel of God. If you want to be successful in your walk with the Lord, you need to be involved in a Bible-believing church that preaches and teaches the whole counsel of God.

Part of the problem in Bible illiteracy is with leaders who are more concerned about sustaining a church growth that looks good on the outward but only serves to feed the rampant consumerism mentality in today's world. But, on the other hand, Paul was conscientious about preaching and teaching the whole counsel of God, as we see in the following Scripture:

Acts 20:26-29 Therefore, I testify to you this day that I am innocent of the blood of all men. ²⁷ For I have not shunned to declare to you the whole counsel of God. ²⁸ Therefore take heed to yourselves and to all the flock, among which the Holy Spirit has made you overseers, to shepherd the church of God which He purchased with His own blood.

The book of Hebrews points out the elementary principles of Christ and how we must establish these truths in our lives before we can go on to maturity. But first, a proper foundation needs to come forth. The foundational principles listed in Hebrews 6:1-2 are repentance from dead works, faith towards God, the doctrine of baptisms, laying on of hands, the resurrection of the dead, and eternal judgment.[139] Then, speaking of going on to maturity or perfection, verse three says, *"And this we will do if God permits."*

In other words, God has to issue you a "building permit" before you can go on to maturity. Obviously, we can continue building something in our works, but it would be wood, hay, straw, or dead works. So, even though saved, our works are burned.

1 Corinthians 3:11-15 For no other foundation can anyone lay than that which is laid, which is Jesus Christ. ¹² Now if anyone builds on this foundation with gold, silver, precious stones, wood, hay, straw, ¹³ each one's work will become clear; for the Day will declare it because it will be revealed by fire; and the fire will test each one's work, of what sort it is. ¹⁴ If anyone's work which he has built on it endures,

---

[139] Workbooks with all of these Bible study subjects and more can be found at: http://kenbirks.com/perspectives-both/

he will receive a reward. ¹⁵ If anyone's work is burned, he will suffer loss, but he himself will be saved, yet so as through fire.

To fulfill your destiny and purpose in God, you must have the foundational truths established in your life. Therefore, it is also essential that you learn to endure sound doctrine. But unfortunately, one of the characteristics of our times is that people will not be able to endure sound doctrine but will give themselves to false teachers with itching ears.

As you are faithful to give yourself to Bible study, you will be complete and thoroughly equipped for every good work with the Word of God. You will have the discernment needed to prove and test everything while holding fast to what is good. Your senses will be exercised to discern the difference between right and wrong and to know the authentic voice of the Holy Spirit vs. the many other voices that are clamoring for your attention.

1 Thessalonians 5:21-22 Test all things; hold fast what is good. ²²Abstain from every form of evil.

God desires to direct our steps through the purity of His Word. As we adhere to the purity of His Word, He does this. Without the purity of God's Word alive and active in our lives, we won't discern what He is saying to us through the Holy Spirit. They must partner together.

The Holy Spirit's Role in the Process

We have seen how God's Word is to be a significant part of our navigational resources. Let's look at the Holy Spirit's role in the process. As the Church and the early disciples exploded into ministry and purpose due to the outpouring of the Holy Spirit, the same can happen to us. The promise of the Holy Spirit is to as many as the Lord our God calls.[140] The exceeding greatness of His power is available to all who believe according to His mighty power.[141]

The early disciples experienced excellent guidance from the Holy Spirit as they went forth, infused by His power, proclaiming the Gospel. God desires to inspire our lives in the same way as we depend on the resources He has granted us through His Word and Spirit.

Significant areas in our lives need guidance to balance the Holy Spirit's input and the Word to agree with each other. Wholeness and destiny are also essential areas, which I will discuss in later chapters. In this section, however, our purpose is to see how the Holy Spirit guides and directs our lives.

---

[140] Acts 2:39
[141] Ephesians 1:19

How the Holy Spirit Guides Us

The Holy Spirit speaks and guides us in many ways, such as dreams, visions, prophecy, the still small voice, our thoughts, intuition, spiritual impressions, circumstances, and even with an audible voice at times. These are all subjective experiences because they distill through our carnal minds. The ability to accurately discern dreams, visions, prophecies, etc., comes when we bring every thought into the captivity of the obedience of Christ and His Word. [142]

Guidance through Dreams and Visions

When Peter began to preach on the Day of Pentecost, he quoted the prophetic passage of Scripture from the prophet Joel, who spoke of dreams and visions.

Joel 2:28 "And it shall come to pass afterward that I will pour out My Spirit on all flesh; Your sons and your daughters shall prophesy, Your old men shall dream dreams, Your young men shall see visions.

This passage implies that dreams and visions will be a common occurrence in the life of believers during the era in which the Holy Spirit is to be poured out upon all flesh. Joel introduces this period, which began on the Day of Pentecost and continues until the Day of the Lord when Jesus returns at His Second Coming.[143]

God desires to fill all of us with the Holy Spirit, which includes an expectation of Him leading us in all we do. Peter mentions spiritual dreams and visions as a source of strength and guidance as we navigate our way through the corruption of the world. Jesus left us with the following promise concerning being led by the Spirit.

John 16:12-13 "I still have many things to say to you, but you cannot bear them now. However, when He, the Spirit of truth, has come, He will guide you into all truth; for He will not speak on His own authority, but whatever He hears He will speak; and He will tell you things to come."

One of the ways He tells us things to come is through visions and dreams. The Bible shows that men and women had dreams and visions of what was to come. Joseph, in particular, had dreams that were a source of encouragement and guidance as he came into the fulfillment of all that God had purposed for his life.[144] Moses had the vision of the burning bush.[145] Daniel had many dreams that revealed things that would occur at the age's end.[146] The apostle Paul spoke of being caught up to the third

---

[142] 1 Corinthians 13:12, 2Corinthians 10:5
[143] 1 Corinthians 1:7
[144] Genesis 37:1-11
[145] Exodus 3:1-4
[146] Daniel 7-9

heaven and heard inexpressible words—a vision that launched him into his ministry to the Gentiles.[147] As Steven, one of the seven deacons, was being martyred, he had a vision of the heavens opening with Jesus standing at the right hand of God.[148] John, the revelator, also had a vision of the Lord Jesus appearing and showing him what would take place at the end of the age.[149]

The above examples are of people who were very committed to God's intended purposes on earth. The more faithful we are to what God is doing by seeking the kingdom first, the more we can expect to have visions and dreams. They solidify our calling and purpose and move God's plans and purposes forward. God always moves with purpose, as seen in the above examples. When He gave these individuals a vision or a dream, it was a part of His overall purpose for humanity.

A good example is Cornelius's story and Peter's vision while in Joppa. Cornelius was a Gentile man who feared God but was not yet a Christian who had heard about Jesus. God, in his mercy, gave him the vision to send for Peter, who was in Joppa.[150] As the men sent to get Peter were on their journey, Peter received a vision from the Lord about eating common or unclean things the Jews were not allowed to eat according to the Law of Moses. God was about to bring the Gentiles into the Church for the first time by giving these two men visions with very explicit instructions as to how this would take place. In the vision, Peter was told to arise and go with them.[151]

Another example is when Paul and Silas ministered to the churches that Paul and Barnabas had planted on their first missionary journey. The Holy Spirit forbade them from preaching the word in Asia as they went through the Galatia region. Instead, they received a vision from the Lord to come over to Macedonia.[152] As a result, God launched the Church in those parts of the world. The Word of the Lord grew mightily and prevailed as they preached and taught in those regions.

As I think back over my life, there were a few occasions in which I received a vision and several dreams. They have proven pivotal while guided by the Holy Spirit into my destiny and purpose.

The only vision I ever had changed the course of my life and woke me up to the spiritual reality I now walk in. It was while serving in the Army in Vietnam during a time in which I had become heavily involved

---

[147] 2 Corinthians 12:2-4
[148] Acts 7:55-57
[149] Revelation 1:9-11
[150] Acts 10:1-8
[151] Acts 10:9-22
[152] Acts 16:6-10

in drugs, including marijuana, LSD, and even heroin. I had to go to the dispensary one day to get a shot of penicillin and went into violent convulsions while experiencing a significant flashback from LSD. All the drugs I was using then must have reacted to the penicillin. It was during a time when I had just started using heroin and had been for a couple of weeks.

Later in the evening of that same day, I felt I was going to go through convulsions again and became frightened. The orderly clerk drove me back to the dispensary to get something to calm me down. On the way, I began to pray and ask God to help me. I was afraid I was going to die. While lying in my bunk much later, I was still terrified I would die. So, I, once again, began to pray. As I was praying, I had a vision from the Lord. I saw my whole life flash before my eyes while God showed me the details of my life from my earliest memories—awakening memories I didn't even know existed. He showed me how He had been with me at every critical stage of my life and directed me to where I was. He then took me into the future and indelibly stamped His calling on me. It had a profound effect on me.

I spent the next three years or so trying to fit the vision into everything except what God had intended for it to accomplish in my life. No matter how hard I tried, I couldn't shake it. Ultimately, I finally surrendered to God and Jesus Christ and have walked in all He showed me ever since.

Over the years, I have had a few spiritual dreams that have been instrumental at pivotal times in my life. The dreams helped confirm what God was doing in my life or gave explicit direction concerning my destiny and purpose.

One of the most crucial dreams I have ever experienced was during the mid-70s while living in Anchorage, Alaska. I was attending a large church that had a two-year Bible College. It was a church responsible for sending out church planting teams throughout the United States, Mexico, the Philippines, and other places worldwide. During 15 years, they sent out close to 100 church planting teams. I sensed that God was leading me to be a part of one of these teams, but I wasn't quite sure. I had already completed the two-year program, had graduated, and was trying to determine my next life phase. While working at a warehouse, I was involved in outreach ministry, ministering in the local jail, rescue missions, and street evangelism.

It was during this season that I had a dream. In the dream, I was driving a forklift, placing a pallet of toys on top of this mezzanine, where it was stored until needed. *(This was one of the jobs that I did in the warehouse.)* The pallet came loose and spilled 15 feet or so below. As the pallet came crashing down, the toys were spread all over, injuring a couple of workers standing around. The Lord quickly revealed to me the interpretation of the dream. I felt a distinct impression that I was supposed to leave and join the newly established church planting team in Chico, California. I sensed that if I didn't respond, there would be accidents. The dream was the sign that I needed to step out in faith into the ministry God was calling me to—another defining moment.

I had made a trip to Chico about six months before gaining a feel for the place and seeing if it would be where the Lord was leading me. The dream resulted in me deciding to discuss it with those who were over me in the Lord. Our church believed in the five-fold ministry taught in Ephesians 4:11 and had apostles, prophets, and pastors on staff. The first person I went to see was the senior leader, who was an apostle. I told him about the dream and how the Lord had been putting it on my heart to join the team in Chico.

He felt good about it and said, "You should go and share with Tom Edmondson and see what he thinks."

Tom was the resident prophet on staff. I shared the dream's details with him and what I thought the interpretation was. He fully agreed and gave me the green light. I then shared with another pastor and my Bible School career counselor. They all agreed and decided to have an official sending-out service, at which time I would share my testimony with the congregation, have the elders lay hands on me, and send me forth with their blessing. Within a few weeks, I was on my way to Chico to join the team. As it turned out, this was an intense kairos moment in the journey toward my destiny and purpose in God.

The Audible Voice of God

Sometimes, God speaks through an audible voice, but they are very few and far between. I can think of at least three instances in the New Testament. First, at the baptism of Jesus, God spoke from heaven that He was well pleased with His Son, Jesus.[153] Another instance was when Jesus allowed Peter, James, and John to accompany Him to the Mount of Transfiguration, where Moses and Elijah appeared. The voice of God from heaven spoke once again, saying He was well pleased with His Son.[154] Another example is when Saul (later named Paul) was on the road to Damascus to persecute the saints when a light suddenly shone around him from heaven.

---

[153] Matthew 3:17
[154] John 17:5

Jesus spoke to him audibly and said, *"Saul, why are you persecuting Me?"*[155]

In Saul's case, the audible voice was used to get his attention and change the course of his life. It was a primary source of direction for his life.

I have heard the Lord's audible voice only on one occasion. It was audible to my spirit but not to anyone around me. It was while I was living in Anchorage, Alaska, as a young Bible School student. I was riding my bicycle one day on one of the many bicycle trails throughout the city when I heard the Lord yell out my name.

He said, "Kenny!" *(That's what my family members always called me.)*

He then said, "What about him?"

He drew my attention to a drunk passed out, with his bottle next to him, in the park I was riding through.

Following that incident, within the next few weeks, I found myself teaching a Bible Study every week at the local rescue mission, where many were in the same condition as the man I saw passed out in the park. Before that, I had spent my Saturday afternoons, for the last couple of years, ministering at the city jail in Anchorage with another individual as my outreach assignment from the Bible College I attended. As that season ended, I was seeking the Lord for another ministry. The experience with the audible voice was very instrumental in pointing me in the direction of the Rescue Mission.

The opportunity to teach the weekly Bible Studies for several months would be very beneficial in the days ahead. The church plant pastor I would join in Chico would eventually ask me to preach during the weekly Wednesday evening services. Had I not had that experience, I don't think I would have been sufficiently prepared to accept the task.

Because we serve a God who sees into the future, He can set up the experiences yet to be revealed for future purposes.

The Prophetic Word through the Gift of Prophecy

The Scripture in Joel that Peter quoted also mentioned that God's sons and daughters would prophesy when the Spirit was to be poured out on all flesh.[156] Prophecy is a vital aspect of being led by the Holy Spirit.

The importance of prophecy is strongly evident throughout the Old and New Testaments. Many prophets in the Old Testament were

---

[155] Acts 9:3-7
[156] Joel 2:28

instrumental in bringing directive and confirming words from the Lord at critical times in the history of Israel. After the Children of Israel arrived in the Promised Land because of Moses and Joshua, people like Deborah, Gideon, Samuel, Elijah, Elisha, and others were instrumental in guiding the nation of Israel to God's purposes. Samuel prophesied to David that he would be King one day. Prophets like Isaiah, Jeremiah, Ezekiel, and Daniel were major prophets who spoke to Israel's purposes during their day and futuristically concerning God's plans and purposes for all ages, including times right up until the second coming of Christ. As the following passage indicates, all God has done and will do will have been spoken through His prophets.

Amos 3:7 Surely the Lord God does nothing unless He reveals His secret to His servants, the prophets.

We live in the New Testament era under the New Covenant God has made with humanity through the blood atonement of Jesus Christ, which Isaiah the Prophet prophesied.[157] As we have already seen, the outpouring of the Holy Spirit that catapulted the New Testament Church into existence was foretold by the prophet Joel.

Throughout the New Testament, we see how the prophetic word comes forth under the New Covenant. The apostle Paul points out in the Book of Ephesians that prophets will be a part of God's plan until we come to the measure and stature of the fullness of Christ.[158] He also tells the Corinthian church that they're not to come short in any gift while waiting for the coming of Jesus Christ.[159] He then encourages them all to prophesy for believers' encouragement, edification, comfort, and exhortation.[160]

It's important to understand there are different levels of the prophetic gift in the New Testament. For example, in the Book of Romans, Paul exhorts the believers to prophesy in proportion to their degree of faith.[161] So we see in the New Testament that prophets and believers were used in the gift of prophecy.

Prophets are used very well in the gift of prophecy because of their diligence in allowing God to use them.[162] They exercise their senses, discerning good and evil, and are set in the body as ordained prophets by those who have observed their gift in operation. They are recognized as operating at a higher level of faith and accuracy in the prophetic gift. The

---

[157] Isaiah 53
[158] Ephesians 4:11-13
[159] 1 Corinthians 1:7
[160] 1 Corinthians 14:1-3, 31
[161] Romans 12:6
[162] Hebrews 5:14

prophet speaks, *"Thus says the Holy Spirit,"* in a more directive way with confidence. We see this in the instance of the prophet Agabus when he prophesied to Paul concerning what would happen to him when we went to Jerusalem.

Acts 21:10-11 And as we stayed many days, a certain prophet named Agabus came down from Judea. [11] When he had come to us, he took Paul's belt, bound his own hands and feet, and said, "Thus says the Holy Spirit, 'So shall the Jews at Jerusalem bind the man who owns this belt, and deliver him into the hands of the Gentiles.'"

Before the prophet Agabus came, other disciples spoke through the Spirit that he should not go up to Jerusalem.[163] They did not prophesy in the specific, directive terms as Agabus did. But, in their spirits, they sensed he shouldn't go because there would be trouble. It took the prophet to speak with authority about what would happen to him if he were to go.

Rather than being blindsided, the gift of prophecy from the above sources helped Paul prepare and respond appropriately to what would happen upon his return to Jerusalem.

Most people who operate in the gift of prophecy speak in the realm of edification, exhortation, and comfort to other believers rather than in a more directive manner.

1 Corinthians 14:3 But he who prophesies speaks edification and exhortation and comfort to men.

Paul encourages us in this same chapter that the gifts of the Spirit are to be done decently and in order. Operating according to our level of faith until our local elders have released us is all a part of allowing the gifts of the Spirit to come forth decently and orderly. None of us are a law unto ourselves but must be connected to the other body members and covered by local elders.

1 Corinthians 14:39-40 Therefore, brethren, desire earnestly to prophesy and do not forbid to speak with tongues. [40] Let all things be done decently and in order.

There has been confusion and abuse with this gift throughout the body of Christ because the Church has not followed the exhortation by Paul. This is especially true in our day and age with the advent of the internet. The internet is full of people prophesying. Who knows what kind of checks and balances they have in their lives?

In prophecy, God's desire towards us is that we would all press into the gift and allow it to work according to our levels of faith. Therefore, we must not despise prophecy but rather embrace and receive it for its extraordinary gift.[164] The gift of prophecy is designed to encourage and

---

[163] Acts 21:4
[164] 1 Thessalonians 5:20, 1 Corinthians 14:5

strengthen us in the faith. It often confirms what God is already doing and saying, which gives us the confidence and assurance that He has been speaking and directing our lives unto Him in a greater way. As a result, we begin to grow from faith to faith.[165] Paul told Timothy that it helps us to fight the good fight of faith. His exhortation to Timothy was to wage good warfare by the prophecies he had received.[166]

I have had quite a few prophecies given to me over the years. They have been very instrumental in the overall direction of my life. Some were kairos moments that solidified my calling and purpose, while others were merely encouraging words that added to my faith and helped keep me moving forward.

During my send-out service, I received prophecies. One, in particular, stood out, which was given to me by the prophet on staff. He said my time with the church planting team would be for a short season, intimating I wouldn't be there long. At the time, I just filed it away because, as far as I was concerned, I was going there fully committed. He said my season there was for training for what God was calling me to do.

As it turned out, within a few months, I was assigned to preach the Wednesday evening services. I did this every week for two and a half years. At the end of this time, our pastor and his family decided to move back to Anchorage and close the church doors. My wife and I decided to move to the Sacramento area, where another church existed, which had been sent from the church in Alaska several years prior.

An unfortunate situation happened after being with our new church for about three years, preaching on several occasions, and teaching in our Bible School. I was asked to take the role of Senior Pastor. The prophecy given to me by the prophet had come to pass and was now giving me the confidence and assurance I was where I was supposed to be. I could do as Paul had exhorted young Timothy—to wage good warfare by the prophecies given me.

A few months after I was set in as the Senior Pastor, we were visited by a proven prophet from New Zealand. Another pastor from our fellowship of churches, who had been mentoring me, suggested we invite this man for a time of ministry as he had been very effective in his church while ministering in the prophetic realm. Our church was still in a period of upheaval due to our pastor resigning and leaving me in charge. Even though our apostle had set me in, I had sensed I wasn't fully received as the new pastor yet.

---

[165] Romans 1:17
[166] 1 Timothy 1:18

When the prophet arrived, he requested no communication with me or anyone else in the body until he delivered the prophetic word to our church. On his first evening with us, he spoke a prophetic word to my wife and me. He spoke directly about our situation, affirming me in taking the new role as Senior Pastor, without having any prior knowledge whatsoever. The pastor mentoring me assured me he had not told him anything about our situation. As a result, I was confirmed in the church's eyes and was very well received from then on.

As you can see, prophecy can be a very encouraging source of faith as we move forward in God's calling and purpose.

Prophecy Can Be Confusing at Times

Prophecy can also be confusing because no one is perfect in the gift nor has complete faith as Jesus did.

Though some did not witness in my spirit, most prophecies I have received over the years have hit the mark. However, I had some in which part of the prophecy hit the mark while other portions were off. How do we respond when that happens?

1 Thessalonians tells us that we are not to despise prophecies but to test everything and hold fast to what is good.[167] The fact that we are to test prophecy indicates room for error. If I'm receiving a prophecy that doesn't witness to me, I won't act upon it. We shouldn't be blown away by the mistake, but instead, discard it and hold fast to the portion that witnessed to our spirit. It may also be that it is for a later time in your life. For instance, when I heard the word from the prophet that my time with the church planting team would be for a short season, I just filed it away. It was constructive and encouraged to me when it did come to pass, and it helped me to process what God was doing in my life during a time of transition.

Prophecy, for the most part, is designed to be more of an encouragement to our faith rather than directional. However, when confirmed, it can be directional by other sources from which we hear from God into our spirits. For instance, when Paul received the directive word from Agabus, it confirmed what he had already heard through the Spirit.

Prophecy can be very helpful as we move forward with the purpose and destiny that God has called us to as we experience authentic Christianity.

---

[167] 1 Thessalonians 5:20-21

The Primary Means of Navigation

Prophecy and visions are essential to us, but the reality is that they are not the primary means of navigation as we move forward on the path of life. Nevertheless, I have found them to be very instrumental at pivotal moments. They help establish our overall direction and purpose, but God prods us daily as we obey His Word and Spirit.

A significant passage of Proverbs says, *"The mind of man plans his ways, but the Lord directs his steps, as we commit our works to the Lord."* Notice the progression of thought in the Scriptures below.

Proverbs 16:1-3 The preparations of the heart belong to man, but the answer of the tongue is from the Lord. ²All the ways of a man are pure in his own eyes, but the Lord weighs the spirits. ³Commit your works to the Lord, and your thoughts will be established.

Proverbs 16:9 A man's heart plans his way, But the Lord directs his steps.

The principle in these verses is that as we are faithful to commit our lives and works to the Lord, He will be faithful to direct our steps. Proverbs 16 goes along with Proverbs 3:5-6, in which we are exhorted not to lean on our understanding.

Proverbs 3:5 Trust in the Lord with all your heart, and lean not on your own understanding; ⁶in all your ways acknowledge Him, and He shall direct your paths.

As we are faithful in committing our ways to the Lord, He will establish our thoughts, enabling Him to direct our steps. It's a total reliance on the Holy Spirit's expertise in our lives to be our guide. In the process, the Lord weighs our motives and convicts us if we have impure motives. Allowing the Lord to convict and challenge our motives keeps our thoughts pure so He can lead us in the direction He has charted out for our lives.

Have you ever wondered how people who prophesy can do it so effectively to the degree they are speaking into the window of your soul? It's as simple as committing their works to the Lord so that God can establish the thoughts coming forth and then trust they are really from God. Then, as they are faithful to speak with pure motives, there is a confirmation in their spirits that releases the prophetic flow. Impure motives such as envy and self-seeking will affect the prophetic word because the mouth speaks out of the abundance of the heart.

God uses this principle daily to direct us as we acknowledge Him in our ways. He does this through spiritual impressions, our intuition, and His still, small voice. We can hear God speaking to our spirits when we shut out all the other voices clamoring for our attention. I'm convinced He's always speaking in one form or another, but we are too busy to quiet our souls before Him.

God Never Speaks in an Anxious Way

It's important to understand God always speaks peaceably and gently, never with confusion or in an anxious way, as we see in the following passage.

James 3:17-18 But the wisdom that is from above is first pure, then peaceable, gentle, willing to yield, full of mercy and good fruits, without partiality and without hypocrisy. ^{18} Now, the fruit of righteousness is sown in peace by those who make peace.

God Never Speaks Contrary to His Word

It's also important to understand that God never speaks contrary to His Word. If we hear something contradictory to God's Word, then His Word takes precedence over what we may be hearing. Remember that none of us are perfect in our understanding, but we must always process what we hear through the purity of His Word.

As we adhere to the Word of God and the Holy Spirit by putting into practice what they say, we will discover more and more about what God has in store for us at each interval in the path ahead.

The bottom line is that God's Word and Spirit are designed to partner as they lead us along this path that holds the keys to our destiny and purpose in Him. As we take on the responsibility of ensuring the Word and Spirit are partnering, it keeps us on track as we pursue our destiny and purpose in God. As a result, we don't fall into deception or error.

Seven Essentials for the Journey

Chapter Six

As His divine power has given to us all things that pertain to life and godliness, through the knowledge of Him who called us by glory and virtue—2 Peter 1:3

As you have discovered by now, you're on the journey of a lifetime that requires you to avail yourself of all God has made available. As you navigate the maze formed by the world around you, you will find several essentials God has given us that are very helpful and necessary for our journey.

The Christian experience is a lifetime event that will take you through many twists and turns filled with joy and sorrows, heartaches and disappointments, trials and tribulations, victories and defeats, and moments of despair to moments of great jubilation. The longer we travel, the more we realize we must pick up a few things to prepare us for what's ahead. By acquiring the essentials along the way, we will make our journey more enjoyable and less stressful when we begin to experience some of the hardships and difficulties.

When the Israelites began encountering hardship in the wilderness on the way to the Promised Land, they began to murmur and complain. Their attitude was so bad they wanted to turn back. Fortunately, God didn't allow them to do so. Instead of giving into the same attitude they had, we can be equipped to continue to move forward despite difficulties.

As we pick up the essentials, our attitudes will change and be one of *counting it all joy* when we allow the perspective of *counting it all joy* to take root by joyfully acknowledging God in all our ways so that He can guide and direct us more perfectly through the process.[168] Jesus didn't promise the journey would be easy. He said, *"In the world, you will have tribulation, but be of good cheer; I have overcome the world."*[169]

---

[168] James 1:2-3, Proverbs 3:6
[169] John 16:33

The apostle Paul experienced many hardships along his journey. On one occasion, after he had been nearly stoned to death while traveling from city to city, he and Barnabas returned to those same cities, strengthening the disciples and encouraging them to continue in the faith.

He told them, *"We must go through many tribulations to enter the kingdom of God."*[170] In Paul's second epistle to Timothy, he wrote, *"You, therefore, must endure hardship as a good soldier of Jesus Christ."*[171]

God's desire is not for us to get caught off guard or blindsided when trying times come upon us but rather to be prepared and equipped as James, the Lord's brother, encouraged us.

James 1:2-3 My brethren, count it all joy when you fall into various trials ³knowing that the testing of your faith produces patience.

We all get blindsided sometimes, but it doesn't have to be as Peter wrote in his first epistle, *"If need be, you have been grieved by various trials."*[172] When he says, *"If need be,"* it depends on our attitude and how grieved we will be.

I recently read an article about the many mistakes tourists make when they visit New York City. The article had many helpful hints on making your stay more enjoyable by knowing a few essentials. The article had many tips, including how to ride subways, get around in a crowded city without a car, visit restaurants, and even walk down a busy sidewalk without getting New Yorkers annoyed with you.

By taking the time to read and study where our journey may be taking us and what the essentials are, we can eliminate many of the bumps and bruises along the way.

Just like many of the video games people play in which they must pick up tools and weapons to deal with the obstacles that come, we, too, must find the tools and other essentials needed for the journey ahead. In addition, they help prepare us for the unexpected and unforeseen events that come upon us as we move forward on a path with many surprising twists and turns.

Essential 1—Baptism of the Holy Spirit

Following the resurrection of Jesus and His ascension into the heavens, one of the first essentials Jesus urged His disciples to acquire was the baptism of the Holy Spirit. He told them to wait in Jerusalem

---

[170] Acts 14:19-21
[171] 2 Timothy 2:3
[172] 1 Peter 1:6

and not to go anywhere until they received it.[173] The disciples were on their journey for three and a half years before Jesus was crucified and put to death. After His resurrection, He made it clear that they would need the baptism of the Holy Spirit and the power that comes with it. It wasn't enough to be just born of the Spirit; they needed to be fully baptized or immersed into His Spirit.

Acts 1:8 But you shall receive power when the Holy Spirit has come upon you, and you shall be witnesses to Me in Jerusalem, and in all Judea and Samaria, and to the end of the earth."

As seen in the Book of Acts, the disciples of Jesus exploded in power after receiving the baptism of the Holy Spirit. They went everywhere, witnessing and preaching the gospel with signs following.

I realize there are differing schools of thought about the baptism of the Holy Spirit and how to receive it. However, I would encourage you to study it out with an open mind before you come to any firm convictions one way or the other.

When the disciples received the baptism of the Holy Spirit in Acts 2 and other places in the book of Acts, they received it with tongues as the initial evidence of having received it.[174] So also, when Paul taught on the use of tongues in 1 Corinthians chapters 12-14, it was assumed that just about everyone spoke in tongues.

Peter said, *"For the promise is to you and your children, and to all who are afar off, as many as the Lord our God will call."*[175]

Has God called you? Then this promise is for you.

When Peter went before the Jerusalem elders, he recounted the experience of the Gentiles receiving the baptism of the Holy Spirit for the first time. He identified the experience with the Gentiles and the one in Acts, where the first disciples received it as the baptism of the Holy Spirit, which John the Baptist spoke of at the baptism of Jesus.[176] In both experiences, speaking in tongues was the evidence they had received it.

The baptism of the Holy Spirit is designed to bring us into greater intimacy with the Holy Spirit as He guides us and disperses things from the heart of the Father into our spirits.[177] As a result, we receive the power and authority of Christ that continually gives us the ability to tackle life's challenging issues. God also imparts Divine and creative abilities as the gifts of the Spirit are released.

---

[173] Luke 24:49
[174] Acts 2:1-4, Acts 10:44, Acts 19:1-6
[175] Acts 2:39
[176] Acts 11:15-18
[177] 1 Corinthians 2:12-16

Just as Jude encouraged us to build up our faith by praying in the Holy Spirit, my prayer is that you would seek the Lord and ask Him to baptize you in the Holy Spirit. The baptism of the Holy Spirit is essential for your journey ahead.[178] God's promises will not be withheld from those who ask, seek, hunger, and thirst for the Holy Spirit.[179]

Essential 2—Prayer

Prayer is another important essential to our journey we must consider. Through prayer, we develop intimacy with the Father and discover His desire to bless us in every conceivable way. So much of His blessing comes from knowing how to pray.

In his book, The Discipline of Grace, Jerry Bridges says, *"When we pray to God for His blessing, He does not examine our performance to see if we are worthy. Rather, He looks to see if we are trusting in the merit of His Son as our only hope for securing His blessing."*

Trusting in the merit of Christ must be continually maintained throughout our journey as we bring our petitions before God. Through prayer, we depend upon the working of the Holy Spirit. As we wait on God, He gives us the grace, encouragement, and strength to continue the journey. The prophet Isaiah says *those who wait upon the Lord shall renew their strength; They shall mount up with wings like eagles. They shall run and not be weary, walk, and not faint.*[180]

The life of Jesus portrays how He continually went to the Father in prayer and supplication. During His seasons in prayer, He found the wisdom and direction He needed for his decisions. He was dependent upon the Father to show Him what to do.[181]

There are many examples of how important prayer was to Jesus. One example is when Jesus called His disciples to Him after spending all night in prayer. He then chose His twelve apostles.[182] Another example is the healing of Peter's mother-in-law and having the whole city gather at His door while healing many sick and casting out many demons. Following this extraordinary time of ministry, He rose very early the following day to find a place of seclusion where He could be alone with His Father. His disciples, wondering where He had disappeared, sought Him out and found Him in prayer. They wanted Him to return and continue ministering to the people because they were all waiting for Him.

---

[178] Jude 1:20
[179] Luke 11:9-13, John 7:37-39
[180] Isaiah 40:31
[181] John 5:30
[182] Luke 6:12-13

He replied, *"Let us go into the next towns that I may preach there also because, for this purpose, I have come forth."*

Just as Jesus renewed His purpose and mission after spending time in prayer, so it is with us. So often, we go about our day without having our purpose renewed. As we spend time in the Word and pray daily, God repeatedly reminds us of our purpose and mission.

If Jesus, who was given the Spirit without measure, needed to have seasons alone with the Father, we would also need to wait upon Him for the instructions and help needed in our journey.

What is Prayer?

The Questions to consider are: what is prayer, and how can we fulfill the admonition to pray without ceasing and losing heart?[183] Numerous books have been written on prayer, giving us glimpses into true prayer. It would be impossible to cover every aspect of prayer in this short section. So, instead, I will try to provide you with a brief synopsis of what I believe prayer to be.

In short, prayer is as much about listening to God's voice as presenting our petitions to Him. In the life of Jesus, the preceding Scriptures show how His time in prayer included this aspect while waiting on the Father for specific instructions and ministry. Just as Jesus had these seasons of extended prayer, so should we as we wait on Him for the direction and wisdom we need for our pilgrimage.

E.W. Kenyon says, *"Prayer is believing in God and His Word while holding it before Him as a mirror with the words that come forth from our lips. As we look to God and His Word for His many promises, it is facing Him to meet our needs as we hold His promises before Him. It's coming boldly to His throne of grace and presence as one who stands in the righteousness of Jesus, expecting He to hear us. Prayer is intimacy and constant communion with the Father through Christ, which enables us to bask in His presence as He illuminates the Word in our minds."*[184] [185]

Prayer involves coming to God with the sacrifice of praise upon our lips.

Hebrews 13:15 Therefore by Him, let us continually offer the sacrifice of praise to God, that is, the fruit of our lips, giving thanks to His name.

When we come before God with a sacrifice of praise and thanksgiving, we come into His presence with our petitions, heartaches,

---

[183] 1 Thessalonians 5:17, Luke 18:1
[184] Paraphrased from "In His Presence" by EW Kenyon
[185] Hebrews 10:19-20, Hebrews 4:16, James 5:16

and burdens as He partakes in the fruit of our lips. Two hearts of love—ours and God's—are joined with a strong desire to give what the other desires.

Prayer is Intercession as well. We are all called to be intercessors to one degree or another. We should be interceding for the needs and concerns the Lord puts on our hearts. Intercession isn't necessarily the idea of coming to Him on our knees as we beg and cry, but instead, as sons or daughters coming boldly into the presence of our Father, who delights in granting us our requests as we make them known to Him.

Scripture encourages us to pray for our secular and spiritual leaders. Paul continually urged the believers to pray for him, one another, and other leaders ministering God's word. He also encouraged us to pray for our governmental leaders. In today's political climate, this is a challenge with the polarization of politics. Nevertheless, we are to pray for them whether we agree with them or not.

Another important aspect of prayer is that of praying according to the will of God, rather than praying for things we use to consume simply upon our lusts, as James the Lord's brother writes.

James 4:3 You ask and do not receive, because you ask amiss, that you may spend it on your pleasures.

When we pray in God's will, we are confident that God hears and gives to us according to our petitions.

1 John 5:14-15 Now this is the confidence that we have in Him, that if we ask anything according to His will, He hears us. [15] And if we know that He hears us, whatever we ask, we know that we have the petitions that we have asked of Him.

When praying in the Spirit by speaking in tongues, I pray according to God's will with greater clarity and purpose. As my heart becomes engaged even though my mind is unfruitful or I do not know what I am praying for, I sense what the Holy Spirit is praying through me in my spirit. I then begin to pray in English in agreement with Him. Praying in the Spirit encourages me to pray more fervently and builds my faith, as it says in Jude's epistle.[186] Who better to agree with than the Holy Spirit, who reveals the Father's will and heart to us?[187]

The disciples of Jesus were very curious about prayer as they observed Jesus in prayer and the results He received. Their curiosity led to asking Him to teach them how to pray. His response has been coined as *"The Lord's Prayer,"* found in Matthew and Luke's gospels.[188] He first exhorts them on what not to do and then goes into How to pray.

---

[186] Jude 1:20
[187] Matthew 18:19
[188] Matthew 7:5-15, Luke 11:1-8

Seven Essentials for the Journey

Matthew 6:9-13 "In this manner, therefore, pray: Our Father in heaven Hallowed be Your name, [10] Your kingdom come, Your will be done on earth as it is in heaven. [11] Give us this day our daily bread. [12] And forgive us our debts, as we forgive our debtors. [13] And do not lead us into temptation but deliver us from the evil one. For Yours is the kingdom and the power and the glory forever. Amen."

In this passage of Scripture, various aspects of prayer are seen. He starts with a prayer focused on who God is and our worship of Him. This kind of prayer can be contemplative or meditative—you concentrate on the various aspects of who God is, which I shared in Chapter One. It can also be declarative as you pray, as David did on many occasions—speaking out how great God is. As you make these faith declarations, you build your faith by being immersed in who God has declared Himself to be.

After encouraging His disciples to pray for God's kingdom to be established on earth, He led them into intercessory prayer. Keep in mind the prayer Jesus gives His disciples is a general outline for us to follow. As you pray for the kingdom of God to come to your friends, community, and life, it should be specific to your harvest field. He also reminds them that He's there to handle daily needs. Confession and asking forgiveness for our sins are also essential as we pray to overcome the temptations that come our way.

There you have it! I sincerely hope this section has encouraged and helped you and that you will take your seasons in prayer more thoughtfully as you engage in this essential to your faith.

Essentials 3, 4, & 5—Faith, Hope, and Love

Faith, hope, and love are three more keys to the Christian life. They are necessary to keep us on the course so that we do not lose sight of the path or get blown off course as we journey toward our final destination in Christ.

In Paul's first letter to the Corinthians, he speaks about our unperfected state on this journey. [189] Then, he compares our lives from what they are now to what they will be like when we see Jesus face to face at the Second Coming, as seen in the following Scripture.

1 Corinthians 13:8-10 Love never fails. But whether there are prophecies, they will fail; whether there are tongues, they will cease; whether there is knowledge, it will vanish away. [9] For we know in part, and we prophesy in part. [10] But when that which is perfect has come, that which is in part will be done away.

In the passage above, Paul mentions several things that are needed until we see Jesus face to face. He then gives three essential ingredients

---

[189] 1 John 3:2

in the passage below that are required in our lives right now—faith, hope, and love.

1 Corinthians 13:12-13 For now we see in a mirror, dimly, but then face to face. Now I know in part, but then I shall know just as I also am known. [13] And now abide faith, hope, love, these three; but the greatest of these is love.

The truth is, there are many potential dangers and pitfalls around us, all of which have the potential to cause us to detour from the path of life. We live in dangerous and evil times with many demonic and destructive forces trying to destroy our faith or detour us. Yet, as we remain in Him, we will continue to walk in faith, hope, and love. Faith, hope, and love are given to us so we can navigate our lives securely until that glorious day of seeing Jesus face to face.

According to the Book of Hebrews, faith is essential to our Christian walk: "*Without faith, it is impossible to please God.*"[190]

Faith is essential because as we catch glimpses of our final destination, we navigate the path of life by faith. We cannot see with our physical eyes where we are going in our spiritual quest for God. Faith goes as far as it can see; when it gets there, it will always be able to see farther.

When amid life's many perplexing dilemmas, faith grasps and seizes that which is ahead. It is the conviction of the reality we see in the invisible realm of all that we cannot see with our fleshly eyes. It is a firm belief in something for which there is no proof. When we respond in this kind of faith to whatever seems impossible or perplexing, it not only brings us to the fruitfulness God has intended but also prepares us for the next adventure with an added dimension as we grow from faith to faith. As a result, we are launched further into our destiny and purpose.

As a young Christian, in my quest to know God and His ways, I found the experience of growing from faith to faith exhilarating with a realization and its importance that continues today. As I responded in faith to where the Holy Spirit was leading me, I would have more motivation and understanding for the next phase of my journey. Growing from faith to faith has sustained me for over 40 years of walking with the Lord. As God continues to breathe into my spirit, I am continually excited about the future with an understanding that my best days are yet ahead. It consistently gives me hope for the future, an anchor to my soul amid all the turbulence of the world.

Hope is also a very important essential. Aside from the hope we have as we journey from faith to faith, there is hope based on God's great

---

[190] Hebrews 11:6

love toward us that helps us seize our eternal destiny in Him. It's an awe-inspiring hope of what we put our faith in—our eternal home in heaven and the Second Coming of Christ.

1 John 3:1-2 Behold what manner of love the Father has bestowed on us, that we should be called children of God! Therefore, the world does not know us because it did not know Him. ² Beloved, now we are children of God, and it has not yet been revealed what we shall be, but we know that when He is revealed, we shall be like Him, for we shall see Him as He is.

As we continue our pilgrimage toward the eternal home Jesus is preparing for us, the hope of our calling often keeps us moving forward despite the obstacles and dangers we may face. Jesus said He is preparing an eternal home and destination for each of us. He continually instills in us hope that is like an anchor to our souls amid the storms of life. We see this in the following Scriptures.

John 14:2-3 "In My Father's house are many mansions; if it were not so, I would have told you. I go to prepare a place for you. ³ "And if I go and prepare a place for you, I will come again and receive you to Myself; that where I am, there you may be also.

We live in a world that has created many turbulences and disorders for itself. The world is on a destructive course. As disciples of Jesus, we must be able to navigate this tide of unbelief, violence, wickedness, and corruption if we are to endure until the end. Knowing that Jesus is preparing an eternal home for us gives us the hope we need in a world that will disappear with the sands of time. We must hold fast to this confession of our hope without wavering.

Hebrews 10:23 Let us hold fast the confession of our hope without wavering, for He who promised is faithful.

When everything seems to be falling apart, hope keeps us steady with our feet firmly holding to the path. When the storms of life begin to rise against us, we throw out the anchor of hope until the storm begins to subside, as seen in the following Scripture.

Hebrews 6:18-19 that by two immutable things, in which it is impossible for God to lie, we might have strong consolation, who have fled for refuge to lay hold of the hope set before us. ¹⁹ This hope we have as an anchor of the soul, both sure and steadfast, and which enters the Presence behind the veil.

Love is included in the essentials because we need to know we are the apple of God's eye. We are loved and treasured by God, who desires to dwell with us intimately. We must understand that our heavenly Father takes great delight in us as His kids. We are the apple of His eye like our children are to us. We need to know we are all His favorite, in the same way the apostle John knew when he referred to himself as the one the

Lord loved.[191] John had a more profound revelation than the other apostles of God's great love towards Him through Jesus Christ. May the Holy Spirit reveal more profound revelations of how much the Father loves and adores us! Our prayer should be like David's when he said:

Psalm 17:7-8 (NIV) Show me the wonders of your great love, you who save by your right hand those who take refuge in you from their foes. ⁸Keep me as the apple of your eye; hide me in the shadow of your wings.

The Father desires to hide us in the shadow of His wings. Jesus expressed this thought as He looked over the people of Jerusalem and said, *"O Jerusalem, Jerusalem, the one who kills the prophets and stones those who are sent to her! How often I wanted to gather your children together, as a hen gathers her chicks under her wings, but you were not willing!"*[192]

The picture of Jesus wanting to gather us as a hen gathers her chicks is a beautiful image of the intimacy and warmth born out of the heart of God's love for us that He desires to engulf us in. Let's not be like those who were unwilling, but rather, let us come boldly to Him. He wants to smother us in His great love. Our prayer should be that of David's—*"to be hidden in the shadow of His wings."*

Love is the greatest of faith, hope, and love because it's the bond that holds everything together. Where would we be without the love of the Father? Where would we be without the love and support of our brothers and sisters around us?

Colossians 2:2 that their hearts may be encouraged being knit together in love, and attaining to all riches of the full assurance of understanding, to the knowledge of the mystery of God, both of the Father and of Christ,

Colossians 3:14 But above all these things put on love, which is the bond of perfection.

God's love springs from the fact that He loves us in our unlovable conditions. While we were still rebelling against Him, He sought us even though we were doing everything we could to hide from Him.

Romans 5:8 But God demonstrates His love toward us, in that while we were still sinners, Christ died for us.

The greatest act of love known to humanity was when God sent His beloved Son, Jesus Christ, to die for our sins so that we could experience the great love God the Father has for us.

John 3:16 For God so loved the world that He gave His only begotten Son, that whoever believes in Him should not perish but have everlasting life.

Luke 19:10 for the Son of Man has come to seek and to save that which was lost.

---

[191] John 21:20
[192] Matthew 23:37

We experience God's love in a myriad of ways. For example, how often has God spoken to your spirit and encouraged you? What about the times in which He answered your prayers in a way in which you knew it had to be God? What about times you were depressed about something? He was there to lift you in times of need. The list goes on. He continually watches over our lives with love and care as He hides us in the shadow of His wings.

We must be able to receive His love before we can adequately love Him in return. I would encourage you to list all the ways God has showered His love and mercy upon you and continue to note them as you travel through life. You may be surprised! Making a list helps you discover the width, length, depth, and height of God's great love toward you.

Our response to God's great love toward us is the "Great Commandment," which is the essence of discovering authentic Christianity. If we fail to get this right, we become nothing more than Christians making much noise without accomplishing much for the kingdom.

As the apostle Paul said, *"If we do not have love, we become sounding brass or clanging cymbals."* [193]

We are to love Him because He first loved us. How is it that God desires us to love Him? The Bible gives us plenty of instruction. The Great Commandment is an excellent place to begin.

Matthew 22:37-40 Jesus said to him, "'You shall love the Lord your God with all your heart, with all your soul, and with all your mind.' (and with all your strength— Mark 12:30) [38] This is the first and great commandment. [39] And the second is like it: 'You shall love your neighbor as yourself.' [40] On these two commandments hang all the Law and the Prophets." [194]

What does it mean to love the Lord our God with all our heart, soul, mind, and strength? Four areas are given here regarding how to show God our love. The Christian position is; *"You shall love the Lord your God with all your mind"*—the intellectual nature; *"with all your heart"*—the emotional life; *"with all your soul"*—the voluntary nature; and *"with all your strength"*—the physical nature. The whole person is to love God—mind, emotion, will, and strength.

When we love God with all our strength of mind, emotion, will, and physical strength, we will have a balanced and strong character, producing a genuine love for God and others as He desires.

---

[193] 1 Corinthians 13:1
[194] Mark's gospel also includes all your strength – Mark 12:29-31

Essential 6—Fruit of the Spirit

When we think about all that we need to pick up along the way, we cannot afford to miss the fruit of the Spirit, which keeps us from stumbling and helps us to hold firmly to the path.

2 Peter 1:5-8 But also for this very reason, giving all diligence, add to your faith virtue, to virtue knowledge, ⁶to knowledge self-control, to self-control perseverance, to perseverance godliness, ⁷ to godliness brotherly kindness, and to brotherly kindness love. ⁸ For if these things are yours and abound, you will be neither barren nor unfruitful in the knowledge of our Lord Jesus Christ.

The above passage mentions things we are to add diligently to our faith. These are character traits we must put some effort into if they are to become a part of our new nature. These attributes take root in our lives as we yield to God's Spirit. As we put on the new man created after Christ, it causes an agreement in the Spirit that allows God to clothe us with these excellent attributes. So, Paul said, *"To this end, I also labor, striving according to His working that works in me mightily."*[195]

For the Holy Spirit to work mightily on our behalf, we must be equally yoked to what He desires to do. Otherwise, we end up frustrating the grace of God, and He is unable to work on our behalf, which is why Paul said, *"To this end, I also labor."*

Have you ever been involved with another person on a project only to discover you must work equally together to complete the task? You were very zealous to get started and do an excellent job, but you soon realized the person appointed to work with you didn't care about the project nor pull their weight. As a result, you could not finish the project as a team with excellence. In the process, the only thing you accomplished was frustrating one another.

I think this often happens in the spiritual realm. In our laboring together with God, He desires to work mightily on our behalf while we are less than diligent and lack enthusiasm. As a result, we frustrate the grace of God, and the work He desires to do in us doesn't get done. [196] It's unfinished! Our lack of enthusiasm quenches or limits what He wants to do in and through our lives. To activate God's grace or supernatural ability, we must agree with Him by yielding wholeheartedly to His desires.

With this in mind, let's look at the attributes mentioned to understand why they are essential.

---

[195] Colossians 1:29
[196] Galatians 2:21 KJV I do not frustrate the grace of God: NKJV I do not set the grace of God aside.

- **Virtue** is voluntary obedience to truth and the strength that comes from straining, stretching, and extending.[197]
- **Knowledge** is understanding the truth of God's word applied to our lives. It follows virtue or willing obedience. When we obey His Word or Spirit, we receive further knowledge and understanding of His ways and purpose.
- **Self-control** is the ability to control your emotions and desires or their expression in your behavior, especially in difficult situations. Self-control requires instant obedience to the initial promptings of God's Spirit.
- **Perseverance** is a continued effort to do or achieve something despite difficulties, failure, or opposition: the action or condition or an instance of persevering: steadfastness.[198]
- **Godliness** is Christian character and much more. It involves pure devotion to God, which results in a life that is pleasing to Him.
- **Brotherly Kindness** is the quality of being friendly, generous, and considerate. It includes being thoughtful, compassionate, warmhearted, and unselfish towards others.

As Peter closes this section, he admonishes us to make our calling and election sure by diligently adding these fruitful characteristics to our lives. If we do, we assure ourselves we will never stumble nor lose our way but will be abundantly guaranteed and supplied an entrance into the everlasting kingdom. All this takes delighting in God, trusting in Him, and resting in Him as you allow these attributes to be worked out. We are to strain, stretch, and extend in doing so.

1 Peter 1:10-11 Therefore, brethren, be even more diligent to make your call and election sure, for if you do these things, you will never stumble; ¹¹for so an entrance will be supplied to you abundantly into the everlasting kingdom of our Lord and Savior Jesus Christ.

Essential 7—Practice of Giving

Another crucial ingredient to our faith is that of giving. Giving ourselves in every area of our lives, including our finances, continually prepares us for the unforeseen events that regularly come our way. As we are faithful to sow bountifully into the kingdom of God, we will also reap bountifully in our lives. As we do, God's grace continually abounds towards us so that we always have sufficiency in all things and an abundance for every good work.[199]

---

[197] Noah Webster's "Definition of Virtue"
[198] Merriam Webster Dictionary
[199] 2 Corinthians 9:6-8

Jesus said, *"Give, and it will be given to you: good measure, pressed down, shaken together, and running over will be put into your bosom. For with the same measure that you use, it will be measured back to you."*[200]

In Jesus' teaching on *The Parable of the Talents,* we discover how important giving is. One of the most necessary ingredients for establishing His kingdom rule and authority is bringing our finances under His Lordship.

In this parable in Matthew 25:14-30, we must ask ourselves, "What is Jesus talking about?" Is it how well we make financial investments or manage and use what He has given us for the glory of His Kingdom?

The Parable of the Talents teaches us the kingdom truth, "We are stewards—not owners." When we fully understand and commit to what this implies, we will experience a more significant measure of God's kingdom authority and power being released. As we welcome this truth wholeheartedly, Jesus becomes the Lord of our lives.[201]

We must see ourselves as caught in the struggle between God and Satan in the area of whose authority gets established in our lives. Satan is using the love of money to establish his rule in the hearts of humanity. God is using the kingdom truth of stewardship to instill His authority and power in our hearts. Both have to do with money because money reveals our heart's condition. When we practice good stewardship, money doesn't get a grip on our souls and causes us to become deceived in our relationship with the Lord.

The Bible tells us in the last days, men shall be lovers of money.[202] Jesus says, *"Do not lay up for yourselves treasures on earth, where moth and rust destroy and where thieves break in and steal; but lay up for yourselves treasures in heaven..."*

An example of this truth is found in the Book of Acts when the disciples gave up complete ownership of their lives, knowing that God's absolute rule and reign would bring them into a much richer blessing. This is because they understood the principle of stewardship.

Acts 4:32-33 Now the multitude of those who believed were of one heart and one soul; neither did anyone say that any of the things he possessed was his own, but they had all things in common. And with great power the apostles gave witness to the resurrection of Jesus. And great grace was upon them all.

God is looking for the heart-attitude of stewardship to be established in His people as we progress toward the culmination of all things. If we

---

[200] Luke 6:38
[201] Matthew 25:14-30 The Parable of the Talents
[202] 2 Timothy 3:1-2

want to see Him work in us as He did in this early church, we must empty ourselves of the ownership of all that we own. We do this by seeing ourselves as stewards and not owners.

Another excellent example of how giving is related to God's authority and power is the heart attitude that went into the foundation for establishing Solomon's Temple with glory and power. As a result, his kingdom rule spread over the whole earth in his day. King David gives a beautiful example of the correct heart attitude in the following Scriptures. He says, *"Of Your own, we have given You."*

1 Chronicles 29:11-12,14 Yours, O LORD, is the greatness, the power and the glory, the victory, and the majesty; for all that is in heaven and in earth is Yours; Yours is the kingdom, O LORD, and You are exalted as head over all. Both riches and honor come from You, and You reign over all. In Your hand is power and might; in Your hand it is to make great and to give strength to all. [14] But who am I, and who are my people, that we should be able to offer so willingly as this? For all things come from You, and of Your own we have given You.

David was not only able to confess that he was a steward and not an owner, but he proved it through his obedience and grateful heart. He understood that this issue was one of God's crucial tests to test man's heart.[203]

The result of David's obedience through the emptying of himself and his possessions was a kingdom established under Solomon's reign that ruled with glory and power throughout the land.[204]

Our ability to allow God's kingdom to be established with power and authority in our midst results from the practice of giving. God must be able to make draws from His earthen and unique treasures on the earth. When we withhold that which belongs to God, His kingdom rule can't be firmly established in our midst.

Our selfish refusal to bring our finances under His lordship withholds His divine power and reign upon the land and our communities. God's absolute kingdom rule won't be established in our hearts until we empty ourselves of personal ownership and accept that we are simply stewards of His goods. The choice is ours, as the parable of the talents so clearly illustrates—we can either be judged as worthy stewards who receive a blessing or as unjust stewards who get cast into the place of outer darkness.

What does it mean to give up ownership? Should we sell our earthly possessions and give them to the poor? How does this play out in 21st-century Christianity?

---

[203] 1 Chronicles 29:17
[204] 2 Chronicles 5:13-14, 9:22-23

Good stewardship begins with giving the tithe or tenth of all that we have towards the work of the Lord. It's the foundation on which the stewardship of our finances rests. When we give the tenth to Him before anything else is bought or paid for, we honor Him as Lord of our finances. By giving God the first fruits of our labor, we are investing in a steady return on our investment. The following Scriptures show when the first fruit is holy, the whole lump is holy.

Proverbs 3:9-10 Honor the LORD with your possessions, and with the firstfruits of all your increase; so your barns will be filled with plenty, and your vats will overflow with new wine.

Romans 11:16 For if the firstfruit is holy, the lump is also holy; and if the root is holy, so are the branches.

Leviticus 27:30 And all the tithe of the land, whether of the seed of the land or of the fruit of the tree, is the Lord's. It is holy to the Lord.

Giving the tithe was a part of the kingdom's blessing in every major covenant God has made with humanity.

- **Abraham** gave a tithe before the Law existed, was incredibly blessed in all he did, and was called the Father of our faith.[205]
- **Jacob** – committed to giving the tithe even when he had nothing. His covenant with God gave birth to the nation of Israel through his twelve sons. Tithing was Jacob's response to the covenant God made with him.[206]
- **Moses** – Tithing was instituted as part of the Law of Moses under the covenant that God made with him.[207]
- **New Testament** – The apostle Paul writes, "In the same way the priests and Levites who ministered the holy things under the law of Moses were taken care of, even so, the Lord has commanded that those who preach the gospel should live off the gospel."[208]

The tithe has always supported those who minister and sow spiritual things to reap material things that enable them to be free to continue to do so.

1 Corinthians 9:11 If we have sown spiritual things to you, is it a great thing if we reap your material things?

Malachi 3:10-11 Bring all the tithes into the storehouse that there may be food in My house, And try Me now in this," Says the Lord of hosts, "If I will not open for you the windows of heaven And pour out for you such blessing That there will not be room enough to receive it. ¹¹ "And I will rebuke the devourer for your sakes so

---

[205] Genesis 14:18-20
[206] Genesis 28:16-22
[207] Leviticus 27:30-32
[208] 1 Corinthians 9:6-12

that he will not destroy the fruit of your ground, Nor shall the vine fail to bear fruit for you in the field," Says the Lord of hosts;

As we have seen, the following benefits come from the principle of tithing the firstfruits or 10% of our income.

- Tithing is our response to God's covenant and divine ownership in our lives.
- It is a significant part of bringing our lives under Christ's Lordship, which is not an option.
- If the firstfruit is holy, the whole lump will be holy. Therefore, God will bless the 90%.
- It blesses the heart by making it receptive to God's will.
- It brings forth God's blessing in every area of our lives—He rebukes the devourer.
- It blesses the church by enabling it to carry out a greater ministry.

Other Ways in Which We Demonstrate Good Stewardship

Stewardship also involves the giving of offerings for various causes, including giving to people experiencing poverty. Many things come up in the church's life that require special offerings to move forward with the vision and purpose for which God has called us. We must be willing to give towards these things as they arise, whether it be time, energy, talents, or finances.

Luke 6:38 "Give, and it will be given to you: good measure, pressed down, shaken together, and running over will be put into your bosom. For with the same measure that you use, it will be measured back to you."

2 Corinthians 9:6-8 But this I say: He who sows sparingly will also reap sparingly, and he who sows bountifully will also reap bountifully. So let each one give as he purposes in his heart, not grudgingly or of necessity, for God loves a cheerful giver. And God is able to make all grace abound toward you, that you, always having all sufficiency in all things, have an abundance for every good work.

To be a good steward, you must first be a good manager of your budget and finances. If you are living beyond your means, running up bills on credit cards, and spending your money on things you don't need, you will never be able to give beyond the tithe.

Charles Swindoll writes, "I have been thinking about why the Scriptures teach 'It is more blessed to give than to receive.'" "Why is it that giving is preferred to receiving? Here are a few reasons that have come to my mind."

- Giving encourages unselfishness within us.
- Giving brings others needed relief and encouragement.
- Giving forces us out of our tight-radius world.

- Giving keeps us from becoming too attached to material things.
- Giving models the life Christ lived.
- Giving results in eternal rewards.
- Giving teaches us the value of servanthood.
- Giving makes us more cheerful, caring people.
- Giving prompts greater sensitivity toward others.
- Giving provides an example for others to follow.
- No wonder the apostle Paul wrote, "God loves a cheerful giver."

It's important to remember that God only expects you to give according to your ability regarding offerings that are over and above your tithe. Giving is equal sacrifice, not equal giving. When your total finances come under the Lordship of Christ, God can bless you in ways so that you can give more towards the work of the kingdom. As you do this, God's blessings continue to abound in your life, and you find yourself as a steward and not an owner of what you have.

Now that you understand some of the essentials of the faith, we are ready to move forward as we continue our journey into the invisible realms of God's kingdom.

May God's blessing and anointing be with you in every aspect of your life!

Into the Wilderness
Finding Purpose in Trials

Chapter Seven

And not only that, but we also glory in tribulations, knowing that tribulation produces perseverance, and perseverance, character; and character, hope—Romans 5:3-4.

Our journey will eventually lead us into wilderness periods at various times, just as it did for Jesus and countless others who have gone before us. The more prepared we are, the better equipped we are to handle these seasons. The key is to have God's Word hidden in our hearts so that we do not sin against Him as the Israelites did.

Before Jesus launched into ministry, the Spirit led Him into the wilderness to be tempted by the devil. However, by relying on the Scriptures stored in His heart, He overcame the temptations. [209]

Just as Jesus had to face the wilderness before He launched into ministry, the same holds true for us. We must go through times of trials and testing if we are to fulfill all that God has purposed for us. The children of Israel were also tested in the wilderness before they could enter the Promised Land. Unfortunately, they were not as successful as Jesus. It took them 40 long years to learn the lessons of the wilderness. The following Scripture shows God's purpose for us during wilderness seasons.

Deuteronomy 8:2-3 And you shall remember that the Lord your God led you all the way these forty years in the wilderness, to humble you and test you, to know what was in your heart, whether you would keep His commandments or not. ³ So He humbled you, allowed you to hunger, and fed you with manna which you did not know nor did your fathers know, that He might make you know that man shall not live by bread alone, but man lives by every word that proceeds from the mouth of the Lord.

---

[209] Matthew 4:1-11

Filled with Faith, Hope, and Love

When we first came to Christ, Jesus filled us with faith, hope, and love with a sense of newness that inspired us. As we began this incredible journey into the invisible realms of God's kingdom, He filled us with anticipation and high expectations of things to come. We may have sensed invincibility as we were shaped and enriched by our new nature and the mind of Christ.

As the newness of the adventure wears off, the enemy steps up his attacks. He knows this is his time to regain the ground he's lost in our lives. We must now be sober and vigilant as the enemy of our faith tries to destroy the work of God in us. It doesn't take long to discover that we have a relentless enemy who doesn't want these kingdom attributes taking root in our lives. He knows once they do, he's lost us for good.

Satan Waits for Opportune Moments

Just as Satan waited for a more suitable time with Jesus, so he does with us. [210] He patiently waits for those opportune moments to drag us down and render us ineffective. As we experience trials, hardships, and tests, he's there to exploit them by bringing accusations against us. He has been called the accuser of the brethren.[211] His purpose is to steal, kill, and destroy all that we've begun to experience in the kingdom realm.[212]

Jesus alluded to this in the Parable of the Sower concerning the seed sown on rocky ground. He said, *"But he who received the seed on the stony places, this is he who hears the word and immediately receives it with joy; yet he has no root in himself, but endures only for a while. He immediately stumbles when tribulation or persecution arises because of the word."*

We all Have A Tendency to Stumble

With our tendency to stumble, we must immerse ourselves in God's Word at the beginning of our journey. It's through the Word that the divine seed gets firmly planted in our hearts and remains incorruptible.[213] As Peter encourages us in the following Scripture, we must continually water and nurture the new seed so that it gets firmly rooted in our lives.

1 Peter 2:1-3 Therefore, laying aside all malice, all deceit, hypocrisy, envy, and all evil speaking as newborn babes, desire the pure milk of the word, that you may grow thereby if indeed you have tasted that the Lord is gracious.

---

[210] Luke 4:13
[211] Revelation 12:10
[212] John 10:10
[213] 1 Peter 1:23-25

Many young believers fall away when they experience hardship by giving in to Satan and his devices. However, those immersed in God's Word and staying in the fellowship continue the journey without getting detoured or drawn off course.

Dealing with Disillusionment

As we begin to experience these newfound trials and tribulations, there is the possibility that a sense of disillusionment will tempt us to give up. But, unfortunately, Satan takes full advantage of our trials and hardships by expanding on the disillusionment. Once we listen to him, we're open to further disappointment, deceit, and whatever else he has up his sleeve.

Trials and hardships are spiritual tests we must go through and eventually pass. Otherwise, we end up like the Israelites—just wandering in circles, not accomplishing much. But, on the other hand, we have many beautiful promises in God's Word that represent the Promised Land in the same way it did for them.

Let's not be like those who become stuck in forms of legalism or walking in the flesh rather than walking in grace. We must continue in the grace of God by allowing Him to be our sufficiency in all things as we navigate through trials that come our way. As Paul mentions, we depart from grace when we walk in our sufficiency rather than God's.[214] We see this in the following Scripture.

Galatians 3:3-4 Are you so foolish? Having begun in the Spirit, are you now being made perfect by the flesh? Have you suffered so many things in vain—if indeed it was in vain?

The diagram on the following page illustrates the process as we journey toward our final destination in God. Bear in mind it is simply a general synopsis of our pilgrimage. We are all individuals before God and experience His dealings in various ways and times throughout our walk with the Lord.

The diagram shows that God initially draws us unto Himself through His Son, Jesus Christ. Then, as we respond to the call of salvation, He fills us with inexpressible joy, resulting in a new-found hope drenched in His rich mercy and grace flowing freely into our lives.[215] Thus begins our new pilgrimage of walking in faith, hope, and love as new-found vision and purpose take root in our lives. Finally, as we repent before God by surrendering to His kingdom authority, we

---

[214] Galatians 5:4
[215] Ephesians 2:4-10, 1Peter 1:8

begin to walk with a new sense of invincibility. We feel the strength of God as He pours it into us.

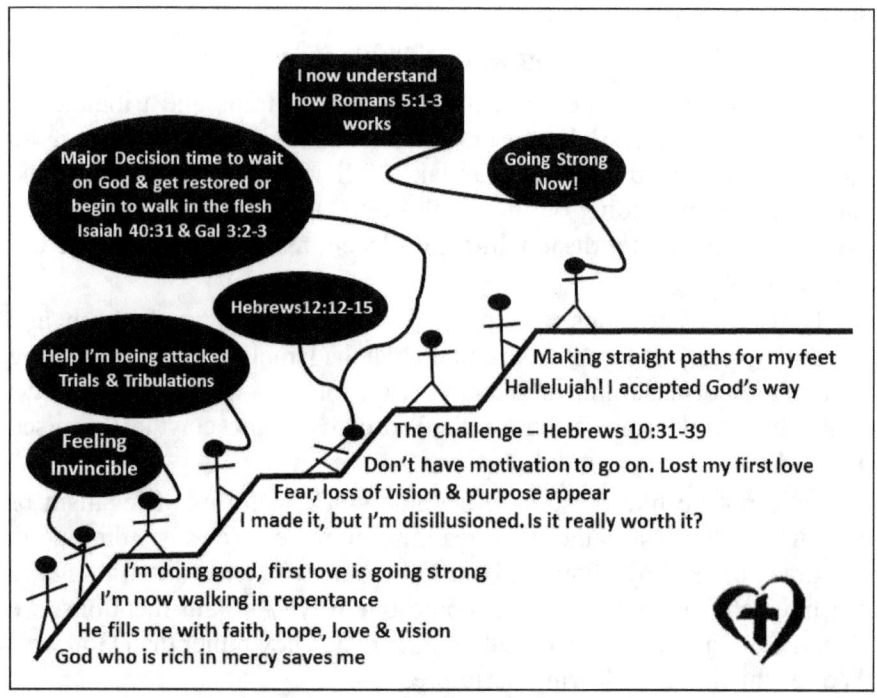

Trials and Hardships

When we think everything is going great, we start getting hit with trials and hardships, which we soon discover are a part of this new life. The Bible says the rain falls on the just and the unjust. Jesus said we would experience trials and hardships. We may have thought we would be exempt from these things, but the truth is, we are not. We are better equipped and prepared to navigate through them if we have immersed ourselves in God's Word and allowed the Holy Spirit to direct our lives.

Some people go through this stage relatively easily, while others get severely wounded. Again, it's about perspective and how we learn to process and perceive how God is working in our lives. Those better prepared and equipped have immersed and aligned themselves with God's Word, responded well during trials, practiced obedience to the Holy Spirit, and stayed in fellowship with other saints.

Those who have not prepared themselves will become tremendously weakened and wounded. These are the ones Satan finds as easy prey while lurking around and looking for weak and helpless Christians. In

Peter's first epistle, he warns about the enemy's tactics, as seen in the following Scripture.

1 Peter 5:8-10 Be sober, be vigilant; because your adversary the devil walks about like a roaring lion, seeking whom he may devour. ⁹Resist him, steadfast in the faith, knowing that the same sufferings are experienced by your brotherhood in the world. ¹⁰ But may the God of all grace, who called us to His eternal glory by Christ Jesus after you have suffered a while, perfect, establish, strengthen, and settle you.

Moses addressed this issue with the Children of Israel during their journey through the wilderness. He spoke of a time of testing that would enable them to do well in their future adventures.

Deuteronomy 8:2-3 And you shall remember that the Lord your God led you all the way these forty years in the wilderness, to humble you and test you, to know what was in your heart, whether you would keep His commandments or not. ³ So He humbled you, allowed you to hunger, and fed you with manna which you did not know nor did your fathers know, that He might make you know that man shall not live by bread alone, but man lives by every word that proceeds from the mouth of the Lord.

Deuteronomy 8:16 who fed you in the wilderness with manna, which your fathers did not know, that He might humble you and that He might test you, to do you good in the end—

Peter expressed this same thought when he said, *"Fire tests our faith."*

*1 Peter 1:6-7 In this you greatly rejoice, though now for a little while, **if need be,** you have been grieved by various trials, ⁷ that the genuineness of your faith, being much more precious than gold that perishes, though it is tested by fire, may be found to praise, honor, and glory at the revelation of Jesus Christ.*

He then reveals trials are to perfect, establish, and strengthen as we settle into the path before us.

1 Peter 5:10 But may the God of all grace, who called us to His eternal glory by Christ Jesus, after you have suffered a while, perfect, establish, strengthen, and settle you.

When trials and testing appear, even for those of us who have been faithful and diligent to stay in God's word and fellowship, they tend to bring things to the surface that are impure. They help us realize we still have past wounds that need healing and sin hindering us. As it says in the preceding Scripture, suffering is to perfect, establish, and strengthen us as we settle into our journey.

For all of us, especially those who have become severely wounded, it is vital to receive the needed healing. It may involve getting good Christian counseling as well. At this journey stage, it's time to wait for the Lord to renew our strength.

Isaiah 40:31 But those who wait on the Lord shall renew their strength; they shall mount up with wings like eagles, they shall run and not be weary, they shall walk and not faint.

Those who try to rush through this process won't get the healing they need and will walk in their sufficiency rather than God's. We have a long sojourn ahead and will continually go through this process until the end of our journey. Therefore, we might as well learn the process from the outset. Otherwise, the weight from your wounds will hold you back from achieving all that God has set before you.

Satan Feeds on our Wounds

You must understand Satan will feed on your wounds. He will compound the problems with disillusionment, fear, and loss of vision, so you no longer have the motivation to move forward. You will probably wonder, "Is this path worth the struggle?" But wait, there is hope!

As we wait on the Lord and soak in God's love, we immerse ourselves in His goodness by remembering His wonderful attributes and excellent benefits, and our strength returns.

Satan will try to get you to focus on the misery instead of looking to God as David did. David would often find himself in this predicament and begin to bless the Lord and bring God's goodness into remembrance. We see this in the following Scripture.

Psalm 103:1-5 Bless the Lord, O my soul; and all that is within me, bless His holy name! ² Bless the Lord, O my soul, And forget not all His benefits: ³ Who forgives all your iniquities, Who heals all your diseases, ⁴ Who redeems your life from destruction, Who crowns you with lovingkindness and tender mercies, ⁵ Who satisfies your mouth with good things, So that your youth is renewed like the eagle's.

We are challenged to move forward as we refocus on God's goodness and mercy. The letter to the Hebrews offers us the encouragement needed as we resolve in our hearts with a solid determination to move forward.

There Must be a Refocus on God's Goodness and Mercy

The preceding passage and the one below reveal to us that it takes two essential elements in our journey with the Lord to move forward. I call them the *guardrails of life*—the goodness of God and the severity of God.[216] I will address these two areas more fully in a later chapter, but it's crucial to understand how badly we need these elements flowing in and out of our lives. We desperately need them to permeate our lives when we become weakened in the faith and don't know how to turn. If we don't take heed to ourselves, we could be on the verge of giving up.

---

[216] Romans 11:22

Finding Purpose in Trials—Into the Wilderness

Hebrews 10:31-39 It is a fearful thing to fall into the hands of the living God. ³² But recall the former days in which, after you were illuminated, you endured a great struggle with sufferings: ³³ partly while you were made a spectacle both by reproaches and tribulations, and partly while you became companions of those who were so treated; **³⁸ *Now the just shall live by faith; but if anyone draws back, My soul has no pleasure in him.*** *" ³⁹ But we are not of those who draw back to perdition, but of those who believe to the saving of the soul.*

When you find yourself in a severely weakened condition, it's similar to those in an *(Intensive care Unit) ICU*. But instead, we are finding ourselves in a spiritual ICU. We are incapable of doing anything but allowing the goodness of God to wash over us. In the same way, a severely injured or sick person in the ICU cannot do anything but lie there and allow the doctors and nurses to take care of them, so we are in the hands of God. As we wait for Him, He nurtures us back to spiritual health.

Eventually, the person in the ICU comes to a time when their body begins to respond to all of the attention and care given to them by the doctors and nurses, and they get better. As a result, they move out of the ICU to a regular hospital room, at which time they are most likely encouraged to begin some physical therapy, even though it may be somewhat painful. Responding to treatment is what it takes to complete the healing process.

In the same way, after the goodness of God washes over us, we begin to respond and get better, at which time God nudges us with a dose of His severity to get us moving in the right direction, even though it may be somewhat painful. He uses it as therapy for our sake. God says, *"My soul will take no pleasure in you if you turn back."* He reminds us that falling into His hands is a fearful thing. It's time to strengthen yourself in the Lord and get back on your feet to continue your journey." The complete healing won't come until you get back on the path and start walking, as we see in the following Scripture.

Hebrews 12:12-13 Therefore strengthen the hands which hang down, and the feeble knees,¹³ and make straight paths for your feet, so that what is lame may not be dislocated, but rather be healed.

Once we have fully submitted our hearts to the Lord, after going through the trial of our faith, God works with us in a whole new way. Just as Jesus learned obedience through the things He suffered, so have we. We are no longer babes in Christ who are unsure of the path ahead. We now have a firm foundation and have begun to experience the reality of Christ tangibly working in our lives. The Holy Spirit has enlightened us; we have tasted the heavenly gift, the good Word of God, and the powers of the age to come.[217] We must now put our hands on the plow without looking back. Instead, we say, "Hallelujah! I'm back on track. I made it through the wilderness. I'm on the way to fulfilling my destiny in God. I'm going strong again!"[218]

Although you made it through this first big test of faith, you will continue to be tested with greater dimensions of grace added to your faith. The difference is you've now learned the process and understand what it says in Romans.

Romans 5:1-5 Therefore, having been justified by faith, we have peace with God through our Lord Jesus Christ, through whom also we have access by faith into this grace in which we stand, and rejoice in hope of the glory of God. And not only that, but we also glory in tribulations, knowing that tribulation produces perseverance; and perseverance, character; and character, hope. Now, hope does not disappoint because the love of God has been poured out in our hearts by the Holy Spirit, who was given to us.

From this point forward, you must keep practicing this victory method as Paul encouraged the Philippians.

Philippians 3:16 Nevertheless, to the degree that we have already attained, let us walk by the same rule; let us be of the same mind.

Now that you understand what it means to go through wilderness experiences, you can avoid the wilderness complex and move forward with purpose and destiny. You will be able to tackle the thorny issues of life without getting bogged down.

May God bless you as you navigate through the wilderness periods of your life! He will be with you to lead you through the process at every juncture. Learn to enjoy the ride by counting it all as joy as you embrace what God has in store for you.

---

[217] Hebrews 6:1-6
[218] Luke 9:62

Breaking Free From Your Past

Chapter Eight

Therefore, strengthen the hands that are weak and the knees that are feeble, and make straight paths for your feet, so that the limb which is lame may not be put out of joint, but rather be healed—Hebrews 12:12-13 (NASB)

In the previous chapter, we saw an overview of the process as we continued to move forward in our spiritual journey. The focus is now on healing past wounds and those from our enemy as he exploits our weaknesses. Our goal is to navigate through this process and break free from the past so that we can serve God without restraints as we continue our pilgrimage.

When we first came to Christ, the joy and anticipation that often results from our first love experience in Christ had a way of overshadowing the wounds of our past. Unfortunately, as we experience hardship, they have a way of resurfacing and compounding the present difficulties. As these wounds resurface, Satan takes full advantage to move in and wreak havoc. Because his purpose is to steal, kill, and destroy the work of God in us, it's of the utmost importance that we apply God's healing ability.[219]

Whether we want to admit it or not, most of us have received emotional wounds from the pathways of our past. From the moment of our birth, the sparks began to fly.[220] We were born and raised in a cruel, imperfect world where wounds came easily. We also have the trial of our faith, which we began to see in the previous chapter. All of this has a way of causing and compounding the pain. We may have even picked up some addictions or bondages along the way, which we must now deal with constructively. It's not God's will for us to be in bondage to our past. We must break free!

---

[219] John 10:10
[220] Job 5:7

We will never have the joy necessary to deal with our current problems and trials until we are free. Remember, it is the joy of the Lord that is our strength.[221] Paul recognized that the weight of his past greatly hindered him, so he let it go. We must do the same. There is so much for us to reach forward to with joy and hope, but we must let go of the past before we can anticipate the future.[222]

Are you ready to deal with your past emotional wounds, broken relationships, addictions, and other areas that keep you in bondage from successfully navigating the path before you? If so, there is hope for you. Jesus came to heal the brokenhearted and the oppressed. Just as the Spirit of God came upon Him to heal the brokenhearted, the Holy Spirit is here today to heal and deliver those in bondage. He is the same yesterday, today, and forever.[223]

Luke 4:18 "The Spirit of the Lord is upon Me because He has anointed Me To preach the gospel to the poor; He has sent Me to heal the brokenhearted, to proclaim liberty to the captives and recovery of sight to the blind, to set at liberty those who are oppressed;

None of us are exempt from being emotionally wounded from time to time. However, God desires to heal us completely. It's part of the reason the Father sent His Son, Jesus, into the world, as the above Scripture says—to heal the brokenhearted, proclaim liberty to the captives, and set the oppressed at liberty. Even King David had wounds he needed healing from. So he said, *"For I am poor and needy, and my heart is wounded within me."*[224]

No matter who we are—businessperson, salesperson, blue collar, construction worker, computer whiz, student, professional, homemaker, mother, father, husband, or wife; life can be ruthless, brutal, and challenging to cope with at times. On the outside, we may look good by putting on a mask to cover the hurt, but the fact remains: the wound is still there and festering.

Some are already healing by openly acknowledging their wounds and moving on. Others have accepted their hurts and heartaches and are dealing with life the best they can but not functioning at full throttle. But then, some can barely perform because of the severity of the wounds inflicted upon them. Is there hope? Is there healing? Is there deliverance from bondages and addictions? The answer is an unequivocal yes because it is God's will and purpose for you!

---

[221] Nehemiah 8:10
[222] Philippians 3:13-14
[223] Hebrews 13:8
[224] Psalm 109:22

Major Causes of Most Wounds

The primary causes of most wounds stem from various areas, including parental wounds inflicted by physical, mental, verbal, or sexual abuse. It could be a general meanness in others, broken relationships, significant disappointments, a nasty divorce, molestation, other crimes against you, or a major moral failure such as adultery or abortion. The list goes on.

These wounds have helped to shape the person you are. But unfortunately, their results have had the potential to produce significant strongholds that can render you ineffective and unproductive as you navigate life. When the injuries are so severe, it helps us to understand why many people turn to drugs and alcohol to numb the pain. The problem is they only compound their issues.

Results of Most Wounds?

You may not know how your wounds have affected you, but you may think everything is okay. Here are some indicators as to how you may have affected you:

- Inability to respond to trials with joy and the proper perspective.
- Wounded people hurt others. Does your behavior often injure others?
- You are often filled with anger, bitterness, hate, and violence.
- You tend to repeat the things that happened to you with others.
- You find yourself filled with shame, guilt, and unworthiness.
- You are full of self-condemnation.
- You have low self-esteem—no confidence.
- You often feel lonely and withdrawn and have very few friends.
- You are unable to respond to others correctly.
- You may have eating disorders.
- You are afraid to show love.
- You cannot trust others.
- You have misconceptions about God.
- You seem passive about life.
- You experience a deep sense of despair and depression.
- You have significant addictions to alcohol and drugs.
- You have suicidal tendencies.

These characteristics are areas that clutter our lives and hold us back from becoming the person God has created us to be. Satan will use them to steal, kill, and destroy what God wants to impart into your life.[225]

---

[225] John 10:10

Seeing yourself in some of these areas indicates that you need healing and possibly deliverance. Otherwise, you are impaired from having a life of adventure filled with God's riches and abundance. As we see in the following Scripture, we must lay aside the weight of these wounds.

Hebrews 12:1 Therefore we also, since we are surrounded by so great a cloud of witnesses, let us lay aside every weight, and the sin which so easily ensnares us, and let us run with endurance the race that is set before us.

Some of these may have become strongholds you are ignoring or not dealing with. Nevertheless, you must forcefully deal with them if you are to break free and get the victory. We must become violent with our faith by taking the kingdom by force.[226]

Webster's dictionary defines a stronghold as a place dominated by a particular characteristic. So you need to ask yourself, "Are any of the characteristics mentioned earlier dominating me?"

In one of his books, Francis Frangipane writes, *"What men call "salvation" is simply the first stage of God's plan for our lives, which is to conform us in character and power to the image of Jesus Christ. If we fail to see our relationship with God as such, we will allow too many areas within us to remain unchanged. Pulling down strongholds is the demolition and removal of these old ways of thinking so that the actual presence of Jesus Christ can be manifested through us."*[227]

The apostle Paul defines strongholds as speculations or lofty things raised against the knowledge of God. It includes any thinking that exalts itself above God's wisdom and gives the devil a secure place to influence our thought life.

2 Corinthians 10:4-6 For the weapons of our warfare are not carnal but mighty in God for pulling down strongholds, ⁵casting down arguments and every high thing that exalts itself against the knowledge of God, bringing every thought into captivity to the obedience of Christ, ⁶and being ready to punish all disobedience when your obedience is fulfilled.

Strongholds are not random thoughts or occasional sins. They're areas you're struggling with because you are in bondage and have lost all hope of breaking free.

Receiving Healing and Deliverance

Remember that Jesus came to heal the brokenhearted and set the oppressed at liberty.[228] Therefore, deliverance is necessary when you find yourself severely oppressed by the enemy in any of the areas

---

[226] Matthew 11:12
[227] The Three Battlegrounds by Francis Frangipane
[228] Luke 4:18

mentioned earlier. You will be unhindered in your journey into the invisible realms of God's kingdom by receiving the healing you need.

The First Step

Whether you require healing or deliverance, the first step is to believe in God's desire and will for you to be whole. He desires this in every area of your life. God's intention in saving us was to heal us, body, soul, and spirit. The apostle Paul makes this abundantly clear in his first epistle to the Thessalonians.

1 Thessalonians 5:23 Now may the God of peace Himself sanctify you completely; and may your whole spirit, soul, and body be preserved blameless at the coming of our Lord Jesus Christ.

Salvation involves more than saving man's soul; it means total salvation for spirit, soul, and body. The Greek words for *"saved"* and *"salvation"* are *"Sozo"* and *"Soteria,"* which reveal God's desire to save us spirit, soul, and body.

These words mean to save, deliver, protect, heal, preserve, do well, be or make whole, and rescue or safety. The chart below shows how these two words are translated in the New Testament.

How the Words "Sozo" and "Soteria" are Translated

Health – Survival	Healed	Preserved	Do Well
Acts 27:34	Acts 14:9	2 Timothy 4:18	John 11:12
	Mark 5:23		
	Luke 8:36		
Be whole	**Made whole**	**Saved – Save**	**Salvation**
Matthew 9:21-22	Mark 6:56	Mark 8:35, 16:16	Romans 1:16
Mark 10:52	Mark 15:30-31	Romans 1:10	2 Timothy 3:15
Luke 8:48-50	Luke 9:56	2 Timothy 3:15	
	Luke 18:42	1 Corinthians 1:21	
		1 Timothy 1:15, 2:15	
		James 5:15	
		Mark 16:16	

Jesus healed all who came to Him when He was here over 2000 years ago and is still willing to heal all who come today. He is the same yesterday, today, and forever. His covenant to heal has not changed. Just as He cast out the spirits and healed all who came to Him so that Isaiah's prophecy could be fulfilled by taking our infirmities and bearing our sicknesses, He still fulfills this divine prophecy about Himself today. His will is the same because it is an irrevocable covenant the Father has made with us through His Son.[229]

Just as Abraham established his faith because of the covenant God made with him, we build our faith when we believe wholeheartedly in the covenant God has made with us through Jesus Christ.

Romans 4:20-22 He did not waver at the promise of God through unbelief but was strengthened in faith, giving glory to God, ²¹ and being fully convinced that what He had promised He was also able to perform. ²² And therefore, "it was accounted to him for righteousness."

The question is, are you thoroughly convinced of God's promise to heal you? We become entirely convinced of God's promise when we know what God's will is in the matter. You need to know that it's God's will to heal you because He established it in the covenant He made with us. **His promise of healing, based on the covenant, is where your faith will come from for healing and deliverance.**[230]

Come Out of Denial

It may be that you have been in a state of denial and have not wanted to face the ugly wounds of your past. If this is so, you will need to acknowledge openly and confess your wounds. It takes courage to face the pain and the ugliness of a wound inflicted upon you, even if you were entirely innocent. You may be trying to smother it with drugs, alcohol, gluttony, eating disorders, or other destructive practices. The problem is the wound is still there and festering.

It's time to make straight paths for your feet by facing the wound's ugliness and receiving the needed healing.[231] The Holy Spirit desires to shine a light on areas you have been hiding or hurting from, but He needs your cooperation. Our stubbornness and refusal to acknowledge and confess the wound will hinder His work in the healing process. As a result, His Spirit gets quenched in this area of your life.

Luke 8:17 For nothing is secret that will not be revealed, nor anything hidden that will not be known and come to light.

Psalm 51:6-8 Behold, You desire truth in the inward parts, and the hidden part You will make me know wisdom. Purge me with hyssop, and I shall be clean; wash me, and I shall be whiter than snow. Make me hear joy and gladness.

As you allow God to uncover wounds festering, you will have the faith to believe with a new sense of freedom as you experience the joy

---

[229] Matthew 8:16-17
[230] For a study on the Healing Covenant, see: http://kenbirks.com/healing-covenant.htm
[231] Hebrews 12:12-13

of your salvation fully restored with a renewed and steadfast spirit. You will now be able to continue your journey unhindered.[232]

Healing and restoration are the works God wants to do for you as you wait on Him rather than giving up and quitting, as we saw in the diagram from the previous chapter. God is faithful toward you with plans to give you a future filled with hope.[233] You can trust Him!

Forgive and Let Go

After openly acknowledging your wounds, you must forgive those who have sinned against you and ask forgiveness of those you may have hurt from your wounding. Jesus is our supreme example of what it means to forgive those who have hurt us. He was wounded more than any of us can even begin to imagine, yet when He was beaten and crucified, He cried out, *"Father, forgive them, for they know not what they do."* Jesus has admonished us to do the same.

Mark 11:25 "And whenever you stand praying, if you have anything against anyone, forgive him, that your Father in heaven may also forgive you your trespasses.

Colossians 3:12-13 Therefore, as the elect of God, holy and beloved, put on tender mercies, kindness, humility, meekness, longsuffering; ¹³bearing with one another, and forgiving one another, if anyone has a complaint against another; even as Christ forgave you, so you also must do.

Bear in mind that the feelings and emotions of unforgiveness will often try to resurrect themselves. However, standing firm in your faith with a forgiving attitude, regardless of your feelings, will increase your confidence to receive healing. Each time this happens, you say, "No! I have forgiven the person and will continue to walk in forgiveness." Eventually, the old emotions of unforgiveness disappear as the new feelings of forgiveness take over. By making this confession, you can let go. As with any of these areas, you may need professional counseling to help you walk in the freedom you need.

When we fail to forgive those who sin against us, Satan takes advantage and causes further wounding. The apostle Paul encouraged the Corinthians to forgive lest Satan should take advantage.[234] We cannot afford to give Satan any advantage. He will wreak destruction if we do. In other words, we must follow Jesus' example and love our enemies by forgiving them.[235]

Just because you have forgiven someone does not necessarily mean you must become their best friend. Some people are not safe people to

---

[232] Psalm 51:10-15
[233] Jeremiah 29:11
[234] 2 Corinthians 2:10-11
[235] Matthew 5:44

be around. You need to know who the unsafe people are in your life. You can still be cordial and kind without bringing them into your inner circle.

Getting Free from Strongholds

As mentioned earlier, some things are so deeply rooted they become strongholds. It takes a little more work, so we are urged to work out our salvation with fear and trembling.[236] If we are to be conformed to the image of Christ, we must be willing to tackle these strongholds. We must become violent about taking the kingdom by force so that the kingdom of God reigns in those areas rather than the kingdom of darkness.[237]

Our allegiance must be to God and His kingdom to completely break free from the past. As a result, we shift our focus to something more important that will now occupy our minds and thoughts. We become more kingdom-focused and make the right choices to bring forth God's blessing and deliverance.

The fruit that comes forth in our lives comprises a series of decisions. When we made choices according to our carnal and selfish appetites, they blocked the flow of God's blessing and abundance in our lives. On the other hand, when we make the right choices concerning seeking the kingdom of God, we release the flow of blessing and abundance into our lives through the law of sowing and reaping.[238]

Listed below are often typical strongholds to give you an idea.

Common Strongholds

Fear	Apathy	Lukewarmness	Greed
Resentment	Unbelief	Sinful Thoughts	Drugs/Alcohol
Bitterness	Depression	Lust	Pornography
Unforgiveness	Anxiety	Pride	Gluttony

Because we all tend to excuse ourselves so readily, it's hard to discern the areas of oppression in our lives. After all, these are our thoughts, attitudes, and perceptions. Moreover, we tend to justify and defend our opinions with the same degree of intensity with which we justify and protect ourselves.

When identifying your strongholds, survey or examine the attitudes in your heart. Every area in your thinking that glistens with hope in God is an area that Christ is liberating. On the other hand, any system of thought without hope but feeling hopeless is a stronghold that needs to be pulled down.

---

[236] Philippians 2:12
[237] Matthew 11:12
[238] Matthew 6:33

When we allow places of darkness to remain, Satan can operate and wreak havoc in our lives. These strongholds become his base of operations from which he launches his attacks. Ephesians 4:27 tells us *not to give place to the devil.* Notice that it says **we are the ones who give him a place of operation**. Are you giving Satan a base to operate by not surrendering to God's authority? The devil flees when we submit to God.[239]

In 1 Samuel chapters 13-14, we find a great example of dealing with a stronghold. The army of Israel could not function because the enemy had control of a stronghold from which they were continually launching attacks upon Israel. The enemy hadn't taken possession of their land yet but could harass and often oppress them because they had control of the stronghold. In the same way, just because we have a stronghold doesn't mean the devil possesses us. Instead, we give him a place to launch his attacks, enabling him to harass and oppress us.

Saul's army was in complete disarray and had been reduced to only 600 men because his soldiers were deserting him in mass numbers. They hid in caves, rocks, thickets, holes, and pits in fear of the Philistines.[240] No one in the army had swords except for Saul and his son, Jonathan. The Philistines had taken all of their blacksmiths, resulting in Israel having to go to them to sharpen their plowshare and other tools.[241] They were immobilized because of the stronghold. Are you immobilized in your journey? If so, it's time to break free!

Confessing the Stronghold to Another Begins the Process

A light has to shine on the dark place in your heart for the darkness to leave. When brought to light, true deliverance begins to come forth. The light dispels the darkness by confessing the stronghold of sin to another person or a group of people. In doing this, you will need a safe environment to remove your mask and be completely transparent and vulnerable without fear of judgment.

James makes this clear in his epistle: *"Confess your trespasses to one another, and pray for one another that you may be healed."* Confession does not mean we confess to anyone and everyone, but rather to someone or a small group of people with whom we trust—people to whom we are accountable. By doing so, it shines a light on the area of darkness. Satan no longer has a good launching site from a place of proximity for his attacks. By submitting to God and His Word, he has to flee. Confessing

---

[239] James 4:7
[240] 1 Samuel 13:6
[241] 1 Samuel 14:19-22

your stronghold could also entail professional counseling or joining a support group that majors on your problem area.

It Takes a Determined Effort

Once you begin the process, the enemy will not leave quickly. Therefore, you must be more determined. We see a great illustration of this when the tribes of Israel were attempting to take possession of the Promised Land. God had given them the command to go forth and to drive its inhabitants out. He not only commanded them but promised them that He would help them.

Joshua 1:9 "Have I not commanded you? Be strong and of good courage; do not be afraid, nor be dismayed, for the LORD your God is with you wherever you go."

With this promise, the children of Israel were to go forth, conquering all of the inhabitants of the Promised Land. But unfortunately, this did not happen in all cases because their enemies were determined to stay.

Joshua 17:12-13 Yet the children of Manasseh could not drive out the inhabitants of those cities, but the Canaanites were determined to dwell in that land. And it happened, when the children of Israel grew strong, that they put the Canaanites to forced labor but did not utterly drive them out.

The children of Manasseh couldn't drive the Canaanites out of the land because they lacked the determination to do so. The Canaanites were more determined to stay. As the tribe of Manasseh got caught up in their ungodly ways, they were filled with a mixture as they mixed with the Canaanites. When we allow strongholds to remain, we experience a mixture and don't completely come out.[242] When this happens, it continually gives the enemy a foothold to reinforce the fortress.

Through a determined effort, we are to drive out our enemies. How many of us give place to the devil because we lack the determination to drive him out? It will take a strong, determined effort to drive out the enemies of your flesh and spirit.

Determination is the inner fortitude and strength of character—being disciplined to remain consistent, steady, and diligent regardless of the odds or the demands. It is deciding definitely and firmly or coming to a firm resolution.

Are you committed to tearing down your strongholds where Satan is still wreaking havoc? As the following Scripture shows, God has given you the authority and power to defeat and drive Satan's influence from every area of your life.

Luke 10:19 "Behold, I give you authority to trample on serpents and scorpions, and over all the power of the enemy, and nothing shall by any means hurt you.

---

[242] 2 Corinthians 6:14-18

If you have strongholds where the enemy is still trying to hold onto you with a determined effort, you will need a revelation and understanding of how great God is and how mighty His power is towards you.[243]

1 John 4:4 You are of God, little children, and have overcome them because He who is in you is greater than he who is in the world.

These Scriptures describe God's ability toward us. Therefore, we must believe, confess and act upon them. A great example is from the above example of *1 Samuel chapters 13-14,* where Jonathan confessed his faith to his armor-bearer. He said, *"Come, let us go over to the garrison (stronghold) of these uncircumcised; it may be that the Lord will work for us. For nothing restrains the Lord from saving by many or by few."*[244]

Jonathan was filled with boldness and courage as he stepped out in faith according to what he knew God's ability was. We must do the same as we step out in faith and take the kingdom by force. Otherwise, His kingdom will be diminished as the strongholds persist. But, as we are faithful to step out in faith, boldness, and courage, it gives us the determination not to give up but to continue pressing forward until we are free.

Aggressive, Focused Behavior is Necessary

If the kingdom is to reign in our lives, even in those areas that are stumbling blocks to us, we must have an aggressive faith that results in a focused intent on dispelling the darkness within us. It's the violent who take the kingdom by force.[245]

Paul said, *"To this end, I also labor, striving according to His working which works in me mightily."*[246] Therefore, aggressive, focused behavior with intent involves bringing every thought into the captivity of the obedience of Christ.

2 Corinthians 10:4-6 For the weapons of our warfare are not carnal but mighty in God for pulling down strongholds, ⁵casting down arguments and every high thing that exalts itself against the knowledge of God, bringing every thought into captivity to the obedience of Christ, ⁶and being ready to punish all disobedience when your obedience is fulfilled.

Notice what verse six says, *"and being ready to punish all disobedience when your obedience is fulfilled."* We destroy our

---

[243] Ephesians 1:19
[244] 1 Samuel 14:6
[245] Matthew 11:12
[246] Colossians 1:29

strongholds when we obey God and His Word. It takes aggressive behavior with focused intent to do so.

Most strongholds continue because our minds do not agree with God's Word but often exalt themselves against the knowledge of God. David said, *"Direct my steps by Your word and let no iniquity have dominion over me.*[247] He also said, *"Your word I have hidden in my heart, that I might not sin against You."*

When Jesus was tempted, the Word quickly came to mind because He had studied and meditated upon it. It was there because He took the time to embed it in His heart. It put the enemy to flight just as it will for us. God gives us the grace to break free from Satan's hold by embedding His Word into the recesses of our hearts.

Our obedience to God's Word brings us freedom and deliverance. It puts us in a position to punish Satan by bringing every thought into captivity to the obedience of Christ.[248]

Satan has nowhere to stand when we apply God's truth. We are pulling the rug out from under his feet, which causes him to be thrown off balance as he hurls his darts at us. They miss the mark, which helps us to break free and continue our journey without being bogged down by our past. The weight is lifted!

The weight is lifted, the wound is healed, the bondage is broken, and we are now ready to pursue our destiny and purpose without weights holding us back.

May God bless you mightily as you deal with the issues holding you back from pressing on with the force of the kingdom. God is with you as you yield to the Holy Spirit in every area the enemy is harassing and oppressing you.

---

[247] Psalm 119:133
[248] John 8:31-32

Immersed Into the Body of Christ

Chapter Nine

For as the body is one and has many members, but all the members of that one body, being many, are one body, so also is Christ. For by one Spirit, we were all baptized into one body—whether Jews or Greeks, whether slaves or free—and have all been made to drink into one Spirit—1 Corinthians 12:12-13.

When God's call to salvation goes out to people; it knows no boundaries. It goes out to people of all races, cultures, backgrounds, genders, personalities, classes, political backgrounds, etc. God's purpose is to create a chosen generation out of all these diversities of people. By going to the cross, Jesus broke down the middle wall of the partition to make this possible.[249] When we experience salvation, we become a part of the chosen generation God is creating, and the fun begins as the work of the cross comes into play.

When we were born again, we were saved and called with a holy calling, not according to our works, but according to God's purpose and grace that was given to us in Christ Jesus before time began.[250] As we allow God to set or place us in the body of Christ, we become a part of His purpose to function in the area He has designated. God sets the solitary in families as it says, *"God has set the members, each one of them, in the body just as He pleased."* [251]

Finding Our Place at the Father's Table

We all have a place at the Father's table, which gives us a place to function with responsibility. Your responsibility begins by finding your niche and operating in it. We are the joints that supply nourishment to the other body members so that they receive strength.[252]

The Church is anemic today because of a lack of harmony in its functioning with one another. The nourishment for the body's growth

---

[249] Ephesians 2:14-16
[250] 2 Timothy 1:9
[251] Psalm 68:6, 1 Corinthians 12:18
[252] Ephesians 4:16

and maturity is missing because its parts are not connected properly to produce the anointing necessary for the body of Christ to be whole and healthy. On the other hand, when we operate in our place, we contribute to and help the body's overall development. As we assume our rightful positions and begin to work and harmonize with one another, the body of Christ is built up and becomes the influence and source of light that God has ordained it to be. His anointing is intended to flow from the head, who is Christ, downward to every part connected through His love for one another.

Functioning together in unity and harmony despite our differences and diversities brings growth. Regardless of where we have come from concerning race, culture, gender, class, or political persuasions, we are all immersed into one body and dependent upon one another for refreshing and nourishment as we drink from one fountain—His Spirit.

No matter what our differences are, we belong to one another. We discover our great need for one another in our differences. God has designed His body so that we are all interdependent upon one another. When we do not fully accept other members for whatever reason, we are not only cheating them but also cheating ourselves of the nourishment and refreshment they offer.

1 Corinthians 12:13-14 (Message) You can easily enough see how this kind of thing works by looking no further than your own body. Your body has many parts—limbs, organs, cells—but no matter how many parts you can name, you're still one body. It's exactly the same with Christ. By means of His one Spirit, we all said goodbye to our partial and piecemeal lives. We each used to independently call our own shots, but then we entered into a large and integrated life in which He has the final say in everything. (This is what we proclaimed in word and action when we were baptized.) Each of us is now a part of his resurrection body refreshed and sustained at one fountain—His Spirit—where we all come to drink.

The day is coming when the body of Christ will arise in maturity and minister as Jesus did in His day over 2000 years ago. Will you be a part of this exciting fulfillment of Scripture, or will you be one of the many who sit by in apathy and unbelief? It's your choice!

Isaiah 60:1-2 Arise, shine; for your light has come! And the glory of the LORD is risen upon you. For behold, the darkness shall cover the earth, and deep darkness the people; but the LORD will arise over you, and His glory will be seen upon you.

Now is the time to take your place by submitting to God's purpose as you pray, meditate, and study His Word. Don't allow anything to stand in the way as you seize your destiny and purpose. It will take you to places you never dreamed possible as you connect with other body members.

Baptism into the body of Christ brings us into a relationship with other members to form one body. Because we now belong to one another, we give up our personal rights to develop relationships with others. It's a one-another gospel, regardless of race, gender, class background, personality, culture, political beliefs, or whatever.

We all have a Measure of Christ's Gift.

God has given to each of us, in His body, a measure of faith and gifting in Him. For the body to come together and be all that He has designed and destined for it, there must be a meshing together that produces the full measure of Christ in our midst.

1 Corinthians 12:21 And the eye cannot say to the hand, "I have no need of you"; nor again the head to the feet, "I have no need of you."

It takes an understanding and revelation of how we fit into the body of Christ to achieve the full potential of who we are in Christ. Without it, we will stagnate and become stuck in a rut with little motivation to continue to move forward in our calling and purpose. We will have lost sight of the path that leads to the wonders of the grace the Father yet desires to bestow upon us.

Because we are groomed in cultures that breed independence, we don't necessarily feel the need to connect to the other members in the way God has designed us. If we remain in this mode, there will be a lack of growth and development in our faith. We will, most likely, produce nothing but wood, hay, and stubble.[253] The truth is, the more we drink from God's Spirit and accept the changes He desires for us, the more we will realize our dependence on one another. His Spirit creates the need within us.

Jesus, the Manifestation of the Body of Christ

When Jesus walked on this earth over 2,000 years ago, He was the perfect representative of God, the Father—the manifestation of God in the flesh. He came in the express image of God the Father with the brightness of His glory indelibly stamped upon His personage.[254] He was given the Spirit without measure to adequately express the Father's image and glory to all who witnessed His coming.

Hebrews 10:5 Therefore, when He came into the world, He said: "Sacrifice and offering You did not desire, but a body You have prepared for Me."

John 3:34-35 (NIV) For the one whom God has sent speaks the words of God, for God gives the Spirit without limit. The Father loves the Son and has placed everything in his hands.

---

[253] 1 Corinthians 3:11-12
[254] Hebrews 1:2-3

John 1:14 And the Word became flesh and dwelt among us, and we beheld His glory, the glory as of the only-begotten of the Father, full of grace and truth.

Jesus was the Anointed One sent to reveal God in His majesty, power, and grace. He showed us the true character of God and what it means to truly love, care, and minister to others as the fruits of the Spirit poured forth from His life. Jesus also showed us God's incredible power and majesty through the gifts of the Spirit manifested through His life. He revealed to us what it is to operate in the authority of God through His anointed teaching, casting out demons and speaking with wisdom to those who opposed Him. Jesus was undoubtedly the embodiment of God in the flesh, who manifested God's power, character, and authority amazingly. He was a man wholly submitted to the fullness of the Spirit working in Him.

God desires His people to express the same attributes that were in Jesus so that His body will continue to bring forth His power, glory, and character to the world's nations without the limitations of space and time. We are now the body of Christ. We are His body that God, the Father, prepared before time existed—eternity.

Philippians 2:5-7 Let this mind (attitude—NASB) be in you which was also in Christ Jesus who, being in the form of God, did not consider it robbery to be equal with God, but made Himself of no reputation, taking the form of a servant, and coming in the likeness of men.

When Jesus came to earth, He never ceased being God. He was and is the second person of the Godhead. But what He did do was this—He made Himself of no reputation by stripping Himself of His right to act as God. He became dependent upon the Holy Spirit working through Him just as you and we must do. It says, *"Let this same attitude be in you."* You see, Jesus came to show us how to be the many-membered body of Christ.

God's ultimate plan is for the many-membered body of Christ to express the full measure of His Spirit in the same way Jesus did. The following passage of Scripture makes this abundantly clear.

Ephesians 4:7-13 But to each one of us grace was given according to the measure of Christ's gift. [9] (Now this, "He ascended"—what does it mean but that He also first descended into the lower parts of the earth? [10] He who descended is also the One who ascended far above all the heavens, that He might fill all things.) [11] And He Himself gave some to be apostles, some prophets, some evangelists, and some pastors and teachers, [12] for the equipping of the saints for the work of ministry, for the edifying of the body of Christ, [13] till we all come to the unity of the faith and of the knowledge of the Son of God, to a perfect man, to the measure of the stature of the fullness of Christ.

The above passage contains God's desire and purpose towards the body He has prepared for today's world.

- We have been given grace according to the measure of Christ's gift.
- When He ascended, He gave gifts unto men.
- He descended and ascended that He might fill all things.
- He gave five-fold ministry gifts for the equipping of the saints until we come into the unity of the faith to the measure and stature of the fullness of Christ.

The Divine Seed was Planted in the Earth

With the divine seed of God planted and coming to fruition in the life of Jesus, it needed to be buried in the earth. It was to bring forth a more glorious expression of God's fullness. We see this again in the following passage.

Ephesians 1: 22-23 And He put all things under His feet and gave Him to be head over all things to the church, ²³which is His body, the fullness of Him who fills all in all.

Space and time limited the ministry of Jesus. God needed a vehicle or an expression of His image that would not be restricted by space and time. For this reason, among others, Jesus had to die—so that the divine seed could multiply and bring forth a greater harvest of sons and daughters. His purpose was to bring forth a many-membered body that would be far more glorious than the single expression of His body in His incarnation.

When Jesus said, *"He who believes in Me, the works that I do he will also do, and greater works than these he will do because I go to My Father. And whatever you ask in My name, that I will do, that the Father may be glorified in the Son,"*[255] He spoke of the many-membered body of Christ.

John 12:23-24 But Jesus answered them, saying, "The hour has come that the Son of Man should be glorified. "Most assuredly, I say to you, unless a grain of wheat falls into the ground and dies, it remains alone, but if it dies, it produces much grain."

What happens when you plant a grain of wheat or a kernel of corn in the ground? It reproduces itself, but only now is it multiplied. One of the reasons Jesus had to die was so He could reproduce Himself in the earth.

Our Sins had to be Purged and Atoned For

The death of Christ was a prominent part of God's overall plan to bring many sons to glory. To be accepted by God, our sins had to be atoned. Before God could breathe His Holy Spirit into us and cause us to

---

[255] John 14:12-14

be born again of the incorruptible seed of God's divine nature, we first had to be cleansed by Christ's blood, as seen in the following Scriptures.

Hebrews 2:10-11 For it was fitting for Him, for whom are all things and by whom are all things, in bringing many sons to glory, to make the author of their salvation perfect through sufferings. For both, He who sanctifies and those who are being blessed are all of one, for which reason He is not ashamed to call them brethren,

Hebrews 1:3 who being the brightness of His glory and the express image of His person, and upholding all things by the word of His power, when He had by Himself purged our sins, sat down at the right hand of the Majesty on high.

The Middle Wall of Partition was Broken Down

Because humanity is made up of many races, tribes, cultures, and other things that divide, the partition wall between us had to be broken down. If we are to be united in Him to bring forth a more glorious body than the body of Jesus, all of the issues that divide humanity must be broken down. Therefore, He broke the wall of partition down by His death!

Ephesians 2:14-16 For He Himself is our peace, who has made both one, and has broken down the middle wall of division between us, having abolished in His flesh the enmity, that is, the law of commandments contained in ordinances, so as to create in Himself one new man from the two, thus making peace, and that He might reconcile them both to God in one body through the cross, thereby putting to death the enmity.

Through Christ's death, God provided the means for the two most significant obstacles to unite us in His fullness—our sins and differences.

God Is Calling for Unity Out of Diversity

Now that Jesus has broken down the middle wall of partition through His death, burial, and resurrection, it's up to us, who have responded to His call, to walk worthy of what He accomplished. We must endeavor or try hard to walk in the unity He made possible.

Ephesians 4:1-7 I, therefore, the prisoner of the Lord, beseech you to have a walk worthy of the calling with which you were called, with all lowliness and gentleness, with longsuffering, bearing with one another in love, endeavoring (trying hard)[256] to keep the unity of the Spirit in the bond of peace.

As mentioned earlier, God has given us a measure of faith and gift in Him. Therefore, if we are to come together as the glorious body that adequately represents Jesus, there must be an intense endeavor to be fitted together. Peter said in his first epistle that we are living stones built together for His purposes.[257] Paul basically said the same thing.

---

[256] Words in parenthesis added to define what the word endeavor means.
[257] 1 Peter 2:5, Romans 12:3-5

Immersed Into the Body of Christ

1 Corinthians 12:13-14 For by one Spirit we were all baptized into one body; whether Jews or Greeks, whether slaves or free; and have all been made to drink into one Spirit. For, in fact, the body is not one member but many.

As we travel along the path of life, we will meet people with all kinds of diversities. We must now learn how to walk together in unity and have the same care for one another. Walking with the same respect and care for one another will knit the body together and cause it to be the magnificent body God has purposed.

We Have Many Differences

Personalities	Class	Giftings
Backgrounds	Gender	Strengths & Weaknesses
Race	Culture	Politics

1 Corinthians 12:25 that there should be no schism in the body, but that the members should have the same care for one another.

Ephesians 4:16 from whom the whole body, joined and knit together by what every joint supplies, according to the effective working by which every part does its share, causes the growth of the body for the edifying of itself in love.

A Body is Being Prepared

In Christ, we are not to know each other after the flesh but after the new creation. Knowing each other in this way enables God to prepare a body for His glory and power—a body that will adequately represent Him in every way and eventually fill all in all—His body, His fullness.[258]

2 Corinthians 5:16-17 Therefore, from now on, we regard no one according to the flesh. Even though we have known Christ according to the flesh, yet now we know Him thus no longer. Therefore, if anyone is in Christ, he is a new creation; old things have passed away; behold, all things have become new.

God's predestinated purpose is to have a fully functioning body continually edifying itself in love. God is doing a mighty work in the hearts of His people all over the earth. He is calling forth His body, the Church, to be the most glorious entity in the world. This body shall usher in the most remarkable revival ever known to humanity and will prepare the hearts of people everywhere for His Second Coming.[259] His body is the Church Jesus is building, of which He says, *"The gates of hell shall not prevail against it."*[260]

Throughout the Bible, the Church is sometimes referred to as the Bride of Christ. Paul mentions that we were espoused as chaste virgins to Christ. As Jesus was the express image of the Father, the royal daughter or the Bride is now being prepared similarly. The day is coming

---

[258] Ephesians 1:23
[259] James 5:7
[260] Matthew 16:18

when she will be in full display with her wedding garments and shall appear in the Father's brightness and glory. Through the power of the Holy Spirit, God is transforming her from glory to glory in His image. She will be a bride without spots or blemishes.

Psalm 45:13-15 The royal daughter is all glorious within the palace; Her clothing is woven with gold. She shall be brought to the King in robes of many colors; the virgins, her companions who follow her, shall be brought to You. With gladness and rejoicing, they shall be brought; they shall enter the King's palace.

Revelation 19:7 "Let us be glad and rejoice and give Him glory, for the marriage of the Lamb, has come, and His wife has made herself ready."

2 Corinthians 3:18 But we all, with unveiled face, beholding as in a mirror the glory of the Lord, are being transformed into the same image from glory to glory, just as by the Spirit of the Lord.

The transformation into Christ's image pertains to us as individuals and the body as a whole. The many-membered and diverse body shall be changed into the image of Christ, bearing the Father's brightness and glory. Therefore, this is where our journey into the invisible realms of the kingdom of God is taking us. The Kingdom is a part of us as the Holy Spirit directs our lives to be changed from glory to glory into the image of Christ.[261] This transformation process is where you are going if you want to experience authentic Christianity rather than a dull, miserable experience in Christianity. It will challenge you as you encounter others on the same path. *Iron will have to sharpen iron* for God's purpose to come forth in His Glory.[262]

Becoming a Functioning Member

Now that we understand how vital immersion into the body of Christ is, it will be significant to grasp how God knits and frames us together to function together in harmony.

Bear in mind that everything we do in the Lord should involve dying to ourselves and embracing the cross of Christ so that Christ is present in our lives. We are to lay our lives down for one another like Jesus laid His life down for us.[263] Race, gender, culture, class, political background, or personality should not affect how we relate. We are all one in Christ and must receive and accept one another accordingly. It takes death to self and embracing the cross for this to happen. In every area of our lives, especially in this area, embracing the cross brings us into God's purpose so that we can bear fruit.

Romans 15:5-7 Now may the God of patience and comfort grant you to be like-minded toward one another, according to Christ Jesus, that you may with one mind

---

[261] Luke 17:21, 2Corinthians 3:18
[262] Proverbs 27:17
[263] 1John 3:16

and one mouth glorify the God and Father of our Lord Jesus Christ. Therefore receive one another, just as Christ also received us, to the glory of God.

If we are to function in harmony and unity with the other members of the body of Christ, we will need the primary ingredient of love to work powerfully in our lives. Every aspect of our walk with the Lord, including our faith, works by love.[264]

Many characteristics in our lives enable the body of Christ to function in the manner God has designed and ordained it, but the primary factor is love. It is the glue that holds everything together. As the apostle Paul said, *"There is a more excellent way—love, which is the bond of perfection."*[265]

What does it mean to love one another and receive one another in the body of Christ? We will want to look more specifically at what this means.

We Belong To One Another

When I think of how perfectly and wonderfully our bodies were fashioned and created by God, with all of our parts functioning in perfect harmony, it gives me faith to believe the body of Christ can operate similarly. All of the elements of my human body belong to each other. Each part is a necessary part of the whole to make it function in how God created it. When part of my body is hurt or wounded, my entire body suffers because all the parts belong to each other and are connected.

1 Corinthians 12:14-18 For, in fact, the body is not one member but many. [15] If the foot should say, "Because I am not a hand, I am not of the body." Is it, therefore, not of the body? [16] And if the ear should say, "Because I am not an eye, I am not of the body," is it therefore not of the body? [17] If the whole body were an eye, where would be the hearing? If the whole were hearing, where would the smelling be? [18] But now God has set the members, each one of them, in the body just as He pleased.

The above passage of Scripture illustrates how the human body is an example of how the body of Christ operates. Every part is needed because they all belong and are connected.

Romans 12:5 So in Christ we who are many members form one body, and each member belongs to all the others (NIV).

Because Jesus bought and paid for us with His blood, we now belong to Him, which means we also belong to His body. Therefore, we cannot say, "I don't need other body members."

When we partake of communion—the Lord's Supper, we partake of His body and blood He poured out for us. We bring to remembrance all that Jesus accomplished when He was crucified on the cross. When He

---

[264] Galatians 5:6
[265] 1 Corinthians 12:31, Colossians 3:14

allowed His seed to be buried in the earth, His purpose in going to the cross was to bring forth a more glorious body.[266]

We read in 1 Corinthians that when we eat and drink the cup in an unworthy manner, many are sick and weak and even die because of a lack of discernment of the Lord's body.[267] Even though it refers to the Lord's physical body when He was here on earth, it also refers to His body of believers—the body of Christ. We bring judgment upon ourselves when we fail to discern the importance of belonging to the body of Christ and what our part and function in it are.

We Must Recognize our Need for One Another

The nourishment and the blessings God desires to pour into our lives often flow through the body's life. The more connected we are to one another through a sense of belonging, the easier it is for us to receive from God. Unfortunately, many go without and don't have their needs met because of an independent spirit that is resisting what it means to belong to one another. We see this in the following Scripture:

Colossians 2:19 and not holding fast to the Head, from whom all the body, nourished and knit together by joints and ligaments, grows with the increase which is from God.

We Must Maintain a Forgiving and Forbearing Attitude

In our relationships, it's important to recognize we are all imperfect and incapable of doing and saying the right thing all the time. As a result, we will offend one another from time to time and even come to dislike certain things about each other. Ecclesiastes says it very well.

Ecclesiastes 7:20-22 For there is not a just man on earth who does good and does not sin. [21] Also, do not take to heart everything people say, lest you hear your servant cursing you. [22] for many times, also, your own heart has known that even you have cursed others.

In other words, we must get over being thin-skinned or easily offended. If you are a person who gets easily offended, you will have a difficult time in your relationships. Unless you are willing to die to yourself in this area, you will have a hard time with forgiveness and forbearance, as we see in the following Scriptures.

Ephesians 4:32 And be kind to one another, tenderhearted, forgiving one another, just as God in Christ also forgave you.

Colossians 3:12-13 Therefore, as the elect of God, holy and beloved, put on tender mercies, kindness, humbleness of mind, meekness, longsuffering; bearing with one another, and forgiving one another, if anyone has a complaint against another; even as Christ forgave you, so you also must do.

---

[266] John 12:23-24
[267] 1 Corinthians 11:29-30

When these things come up, the natural thing to do is to withdraw or put up walls in the relationship. But God's way is to continue to build the relationship in a godly way with an understanding that *iron sharpens iron, so a man sharpens the countenance of his friend.*[268]

Jesus was able to look beyond our sins and shortcomings when He received us, and we must do the same for each other. We are no longer to focus on the natural man but rather on the new man that God is creating.

2 Corinthians 5:16 Therefore, from now on, we regard no one according to the flesh. Even though we have known Christ according to the flesh, yet now we know Him thus no longer.

Many hurt people come into the Church after years of abuse from the world. Hurting people tend to harm others. As you love and forgive them during their pain, you become an agent of healing by continually receiving and accepting them. You are not only helping them along in their journey, but you are also helping yourself as well. What you sow, you will reap.

Esteem Others More Important Than Yourself

One of the most incredible things we can do in our relationship with others is to esteem others more significant than ourselves. Can you imagine what it would be like if we all practiced this? We would be continually encouraged.

Philippians 2:3-4 Let nothing be done through selfish ambition or conceit, but in lowliness of mind let each esteem others better than himself. Let each of you look out not only for his own interests but also for the interests of others.

By regarding the needs and concerns of others more than your own, you automatically enter into a relationship of receiving and accepting others.

Be Hospitable To One Another

Aside from being hospitable to those we enjoy being with, there are many times in our journey when a situation demands that we be gracious and kind to one another. Sometimes, these things happen at the most inconvenient times. It could mean bringing someone into your home that would involve giving up some of your independence, or it could be as simple as providing a meal or a ride to someone in need.

I have had to make adjustments so many times that I've finally gotten to the point where I've learned to do it with the right attitude. My wife was the benevolence outreach pastor in our church and is the kind of person whose heart continually goes out to people in need. She often

---

[268] Proverbs 27:17

called on me to help her give a ride to someone or help move furniture or something with my truck. Sometimes, I encountered people who grated against my personality, but I've learned to die to my feelings and be hospitable without grumbling or complaining. It's a growing experience we must all go through.

1 Peter 4:8-10 And above all things have fervent love for one another, for "love will cover a multitude of sins." Be hospitable to one another without grumbling. As each one has received a gift, minister it to one another as good stewards of the manifold grace of God.

As I conclude this chapter, I want to remind you that we must be committed to seeing the body of Christ come to the stature of the fullness of Christ. Because of what Christ has already accomplished for us, we should be willing to make the necessary sacrifices to help make this happen. As Paul said in Romans, *"It's only reasonable that we present our bodies as living sacrifices, holy and acceptable unto God."*[269]

---

[269] Romans 12:1

Spiritual Gifts and the Body of Christ

Chapter Ten

Now, there are diversities of gifts, but the same Spirit. There are differences of ministries, but the same Lord. And there are diversities of activities, but it is the same God who works all in all. But the manifestation of the Spirit is given to each one for the profit of all—1 Corinthians 12:4-7.

As seen in the previous chapter, Jesus was the complete expression of the body of Christ with the full measure of God's Spirit working in and through Him during His time on earth. He expressed God's image in character, power, and authority. Jesus had all the gifts working in Him with the fruit of the Spirit fully developed in His life.

Our discussion now revolves around the importance of operating with the gifts of the Spirit. The gifts of the Spirit are an integral part of our spiritual growth and function within the body of Christ. Paul said concerning spiritual gifts, *"I don't want you to be ignorant nor come short in any gift while eagerly waiting for the second coming of Christ."*[270] We must understand God's will and purpose to discover our particular gift or gifts. Rather than pushing the default button through unbelief, ignorance, or apathy, we must press into spiritual gifts. Involvement with the gifts brings excitement, fun, and challenge to your journey.

Ephesians 4:7 But to each one of us grace was given according to the measure of Christ's gift.

We're to Desire Spiritual Gifts

Through the gifts, the manifestation of the Spirit is freely given for the profit of all.[271] We are encouraged strongly to desire spiritual gifts.[272]

---

[270] 1 Corinthians 1:7 and 12:1
[271] 1 Corinthians 12:7
[272] 1 Corinthian 14:1

We all have a measure of the fullness of Christ's Spirit and faith.[273] Having gifts differing according to the grace given to us, we are to use them as the following passages of Scripture encourage us.

Romans 12:5-6 So we, being many, are one body in Christ, and individually members of one another. Having then gifts differing according to the grace that is given to us, let us use them.

1 Peter 4:10 As each one has received a gift, minister it to one another, as good stewards of the manifold grace of God.

Notice that it says, *"As each one has received a gift according to the grace given to us, we are to use them by ministering one to another."* We are good stewards of the manifold grace of God when we take to heart the admonition to discover and develop the gift or gifts freely given to us. As we do, we make a contribution to the whole, which will have an effect on the world around us.

Through the gifts of the Spirit, God releases His power to the world in which we live. Just as the world needed to see displays of God's power throughout the ages, it is equally important in our lives today. Today's world is experiencing as much decay and degeneration as ever. It needs to experience an impressive display of God's power and anointing. Otherwise, it will be carried away by the tide of violence and wickedness currently sweeping through nations of the world. The Church—the body of Christ is the pillar and ground of all truth—a city set on a hill with its lights brightly shining for all to see.[274]

It's up to us as His body to rise and be all God has ordained in this critical hour of the Church's destiny. Without the gifts of the Spirit operating in our lives, it will never happen. However, there is hope because God is positioning each of us to be a part of the end-time anointing that shall sweep the world as we allow His gifts to emerge.[275]

The Gifts are for the Benefit of the Whole.

The gifts of the Holy Spirit are for the common good or the profit of all. When the Holy Spirit manifests Himself through a gift to someone, it's not for the person's sake but for the good or gain of the whole body. Spiritual gifts are given wholly for ministering to others, though the ministry may be to one or several or the entire body. We see this in the following passage of Scripture.

1 Corinthians 12:4-7 Now there are diversities of gifts, but the same Spirit. There are differences of ministries, but the same Lord. And there are diversities of

---

[273] Romans 12:3
[274] 2 Timothy 3:15 & Matthew 5:14
[275] 1 Corinthians 4:20

activities, but it is the same God who works all in all. But the manifestation of the Spirit is given to each one for the profit of all:

With an understanding that God is always working, we realize God knows how and when to meet needs because He is omniscient. He knows where His servants are, at any given time, with the particular gift to meet their needs and will use them accordingly. Our part is to open the eyes of our understanding to the field of harvest we are laboring to see where and how God is working.[276]

John 12:26 If anyone serves Me, let him follow Me; and where I am, there My servant will also be. If anyone serves Me, him My Father will honor.

It is through our faithfulness as servants that God uses us, which is why we need to be good stewards of the gift He has given to us. When we are faithful and steadfast, it allows God to set up divine appointments. Because God is always aware of the need where His servants are, He can manifest His glory as He works all in all.

In the passage below, two words help us see God's intent and purpose for the gifts and how He expects them to operate in our lives.

1 Corinthians 12:6-7 And there are diversities of activities, but it is the same God who works all in all. ⁷ But the manifestation of the Spirit is given to each one for the profit of all.

God Who Works All in All to Manifest His Spirit

The word *"works"* in verse six means active operation, effectual, powerful, active, efficient, fervent, and mighty in showing forth—the word *"manifestation"* in verse seven means to make visible, clear, and known. According to Vine's Greek Dictionary, the meaning is to uncover, lay bare, or reveal.

With these two definitions in mind, we can see it's God's desire for us to be fervent and mighty in showing forth and making His power visible through the gifts of the Spirit. As members of His body, we are to be zealous, active, effectual, efficient, and mighty in manifesting the gifts of the Spirit to benefit the body as a whole—authentic Christianity in action.

Jesus gave examples of operating in the gifts as He ministered in all of them with the full measure.

Definition of a Spiritual Gift

A spiritual gift is a divine attribute given by the Spirit to every member according to God's grace for use within the context of the body of Christ for specific times and places. Spiritual gifts are not latent talents or trained abilities brought to heightened expression. Instead, they are

---

[276] John 4:35-36, Ephesians 1:17-18

supernatural manifestations of God's authority and power given to members of His body to act on His behalf.

As members of His body with God's divine nature, we act in the name of Jesus, doing the Father's will. We are supernatural beings with His divine ability and indwelling presence. Because we belong to Him, we are linked with His capacity and omnipotence and can draw from it as needed. It's a two-way street. We draw our anointing from Him as He draws from our willingness to serve as His vessels of honor—an agreement that produces a powerful explosion in the Spirit. Paul had this agreement in that *which was working in Him mightily."*[277]

Each member has at least one gift to use for His glory and the growth and care of His Church, the body of Christ. Manifestations of the Holy Spirit occur in and through all believers regardless of background, experience, or education. Our part is to press in and receive and use the gift given.

1 Corinthians 12:7-11 But the manifestation of the Spirit is given to each one for the profit of all. ⁸ for to one is given the word of wisdom through the Spirit, to another the word of knowledge through the same Spirit, ⁹ to another faith by the same Spirit, to another gifts of healings by the same Spirit, ¹⁰ to another the working of miracles, to another prophecy, to another discerning of spirits, to another different kinds of tongues, to another the interpretation of tongues. ¹¹ But one and the same Spirit works all these things, distributing to each one individually as He wills.

Notice it says, *"distributing to each one individually as He wills."* The Father is intimately acquainted with each of us.[278] He created us in His image to function with a designated purpose. The Spirit distributes the gifts needed to fulfill our destiny and purpose. We may all desire whatever gifts we want, but our primary gift will be what the Father chooses.

If it's God's will for us to desire spiritual gifts, then it's also true that each of us has already received a spiritual gift, whether dormant or functioning. It's up to us to discover and develop them. As we do, we become faithful stewards of the manifold grace of God.

1 Peter 4:10 As each one has received a gift, minister it to one another, as good stewards of the manifold grace of God.

Our spiritual gifts are needed to help the body come to the stature of the fullness of Christ. As we are faithful to minister to one another, we add dimensions of faith to us and those we serve. By faithfully operating in our gifts, we add to the increase and growth of the body.[279]

---

[277] Colossians 1:29
[278] Psalm 139:2-3
[279] Ephesians 4:16

Spiritual Gifts and the Body of Christ

Let's look at the gifts to see how they operate in us and the body of Christ. First, however, I will give you a brief description of each gift as an introduction. After that, I am merely attempting to whet your appetite for further study.

Spiritual gifts are broken down into four areas: Revelation, Power, Vocal, and Service gifts found in 1 Corinthians 12 and Romans 12.

The Revelation Gifts

The revelation gifts are the word of wisdom, knowledge, and discerning of Spirits. Through them, we may know anything God chooses to reveal. They are fragments of God's knowledge, wisdom, and discernment to meet specific needs, answer challenges, or determine the source of spiritual activity in a person's life, whether human, demonic, or divine.

The word of wisdom is the unique ability to speak forth the wisdom of God in almost any situation. For example, it could come as you pray for a particular person and receive a word of wisdom that is precisely right for how you should be praying and handling the situation. You know because your spirit immediately agrees. It could also come forth in counseling, opening the door for active ministry into the person's life as the two of you recognize it as divine intervention. We all encounter many situations in the everyday routines of life where the word of wisdom coming forth is of great value. Learn to ask and look for it with a heart of expectancy.

Jesus gave many examples of how to use these gifts. First, we have the account of the woman caught in adultery.[280] Then, in this story, we see His example of being slow to speak and quick to hear while listening for the word of wisdom coming from the Father.[281] Jesus' confession was that He only did what He saw and heard the Father doing.[282]

While looking to Jesus as our example in all things, we must never forget that even though He was God, He made Himself of no reputation by not acting as God. Instead, Jesus ministered as a man fully empowered by the Holy Spirit within Him.

Jesus used the gift of the word of wisdom here to confound those accusing the woman. As a result, the woman was led to repentance while her accusers sheepishly backed away and disappeared.

We often do not lead people to repentance because we are too quick to speak and condemn rather than wait on God. Instead, we need to be

---

[280] John 8:2-11
[281] James 1:19
[282] John 5:30-31

like Jesus, who was slow to speak and quick to hear the perfect word of wisdom that brings reconciliation to those listening.

Proverbs 25:11 A word fitly spoken is like apples of gold in settings of silver.

As we are faithful to minister one to another, we will encounter innumerable opportunities to use the gift of wisdom in conversations, counseling opportunities, and even in exceptional situations, as seen in the above example of Jesus when confronting the scribes and Pharisees.

The word of knowledge is the unique ability to declare a fragment of God's knowledge only revealed supernaturally. Wikipedia defines it as follows: *Among Pentecostal and Charismatic Christians, the word of knowledge is often defined as the ability of one person to know what God is currently doing or intends to do in another person's life. It is also defined as knowing the secrets of another person's heart.*

The gift of the word of knowledge enables us to minister efficiently and understand the enemy's situations, circumstances, and strategies. It allows us to know how to speak in the above conditions with the knowledge that can bring healing and understanding to others. As we wait on God in various situations, He can speak into our spirits a word of knowledge that addresses the issue and opens their hearts to what the Lord desires to do.

In John's Gospel, the account of Jesus with the woman at the well illustrated how He used this gift to see into the window of her soul. With it, He addresses an area in her life that brought her to repentance.

In a lengthy conversation with her, Jesus reveals things about her failed marriages and the man she was currently living with. As a result, she perceived Him as a prophet and then realized He was the Messiah. She then goes and tells the whole city, and they all come to hear Jesus as well. As a result, many become believers in Him.[283]

John 4:42 Then they said to the woman, "Now we believe, not because of what you said, for we ourselves have heard Him and we know that this is indeed the Christ, the Savior of the world."

This passage shows the importance of taking the gifts into our sphere of influence, small group, or congregational settings. The word of knowledge from Jesus opened the door for many to believe in Him. What would happen if we used the gifts as we go into the world and marketplaces with a heart of expectancy? Revival would most likely break out with people convinced as the Samaritans were—that Jesus is the Messiah, who has come to deliver them from their sins.

---

[283] John 4:1-42

Discerning Spirits distinguishes between genuine and false doctrine and between what is of the Holy Spirit and what isn't. Satan can appear as an angel of light with a false and tempting deception.[284] The Bible makes it clear there can be lying spirits in the mouths of prophets. Satan can speak right after God speaks, as in the case of Peter when he had the incredible revelation of proclaiming Jesus as the Messiah.[285]

The gift of discernment is very much needed in the Church today! But unfortunately, the Church is full of deceptive practices and influences. Satan has had his day, but his time is coming to a close as Jesus continues to build His Church, a Church that will prevail against the enemy.

The Power Gifts

The power gifts are the gift of faith, working miracles, and gifts of healing. God gives supernatural manifestations for a particular time in a specific place. These gifts show God's glory, power, greatness, majesty, and victory over sickness and disease. They're for deliverance and overcoming nature itself.

The gift of faith is miraculous, like all other gifts of the Spirit. It is a supernatural manifestation that miraculously gives a surge of assurance and confidence, which sometimes arises in a person facing a particular situation or need.

All Christians have a measure of faith that is essential to their journey in the Lord. The gift of faith, however, is the unique ability to trust God and exercise faith in individual circumstances, as Peter did when he walked out of the boat onto the water.[286]

An example of the gift of faith is when Jesus cursed the fig tree. As a result, it immediately withered and died.[287] Jesus used the fig tree as a lesson to show us we can also have this kind of faith. He said, *"Therefore I say to you, whatever things you ask when you pray, believe that you receive them, and you will have them."*[288]

Another example of the gift of faith in action is when Peter and John spoke the word of faith to the lame man who was healed.[289] Their burst of faith resulted in 5,000 people getting saved and coming to the Lord. Just as these people turned to Jesus due to the gift of faith producing miracles and healings, the hearts of people everywhere are turned

---

[284] 2 Corinthians 11:14, Genesis 2:16 – 3:5
[285] Matthew 16:23, Acts 13:6-1-2, 16:16-18, 1 John 4:1-3
[286] Matthew 14:22-33
[287] Mark 11:12-14, 20-24
[288] Mark 11:24
[289] Acts 3:1-10

towards the Lord when we step out in gifts of faith, miracles, and healings.

The gift of miracles comes when the Holy Spirit chooses to "override" the laws of nature working in or through an available person. They are supernatural manifestations of the Spirit to perform miracles.

There are many examples of miracles in Scripture. We know Jesus performed many miracles, such as turning water into wine, raising the dead, healing the blind, walking on water, and many others during His three-and-one-half years of ministry. The Apostles also performed all kinds of miracles. They were able to cast out demons, heal the sick, raise the dead, strike people dead, cause blindness, and much more.[290] As did Steven before his persecution in Jerusalem, Philip had extraordinary results in Samaria with miracles.[291] Peter's shadow healed people as he walked the streets of Jerusalem.[292]

When God moves, it is always with purpose. Miracles are no different. God often uses Miracles to move the Church in a particular direction. For example, when God performed miracles through the hand of Moses, it was to lead the people of Israel out of Egypt. In the New Testament, there was a magnificent display of God's power through the hands of Jesus and his early disciples. Miracles through their hands helped to launch the New Testament Church. They're always happening in various places, but there are seasons in which they are much more abundant.

It appears we may be entering into the latter days before Jesus' return—another significant event in the Church—a time when He desires to bring His Church to the stature of the fullness of Christ as His glory fills all in all.[293] As God poured out the early rain upon the Church to moisten the ground, the seed of the gospel was planted during the ministry of Jesus and the first disciples.

The latter rain brings the harvest to a place of complete maturity![294] The prophets Haggai and Joel spoke of the latter house as greater than the former, with the early rain pouring out moderately.[295] The latter rain will cause the Church to become a great army with authority as Jesus cleanses His Church and prepares it for the awesome day of the Lord. Miracles will be everywhere, with God's people filled with the Spirit going forth with the same zeal as the early disciples—a zeal that caused

---

[290] Acts 2:43; 3:1-10;5:1-16; 9:36-43; 13:4-12; 19:11-12
[291] Acts 6:8, 8:4-8
[292] Acts 5:14
[293] Ephesians 4:13, 1:22-23
[294] Joel 2:23
[295] Haggai 2:7-9, Joel 2:23 KJV

their known world to be filled with the gospel of Jesus Christ. As a result, multitudes upon multitudes will be saved in this coming harvest.[296]

The final harvest is coming. Jesus said, *"The harvest truly is plentiful, but the laborers are few. Therefore, pray the Lord of the harvest to send out laborers into the His Harvest."*[297] Will your journey be such that it causes you to press into the gifts of the Spirit and to be used by the Lord in remarkable ways, or will you press the default button in unbelief or apathy and miss out on grand adventures in the faith? The choice is yours. Ask the Lord for rain in the latter rain, and He will give it to you.[298] A double portion is awaiting you!

John 4:35 Do you not say, "There are still four months, and then comes the harvest?" Behold, I say to you, lift up your eyes and look at the fields, for they are already white for harvest!

The gifts of healing are supernatural abilities or manifestations of the Spirit for various kinds of healing and restoration to individuals through the power of the Holy Spirit. The New Testament is filled with examples of the apostles going forth with power as they received the gift to cure diseases.

Gifts of healing and working of miracles often operate in conjunction with the gift of faith, as with Peter and John in Acts 3:1-8 where the Holy Spirit prompted and gave them the gift of faith to heal a lame man.

Another great example is when Paul was at Lystra and perceived a man in the audience had faith to be healed. However, even though the man had faith to be healed, his faith wasn't enough until it was joined with Paul's faith to perform the healing.

Acts 14:8-10 And at Lystra a certain man without strength in his feet was sitting, a cripple from his mother's womb, who had never walked. This man heard Paul speaking, Paul, observing him intently and seeing that he had faith to be healed, said with a loud voice, "Stand up straight on your feet!" And he leaped and walked.

In this situation, it wasn't faith and the miracle alone that produced the healing—a word of knowledge also came. So Paul received a word of knowledge that the man had faith to be healed.

The Vocal Gifts

The vocal gifts are tongues, interpretation of tongues, and prophecy. They are supernatural manifestations of the Spirit, through which God speaks through His vessels about anything He chooses to tell. The gift of tongues and the interpretation of tongues are inseparable. Therefore, the

---

[296] Joel 2:28-32, 3:14
[297] Matthew 9:37-38
[298] Zechariah 10:1

gift of tongues must be interpreted when it comes forth in the congregational or small group setting.

1 Corinthians 14:27 If anyone speaks in a tongue, let there be two or at the most three, each in turn, and let one interpret.

The gift of tongues is a congregational gift, not all believers possess, as implied in 1 Corinthians 12:30, where it asks the rhetorical question, *"Do all speak with tongues?* The answer is, obviously, no. In the same way, not everyone has the gift of miracles, healings, or interpretation of tongues. This particular passage is in the context of how the gifts are used when the church meets as an assembly or in small groups.

On the other hand, there is also the gift of tongues that comes from receiving the baptism of the Holy Spirit. In the following passage, Paul writes about this difference between the two and encourages all believers to accept it.

1 Corinthians 14:3-5 But he who prophesies speaks edification and exhortation and comfort to men. He who speaks in a tongue edifies himself, but he who prophesies edifies the church. I wish you all spoke with tongues, but even more that you prophesied; for he who prophesies is greater than he who speaks in a tongue, unless indeed he interprets, that the church may receive edification.

The gift of interpretation of tongues is the God-given inspiration to speak in the listeners' language, giving them the dynamic equivalent of what was expressed in tongues. However, the interpretation of tongues is just that, an interpretation. It is not a translation.

Prophecy is also the God-given inspiration that speaks to the congregation a particular word from God that communicates and reveals His will, mind, and purpose through a Spirit-filled individual. Prophecy can also come to specific individuals, such as the prophet Agabus prophesying to Paul about going to Jerusalem. Prophecy to particular individuals is often called *personal prophecy,* which can be very helpful in a person's life. [299] I have already covered this aspect of prophecy more explicitly in chapter five of *"Navigational Tools—Word and Spirit."* Please see that chapter for further explanation.

The Service Gifts

The service gifts build us in love, prepare us for effective kingdom service, and enable us to live between the miracles. These gifts have a greater capacity for consistently building the church.

Some gifts listed in the following passages were included in the previous section, but others listed below were not on that list, which can be called service gifts. The two passages on the next page are as follows:

---

[299] Acts 21:9-12

ministry, teaching, exhorting, giving, leading, showing mercy, helps, and administration.

Romans 12:6-8 Having then gifts differing according to the grace that is given to us, let us use them: if prophecy, let us prophesy in proportion to our faith; or ministry, let us use it in our ministering; he who teaches, in teaching; he who exhorts, in exhortation; he who gives, with liberality; he who leads, with diligence; he who shows mercy, with cheerfulness.

1 Corinthians 12:28 And God has appointed these in the church: first apostles, second prophets, third teachers, after that miracles, then gifts of healings, helps, administrations, varieties of tongues.

The gift of ministry involves all church service areas that require someone with a special grace that goes above and beyond the average ability to serve. We are all called to serve, but some excel in ministering to others because of their gifting. They are gifted in functional areas like the select group in Acts 6, where they are called deacons. The gift of ministry isn't relegated to the office of deacons only but can refer to any serving done in the name of the Lord Jesus Christ where their gifting takes them above and beyond the normal.

The gift of teaching is the spiritual ability to take the truth from God's Word and explain it clearly so that God's people can understand and apply it to their lives. The teaching gift is expressed within various ministries in the church, such as small groups, children, teachers of women, or one who teaches the whole congregation. It communicates biblical truth and motivates God's people toward a life of godly obedience to that truth.

The gift of exhortation and encouragement is the spiritual ability to come alongside a person who is hurting spiritually or emotionally to offer a word of comfort or encouragement that would enable the person to continue to move forward despite the wound. It could also come as a word of admonishment—truth in love—in a challenging manner that gives them the nudge they need in their spiritual journey.

The apostles renamed a man called Joseph to Barnabas (son of encouragement) because of his ministry to the early church in Jerusalem.[300] For example, Barnabas found Saul in Tarsus and brought him to the church in Antioch. Up until then, the Church, for the most part, had ignored Paul. Because of Barnabus, Paul was fully received into fellowship.

Barnabas saw something in Paul and was determined to draw it out of him. We all need people in our lives who will discern the gift of God in us and draw it out. What would have happened if Paul had been left to

---

[300] Acts 4:36-37

his own devices without a son of encouragement coming to him? Where would the Church be?

Many Christians fall by the wayside because there is no one with the gift of encouragement to help them on their way. The body of Christ needs people who encourage and exhort for the benefit of the whole. The example of Barnabus and Paul shows how the gifts of the Spirit relate to God's overall plan and purpose. Paul became very strategic in spreading the gospel of Jesus Christ in the early days of Christianity, taking the gospel as far away as Rome. Many accused him of turning the world upside down with the gospel's message.[301] Nevertheless, all of Asia Minor heard the gospel because of his ministry.[302] He wrote one-third of the New Testament.

Giving with liberality is the spiritual ability to give financially or materially to the Church and the needs of others within the body of Christ or the community in which they live. It is a gift to be shared in simplicity for the glory of God without drawing attention to one's self. Barnabas is also an example of this gift in that he sold a field and gave the money to the apostles for the sake of the Church.[303]

We all have the responsibility to give—everybody—nobody is excluded! We are all to give as we purpose, not grudgingly or of necessity, for God loves a cheerful giver.[304] The giving should be systematic, not haphazard, not according to whether you feel you can or can't, but each is to lay aside as the Lord has prospered.[305]

The gift of leadership is the spiritual ability to stand before a group and lead, such as a mission project, an elder's meeting, or the building of a new community of Christians.

James, the Lord's brother, is an example. Even though he wasn't one of the original apostles, he eventually became the leading apostle of the church in Jerusalem because of his ability to lead and make hard decisions.

He is seen in action with the leadership gift when he made the final decision to the council of the Jerusalem elders following the heated discussion on whether the Gentile believers should be circumcised.[306] After hearing all the arguments, he was the deciding voice as to what should happen.

---

[301] Acts 17:6
[302] Acts 19:10
[303] Acts 4:36-37
[304] 2 Corinthians 9:8
[305] 2 Corinthians 16:2
[306] Acts 15:13-19

The word *rule* associated with leadership means it can vary in many ways. When it says, *"He that rules, let him rule with diligence."* It implies the church's eldership, as the word *rule* means "to be able to stand before individuals." The idea of ruling with diligence suggests doing it with eagerness in a business-like manner. One of the qualifications of elders is that they are to rule well.[307] However, eldership is not the only manifestation of the gift. The gift of leadership needs to be in operation in many areas of church life. Many ministries within the church need someone operating with the gift or skill to lead.

The gift of mercy is the spiritual ability to manifest pity and aid those physically, emotionally, or spiritually helpless. It is the capacity to express compassionate, loving action and lift the downtrodden while doing it joyfully. The example of Tabitha in the Book of Acts is an excellent example of the gift of mercy.

Acts 9:36 At Joppa, there was a certain disciple named Tabitha, which is translated Dorcas. This woman was full of good works and charitable deeds, which she did.

The person with the gift of mercy can aid an individual who is hurting emotionally or physically. They have an understanding that exudes compassion that allows others to open up. In their mercy, they speak words of truth that can touch the heart of the matter, *like apples of gold in settings of silver.*[308] They recognize a genuine need or concern without being asked to respond. Instead, they answer out of heartfelt concern.

The gift of helps is the ability to help by aiding and assisting others with compassion and grace. The word translated as "helps" means literally "to relieve, succor, participate in, and support." These are those gifted with helps that are beyond what most of us are willing or able to do. Yet, they can freely give of themselves in various ways that encourage the body of Christ.

Countless things come up that make this gift necessary and needed. People with this gift are more than willing to pitch in and help, even if it's for the most mundane or repulsive jobs. Whether working with the church, projects, helping widows, single moms, or whatever, they offer their help with a spirit of humility and grace as they volunteer anonymously.

The gift of administration is the ability to organize, implement, plan, and keep track of various duties and records as a help to the organizational structure of a church. It would involve being a strategic thinker who thinks outside the parameters of situations. They have good leadership skills, manage people, projects, finances, and information,

---

[307] 1 Timothy 5:17
[308] Proverbs 25:11

and stay on task, while others might get lost in the details. They might even be able to help others accomplish tedious or difficult tasks and multitask different projects or prescribed duties of individual plans and meetings. They are likely computer-savvy and might even have excellent people skills.

There are no major or minor gifts in the charismatic outpouring with the gifts of the Spirit. All gifts are to be cherished, coveted, faithfully stewarded, and graciously utilized as products of God's unmerited favor. These are all God-given abilities to do what the gift suggests.[309]

Three Keys to Developing Spiritual Gifts

We should earnestly desire the best gifts, especially that of prophecy." The Scripture says, "earnestly desire to prophesy."[310] The best gifts are the ones God will pour into your heart, whatever they may be.

There must be holy ambition and desire. With the Holy Spirit's baptism, an explosion occurs within us. *"Dunamis"* is the Greek word for power mentioned in Acts 1:8. When the disciples received the baptism of the Holy Spirit as prophesied by John the Baptist and Jesus, they exploded with a holy ambition to fulfill the "Great Commission." They went everywhere with signs following. If we are serious about desiring spiritual gifts, it will take this same holy ambition within us as we receive the baptism of the Holy Spirit and pray in tongues daily.[311] The book of James urges us that faith without works is dead. Unless we have an active response to go along with our desire for spiritual gifts, it will always remain an unfulfilled desire. Romans 12:6 reminds us to *"use them."*

There must be an attitude of expectation. If God, through His word, has encouraged us to desire spiritual gifts, then we should expect to receive a spiritual gift. It's part of the package to equip us for the journey ahead. Unfortunately, many people never discover their spiritual gifts because they're not looking for them with a heart of expectation.

You need to know that it is in God's best interest for you to discover what He is pouring into your life. Spiritual gifts are like grace. You don't receive them because you deserve them. It has nothing to do with that. They belong to you because you are a child of God. Therefore, you need to diligently seek the gift God has for you.

---

[309] Most of these definitions I picked up over the years, but do not know where they originated from.
[310] 1 Corinthians 12:1 and 1Corinthians 14:1,39
[311] See Chapter 6 on "The Seven Essentials" for more information on the Baptism of the Holy Spirit.

Spiritual Gifts and the Body of Christ

Hebrews 11:6 But without faith it is impossible to please Him, for he who comes to God must believe that He is and that He is a rewarder of those who diligently seek Him.

Practice, Practice, Practice. No one will be perfect when attempting to function in spiritual gifts. However, the more you use them, the more you understand how they work in life and ministry.

Romans 12:6-8 Having then gifts differing according to the grace that is given to us, let us use them: if prophecy, let us prophesy in proportion to our faith; [7] or ministry, let us use it in our ministering; he who teaches, in teaching; [8] he who exhorts, in exhortation; he who gives, with liberality, he who leads, with diligence; he who shows mercy, with cheerfulness.

Ephesians 4:16 from whom the whole body, joined and knit together by what every joint supplies, according to the effective working by which every part does its share, causes growth of the body for the edifying of itself in love.

When I first received the baptism of the Holy Spirit, I would shut myself in my room and pray for hours. I wanted to develop the new tongue the Lord had given me. When I first started prophesying, I would expect God to use me at every opportunity. He was always faithful. 11He worked in my life. It took lots of practice.

Spiritual gifts are crucial to our journey and calling in God and God's purpose and destiny for His Church—the body of Christ. When we are faithful to function in the gift and the ministry God has given us, it helps the body of Christ be more active and efficient.

May God bless you as you discover and press into the spiritual gift or gifts the Father has in store for you.

Discipleship and Ministry

Chapter Eleven

And Jesus came and spoke to them, saying, "All authority has been given to Me in heaven and on earth. Go therefore and make disciples of all the nations, baptizing them in the name of the Father and of the Son and the Holy Spirit, teaching them to observe all things that I have commanded you; and lo, I am with you always, even to the end of the age." Amen—Matthew 28:18-20.

Works do not save us, even though God created us in Christ Jesus for good works. We are His workmanship.[312] Our relationship with Jesus is based solely on what He accomplished on the cross. Jesus saved us by grace and not by works. However, as we grow and mature in our relationship with Him and continue to move forward in our journey, we discover He has work for us to do. Paul speaks of this when he mentions that the saints are equipped for the work of the ministry.[313]

In ministry, discipleship, and serving, the excitement and adventure of being a Christian take off with a heightened effect upon us. As we get involved in church ministry, we experience God working in and through us as He gives us the grace to do various tasks and ministry purposes. We come to a greater understanding of what grace is. It is multifaceted, expressing God's divine ability working in us. Serving and Ministry take us into a deeper relationship with Jesus Christ as the Holy Spirit communicates the Father's heart and desire in all that we do. As the Holy Spirit leads us to more remarkable revelations of grace, work, and ministry the Father has for us, He shows us our place at His table. In this, we learn what it means to be a disciple of Jesus Christ.

Ministry and serving all evolve around the concept of being a disciple of Jesus Christ in the same way that the early disciples were followers of Jesus. With this in mind, it will be essential for us to understand the concept of discipleship more fully.

---

[312] Ephesians 2:6-8
[313] Ephesians 4:13

What it Means to Be a Disciple

Becoming a true disciple of Jesus involves understanding that discipleship is at the core of all we do as Christians. Everything we do, including evangelism, ministry, and serving, flows out of our calling as disciples of Jesus. We are all called to be disciples—there are no exceptions. If we get this wrong, it will affect everything we do. Discipleship is the foundation we must build on, as no other foundation is established other than the Lordship of Christ. Therefore, we are to take heed of how we build.[314]

A Disciple is a Disciplined Follower of Jesus Christ

Discipleship is how we grow in our walk with the Lord. We become more Christ-like as we continually depend upon the Holy Spirit to lead us in our ministry, work, and through the pressures and trials we encounter. We are to become disciplined followers who continually abide in Christ. We are to be imitators of Christ who strive to be like Him in every way. Our goal is to be molded to His image.[315]

Luke 6:40 A disciple is not above his teacher, but everyone who is perfectly trained will be like his teacher.

Followers of Jesus are more than students. They are strict followers of Jesus Christ in every aspect of their lives. They are in a continuous learning process throughout their journey with the Lord. They adhere to the teachings of Jesus Christ by living according to the standards He and the other writers outlined in the New Testament.

A Disciple Embraces the Cross of Christ

A disciple of Jesus must willingly embrace the cross of Christ and all that it represents. In the life of Jesus, it represented obedience, pain, suffering, humiliation, and death. As it says in the Book of Hebrews, *"It was for the joy that was set before Him that He endured the cross and its shame."*[316] As followers of Christ, we are to maintain the same attitude toward Christ as we embrace the cross.

Hebrews 12:3-4 For consider Him who endured such hostility from sinners against Himself, lest you become weary and discouraged in your souls. You have not yet resisted to bloodshed, striving against sin.

Paul's testimony was that he desired to know Christ in the fellowship of His sufferings.[317] Throughout his journey, it was evident he lived this out. We will most likely not suffer in the manner that he did, but as we

---

[314] 1Corinthians 3:9-15
[315] Romans 8:29
[316] Hebrews 12:2
[317] Philippians 3:10

Discipleship and Ministry

purpose to live godly lives in a sinful world, we will find, at times, being ridiculed and even persecuted.[318] We see in the following Scripture how Paul suffered in some ways.

2 Corinthians 11:26 (NIV) I have been constantly on the move. I have been in danger from rivers, in danger from bandits, in danger from my fellow Jews, in danger from Gentiles; in danger in the city, in danger in the country, in danger at sea, and in danger from false believers.

Jesus made it abundantly clear that we can't become His disciples unless we are willing to bear His cross. He says, *"Whoever does not bear his cross and come after Me cannot be My disciple."*[319] It doesn't get any clearer than that.

The idea of getting involved in ministry is usually an exciting thought. So much of ministry is very exciting, though it can be quite a grueling experience. It will cost you your life. Are you prepared for all that the cross may demand from you? A wise man will sit down and count the cost before he begins.

At some point, you realize embracing discipleship is the only way forward in the journey you have begun with the Lord. Of course, there are different levels of commitment and responsibility as we move forward, but no matter what level we enter, there will always be dying to self as we pick up the cross and follow Jesus.

Attempting to get involved in ministry, serving, or evangelism without embracing the cross won't produce the fruit and the character Christ desires from us. Instead, we will only create dead works.[320]

Discipleship Requires Total Commitment

Jesus was quite explicit about the cost of following Him. Discipleship requires a committed life. He said, *"Any of you who does not give up everything he has cannot be my disciple."*[321] The sacrificial life is expected! Jesus told his disciples, *"If anyone would come after me, he must deny himself, take up his cross, and follow me."*[322]

What does this mean? Does it mean we sell all that we have and follow Jesus? I don't think so! Instead, it means we consider ourselves as stewards rather than owners. We are to live as He has called us, which means we must acknowledge Jesus in all our ways, whatever they may be. In other words, Jesus must be the King and Lord of our lives. Nothing is to take precedence over Him and His will for us.

---

[318] 2 Timothy 3:12
[319] Luke 14:27
[320] 1 Corinthians 3:13-15
[321] Luke 14:33
[322] Matthew 16:24

The cost of discipleship required by Jesus caused many to turn from following Him.[323] His goal wasn't to attract large crowds. He wanted disciples! The problem with some churches today is that they're more concerned with drawing large crowds than making disciples. Let's choose to be involved with churches interested in building missional communities through discipleship.

As great multitudes followed Jesus, He turned to them and challenged them with what it meant to be a disciple and count the cost.[324] So, in the following passage, Jesus challenges them to calculate the cost before building.

Luke 14:28-30 For which of you, intending to build a tower, does not sit down first and count the cost, whether he has enough to finish it— ²⁹ lest, after he has laid the foundation, and is not able to finish, all who see it began to mock him, ³⁰ saying, "This man began to build and was not able to finish?"

Will you be one of those who have counted the cost and become a true disciple of Jesus? Or will you press the default button because of a lack of faith and understanding of what being a follower of Jesus requires? Pressing the default button may seem easy and painless now, but what will it earn you in the end? By embracing the cost of discipleship, you will receive significant rewards in this life and the future.

As we are faithful to commit our ways unto Him daily, we die to ourselves as Paul encouraged us to do.[325] When we die daily, it will cause us to be missional in our approach to our day-to-day activities rather than seeking what we can get out of them.

Does discipleship mean we never take the time to enjoy ourselves? No! God is faithful in giving us plenty of time to rest and enjoy ourselves as we commit our lives to Him and His purposes.

Following Jesus' dissertation on what it means to be a disciple and counting the cost, He said, *"Salt is good; but if the salt has lost its flavor, how shall it be seasoned? It is neither fit for the land nor the dunghill, but men throw it out. He who has ears to hear, let him hear!"*

Discipleship Causes Our Light to Shine

Discipleship affirms the fact that our salt will not lose its flavor. Hopefully, we will have ears to hear what Jesus is saying to us about what it means to become a true disciple of His. Once we have counted the cost, we are ready to move forward into the ministry and calling He has for us. His calling will lead us into ministry and missional purposes

---

[323] John 6:63-68
[324] Luke 14:25-28
[325] 1 Corinthians 15:31

while serving and being a witness for Him. By becoming true disciples, the Scriptures assure us that our works will not be burned.

I remember the day I committed to being sold out to Jesus Christ as His disciple. I had just been saved for a few months when a friend gave me the book, *"The Cost of Discipleship,"* by Dietrich Bonhoeffer. As I read the book, I came across the chapter challenging the readers from the passage in Isaiah about being the one the Lord would send.

Isaiah 6:8 Also, I heard the voice of the Lord, saying: "Whom shall I send, and who will go for Us?" Then I said, "Here am I! Send me."

As I read this portion of the chapter more than 40 years ago, the presence of the Lord came over me very strongly. At that moment, I knelt and said, "I will go! Send me." It was a decisive defining moment in which I sensed total consecration unto the Lord. Shortly after that, the Lord opened the doors for me to travel to Alaska and begin Bible College.

There should be a time in our lives after we have tasted the Lord's goodness and counted the cost that we commit to following Him as wholehearted, faithful disciples.

John 8:31-32 If you abide (continue-KJV) in my word, you are my disciples indeed; ³²and you shall know the truth, and the truth shall make you free.

As we take this step of faith, the Father fills us with a more profound revelation and understanding of who He is and how He desires to work in our lives. For me, it was as if the windows of heaven opened with the revelation of God's Word, filling my spirit and soul in a much deeper way than I had previously experienced. Excitement and passion for His calling formed in me and catapulted me forward enormously. I became consumed with the new-found passion for God's kingdom and the calling He had placed in my life. It has led me through many avenues of ministry these past 40 years.

Even now, as I write this book, I sense the Holy Spirit breathing life and revelation into me as I write. Discipleship brings us to an understanding of the kingdom that is ever increasing, as Isaiah 9:7 says, *"Of the increase of His government or kingdom there shall be no end."* Becoming a disciple causes us to know the truth in a way that sets us free from the burdens and cares of this life, bringing healing and deliverance as we cast all of our cares upon Him.

Discipleship Gives Birth to Ministry

Most of the work that gets done in the kingdom is by saints whom God calls to do the work of the ministry. That's you! We need to get over the concept that it's just those who are in full-time ministry to whom God calls to ministry. Ministry is for every saint of God—that's you! We are all called to serve in some capacity. By accepting the call to be a disciple, you need to know you will be in a ministry of some sort. In any given church or body of believers, there is plenty of work to go around.

You may think, "I'm not sure what my ministry is!" Just get involved and start serving wherever there's an opening. You will discover your passion and gifting as you serve and get involved.

As a young Christian, one of my first service areas was in a bus ministry. As an introvert, this was a big challenge for me, but I decided to face my insecurities and do it. I would go out each Saturday, meet the parents, and talk to the kids riding my bus. It wasn't long before I began to enjoy doing this each week as I started to sense the grace of God leading me out of my insecurities and giving me favor with the kids and their parents.

My next area of service was teaching the single adults in our church during our Sunday morning classes before the service. I had never done anything like this before, but there was a need, and I responded to it. Again, my obedience led me to more significant study times in God's Word.

During this season, I also felt compelled to be involved in evangelism, which also went against my introverted personality. I, therefore, became God's secret agent and started planting evangelistic tracts everywhere. It was my way of doing something despite my introverted nature.

God showed me how to get involved in ministry as a young believer in all these service areas. It was very exhilarating and life-changing! Then, the transformation process began to take root as I willingly offered myself as a living sacrifice in those areas that weren't in my comfort zone.[326]

The next stage of my Christian experience took me to Bible College at a large church in Anchorage, Alaska. During this time, I became involved in all kinds of evangelistic endeavors, from witnessing on the streets and in bars to picking up hitchhikers and spending Saturday afternoons witnessing and counseling with guys in the city jail in downtown Anchorage. I also had a small group Bible study in my home every week. My last area of service during this phase of my life was teaching Biblical foundations at the local mission weekly. They all had to listen to me before getting their free meal for the day.

At this juncture, I knew God had called me to ministry but was unsure about what aspect. As I was faithful to serve wherever the need was, God began to reveal what my primary gift was. At first, I thought it was

---

[326] Romans 12:1

evangelism, but I soon discovered that teaching was where my passion and anointing seemed to be.

If you desire to learn who you are in Christ and what your area of gifting is, start serving and allow the Lord to lead you and reveal your true passion and gifting. Eventually, you find your place. Don't wait for someone to seek you out; begin to do it, and you'll discover the faithfulness of God in relationship to who you are in Christ.

The Church has all kinds of ministries that need everyday people with a heart to serve. Places like greeters, children's ministry, ushering, benevolence, hospitality, small group leaders, singers, musicians, youth workers, visitor follow-up, evangelistic outreach events, office help, building and grounds maintenance, intercessors, and many more are always in need of faithful followers of Jesus to serve.

Disciples in Action

I recently attended our Sunday 11:00 am service and was sitting in the back of the church because I had broken my foot. I was using crutches, so I wanted a spot near the back where there wasn't too much traffic. The service was quite full, and I watched Monte, the usher, trying to find seats for all the latecomers. He's a man about 75 years old who walks with a limp. Even though our church caters to a much younger crowd, an older man served God with all his heart.

As I watched Monte find seats for everyone, I was impressed with his diligence. He would walk down the aisle several times during the service, noting where all the empty seats were. Unfortunately, many of them were in the middle of the rows, which meant asking the people at the end of the rows to scoot over or step out to let in the latecomers.

As I observed how effortlessly he did this with an expression of joy, I thought to myself, "There's a real servant of God enjoying his ministry—a disciple in action." You see, because he was in his place of ministry and doing it with joy, he was helping and ministering to others who needed to feel comfortable as they worshiped the Lord. His joint supplied what was necessary for the body to edify itself and grow in love. He was a saint doing the work of the ministry.

I have a friend named Charlie, a greeter at our Saturday evening service. He's in his early 50s, has long blond hair, and has an upbeat personality—a natural extrovert. Charlie's gift is his personality. He's not afraid to talk to anybody. He's always warm and friendly to whomever he speaks to, no matter who they are. He can draw out even the shyest person. He faithfully ministers every week, whether scheduled or not. Everyone knows him in a church of over 1500 because he has greeted them at one time or another. He is a faithful servant who takes his gift of hospitality and the responsibility with it very seriously.[327] He provides that first touch to everyone who walks through the doors, especially those visiting for the first time. He's a saint doing the work of the ministry—a disciple in action—his joint supplying to the whole. He's fulfilling the following Scriptures just as Monte was.

Ecclesiastes 9:10 Whatever your hand finds to do, do it with your might; for there is no work or device or knowledge or wisdom in the grave where you are going.

Ephesians 4:16 from whom the whole body, joined and knit together by what every joint supplies, according to the effective working by which every part does its share, causes growth of the body for the edifying of itself in love.

Several years ago, after being the senior pastor of a church for 12 years, my wife and I felt it was time to step aside and pursue a different avenue of ministry. We had no guarantees as to what our future would hold. During this season, we did all sorts of things to make ends meet, including being the custodians of the church to whom we had sold our building. We had become a part of this new church plant and were excited about starting over.

One evening, as I was vacuuming between the rows of seats, I sensed the Lord saying, "What you're doing right now is just as important as every sermon you've ever preached." It was another defining moment for me as I approached this season of my life. It helped me walk in humility towards the Lord and others as I followed the advice of the scripture above that says, *"Whatever your hand finds to do, do it with your might."*

It has been 19 years since stepping aside, and my wife and I are walking in God's blessing in every way. God has been faithful to us as we have continued to serve and involve ourselves in Kingdom ministry. I ministered for 15 years in my primary gifting, which is that of a teacher to our first and second-year interns—a group of 18-25-year-olds—performing many other functions while being on staff at the new church plant. I am now semi-retired with a writing ministry and have a business as a wedding officiant. I have also led small groups for the last several years that have seen many saints of God discipled and brought into Kingdom truths—my website ministers to many pastors and saints worldwide who need equipping for the ministry. The site reaches over 1500 unique visitors a week. My wife is the pastoral assistant to the senior pastor and benevolence outreach pastor at the church we attend. Instead of sitting idly by, we have kept ourselves busy building the kingdom. There is no retirement from that.

---

[327] 1 Peter 4:9-10

When we allow God to use our talents and gifts to disciple others, He is faithful! The examples above and my story illustrate the importance of getting involved and doing what we can, no matter who we are. As we are devoted to becoming disciples and disciple others with the gift God has placed in us, He is faithful to move us forward on our journey. We may not see everything clearly, but as we step out in faith, we begin to see with greater clarity. Through our example, we leave a path that is visible to others. Ministry avenues open up as we commit ourselves to be faithful disciples of Christ. As we serve with willing and obedient hearts, we find ourselves positioned as faithful laborers in the harvest where the Lord is working.

John 12:26 If anyone serves Me, let him follow Me; and where I am, there My servant will also be. If anyone serves Me, him My Father will honor.

As we are faithful to serve in this manner, the invisible path opens up before us with greater clarity while God continually reveals His plans and purposes to us. We see ourselves as lively stones fitted and framed into the building God is raising and vessels unto honor rather than dishonor.

1 Peter 2:2-5 As newborn babes, desire the pure milk of the word, that you may grow thereby, ³ if indeed you have tasted that the Lord is gracious. ⁴Coming to Him as a living stone, rejected indeed by men, but chosen by God and precious; ⁵you also, as living stones, are being built up a spiritual house, a holy priesthood, to offer up spiritual sacrifices acceptable to God through Jesus Christ.

2 Timothy 2:20 But in a great house, there are not only vessels of gold and silver but also of wood and clay, some for honor and some for dishonor.

My prayer for you is that as you continue your journey, you will open your heart to all God has for you and become a vessel unto honor. May God bless you richly as you press into discipleship and ministry!

The Need for Guardrails

Chapter Twelve

For if God did not spare the natural branches, He may not spare you either. Therefore consider the goodness and severity of God: on those who fell, severity; but toward you, goodness, if you continue in His goodness. Otherwise, you will also be cut off.
Romans 11:21-22

As you travel south along the Pacific Coast on Highway 101, there are many places where you are very thankful for guardrails. The guardrails are there for your safety and protection because of the many places where the road is very narrow and winding. It would not be very comforting if it weren't for the guardrails. Even with the guardrails, it can be pretty scary. On a trip there last year, my wife informed me this was the last time she would ever come on this road. Sometimes, it feels like you could end up down a cliff and into the ocean if you make the slightest mistake. On the other side of the road, the steep hills act as guardrails for your protection.

I live in Northern California, about two hours from South Lake Tahoe. When traveling East towards Lake Tahoe on Highway 50, there's a place where you are about 7250 feet in elevation on a winding two-lane road with a deep canyon to your right. From the passenger side, looking out your window, it seems like an abyss below. However, on the driver's side, you have the mountain for your protection, which acts as a natural guardrail. If it weren't for the guardrails, you would, most likely, be traveling slowly with much precaution and trepidation. The guardrails are there for your protection and safeguard so that you feel safe and secure.

As we continue our journey with Christ, we need spiritual guardrails in place for our security and protection. There will be innumerable occasions along the way where we will need them to keep us on track with God and His purpose for our lives. Without them, we could easily injure ourselves and end up emotionally wounded, potentially causing us to shipwreck our faith in God.[328] In addition, because we all have a propensity towards foolishness and stubbornness at times, we desperately need these guardrails.

There are two significant guardrails in the Christian experience designed to keep us on the straight and narrow path so we don't lose sight of our eternal destiny and purpose. They are God's goodness and severity, as we saw in the opening Scripture.

For the most part, God's goodness keeps us safe and secure. The goodness of God leads us to repentance and then keeps us in a continuous state of repentance. However, there are times when we also need a healthy dose of the severity or the fear of God to keep us safe and secure.

The Goodness of God

We experience the goodness of God in many ways. It comes from being redeemed from the hand of the enemy, delivered in times of trouble, led by the Spirit, satisfying our hungry souls, comforted during times of distress, deliverance from our destructive ways, blessings beyond measure, successful seasons, and much more.[329] God desires to pour His goodness into us in ways beyond our imagination. He has given to us all things that pertain to life and godliness.

The goodness of God is one of the Father's divine attributes that helps us to understand His nature and who He is. In coming to the Lord and being drawn to Him through His goodness, we soon discover He is inherently good. As a result, we take refuge in Him, knowing He will always be there to protect us and act as a guardrail while keeping us from the harmful tactics of the enemy.

Psalm 34:8 "Taste and see that the LORD is good; blessed is the one who takes refuge in him."

Over and over in the first chapter of Genesis, God describes His works. He saw all that He had made, and it was excellent.[330] In the same way, God displayed His goodness in all He created; His goodness appears to us as His created beings. We are products of His goodness or the fruit of His works. It doesn't matter who we are or what we do; we cannot earn His goodness. It's simply freely made available to us despite ourselves. God is good to all and has compassion for all He has made. That's you and me! His tender mercies can't be denied nor stopped.

Psalm 145:9 The Lord is good to all, and His tender mercies are over all His works.

---

[328] 1 Timothy 1:19
[329] Psalm 107
[330] Genesis 1:31

The Need for Guardrails

Because of God's goodness, we can put our trust in Him in a way that enables our hearts to respond with a resounding, "Yes, I'll receive it!" As we receive His goodness that endures forever, it becomes a stronghold or a guardrail to us in times of trouble, hardship, and discouragement.

Nahum 1:7 The Lord is good, a stronghold (guardrail) in the day of trouble; and He knows those who trust in Him.[331]

As seen here, the goodness of God is a strong guardrail for us. It offers us the security and encouragement we need during difficult and trying times. It is continually there for us in that God's character never changes. Through His goodness, He constantly provides for us according to His plans and purposes.

Jeremiah 29:11 For I know the thoughts that I think toward you, says the Lord, thoughts of peace and not of evil, to give you a future and a hope.

James 1:17 Every good and perfect gift is from above, coming down from the Father of the heavenly lights, who does not change like shifting shadows.

God's goodness never changes with the shifting shadows of time. However, good things are sometimes disguised as adversity or hardship. But don't worry! God even causes those things to work together for our good. He cannot deny who He is. It's impossible! In all circumstances, His goodness keeps us from going over the edge and continually acts as a guardrail to protect us.

Romans 8:28 And we know that in all things work together for good to those who love God, to those who are called according to His purpose.

As stated earlier, God's goodness initially draws us unto Him and begins to produce the repentance that continually brings us into a deeper relationship with God, the Father. The goodness of God is at the core of our faith as we mature and move forward. As we keep our eyes and hearts open to God's goodness, it becomes the stronghold of righteousness and the guardrail God intended it to be.

We keep our hearts open by praising God for His goodness. David had a revelation of God's goodness and often praised and thanked Him for it.

Psalm 107:1-2 Oh, give thanks to the Lord, for He is good! For His mercy endures forever. Let the redeemed of the Lord say so, Whom He has redeemed from the hand of the enemy.

Psalm 107:8 Oh, that men would give thanks to the Lord for His goodness and for His wonderful works to the children of men!

David repeated this phrase three more times in this chapter after writing about the wonderful works of the Lord.[332] He then sums it up in

---

[331] I added (guardrail)
[332] Psalm 107:15, 21, 31

verse 43: *"Whoever is wise will observe these things, and they will understand the lovingkindness of the Lord."*

The more we thank and praise God for His goodness, the greater the revelation we receive of how it affects us, becoming more of a stronghold for protection.

Do you understand the goodness of the Lord towards you? If not, give yourself to Him in thanksgiving. I would encourage you to read and meditate on this chapter in Psalms over and over until it gets lodged deep in the recesses of your heart: *"Oh that men would give thanks to the Lord for His goodness, and for His wonderful works to the children of men!"*

Gratitude is what is required as we contemplate how great God's love and goodness are. We often lightly esteem His goodness or take it for granted by withholding our thanksgiving because it's a common occurrence with God. It is through our gratitude that we don't take it for granted and even come to despise it.

You may say you'd never come to the place of taking it for granted, but it happens so quickly through the hardness of our hearts. An indicator that His goodness is despised is when it no longer leads us to repentance. If our hearts have grown cold toward Him, it's a good sign that we have grown cold in our appreciation of His goodness toward us. So, a heart examination may be in order.

Romans 2:4 Or do you despise the riches of His goodness, forbearance, and longsuffering, not knowing that the goodness of God leads you to repentance.

As a young Bible College student, I had acquired a job working at a warehouse. We had a large break room where we gathered during our breaks and lunchtime. One day, while hanging out and eating lunch with everyone, some were shooting pool and playing ping pong; the conversation shifted to what everyone had done over the weekend. They told stories about their wild escapades while laughing, cursing, and swearing. Amid this, I had an overwhelming sense of gratitude and joy. I began to thank the Lord for bringing me out of all that and thinking, "Who am I that God would pour out His mercy, grace, and goodness toward me?" I had such an overwhelming sense of the deliverance God brought me that my heart began to swell with gratitude and joy. Some 40 years later, I still remember it like it was yesterday.

I often still find myself taking a few minutes here and there to think about all that God has done for me over the years. His faithfulness and goodness have always abounded towards me. I am so thankful that He sought me out—a poor, helpless sinner to pour forth His goodness, mercy, and grace.

I desire to be like David, who prayed, *"Oh, that men would give thanks to the Lord for His goodness and for His wonderful works to the children of men!"* My prayer is that this is your heart cry as well. *"Let the redeemed of the Lord say so."*

The Severity of God

Now that we have discussed the goodness of God and how wonderful it is, we must also look at the severity of God—the other guardrail that is necessary for our protection. This guardrail is required for when we begin to take for granted the goodness of God and lose sight of all that God has done for us. Losing sight of God's goodness can produce a recklessness in us that could cause us to crash hard.[333] Because God is a faithful and merciful God, He has put the guardrail in place to keep us from going over the edge and crashing into the abyss below. It is also called the fear of God.

Jesus spoke of it when He said, *"Do not fear those who kill the body but cannot kill the soul. But rather fear Him who can destroy both the soul and body in Hell."*[334] Solomon said, *"The fear of the Lord is the beginning of wisdom, and the knowledge of the Holy One is understanding."*[335]

I understand that the fear of the Lord is a tremendous respect and reverence for God, but it also entails what Jesus said when He said, *"Fear Him, who can destroy the soul and body in Hell."* With this comes the necessity of a healthy Biblical understanding of what Hell is and who's going there.

The Reality of Hell

There is much to say in the Old and New Testaments concerning Hell and the Lake of Fire. The Bible teaches that life continues after the physical death of the body. God created man with a natural, physical body and an eternal soul. The soul of man consists of who we are. It is the center of our mind, will, and emotions. The Bible teaches that life is eternal. Because the soul is immortal, we will spend eternity in Heaven or Hell.

Daniel 12:2 And many of those who sleep in the dust of the earth shall wake, some to everlasting life, some to shame and everlasting contempt.

God created Hell for the devil and his demons to inhabit. It is such an awful place that Jesus said cutting off your hand or gouging out your eye would be better than going there. There will be crying and total darkness

---

[333] Romans 11:22
[334] Matthew 10:28
[335] Proverbs 9:10

in Hell—a lake of unquenchable fire and brimstone with intense pain and agony.

Mark 9:43 And if your hand makes you sin, cut it off. It is better for you to enter into life maimed than having two hands, to go to hell, into the fire that shall never be quenched.

Mark 9:45 And if your foot makes you sin, cut it off. It is better for you to enter life lame, than having two feet, to be cast into hell, into the fire that shall never be quenched.

Indeed, people can partially experience hell on earth. Those who live in rebellion against God and His ways do experience, to a small degree, some of the things that those in Hell are suffering. This experience is, however, only a slight foretaste of the miseries that the occupants of hell will experience forever.

Hell will be a place of intense torment, pain, and weeping, described as a furnace of fire where there will be wailing and gnashing of teeth.[336] The example that Jesus gave of the *"Rich Man and Lazarus"* illustrates the intensity of the pain in Hell. The rich man tormented in the flame did not wish this place of torment upon anyone.[337] Instead, he cried out, saying, *"Father, Abraham, have mercy on me, and send Lazarus that he may dip the tip of his finger in water and cool my tongue, for I am tormented in this flame."*[338]

People say they would rather party in Hell with their friends at various times than walk in gardens with their enemies. What an absurd statement! If they only realized how ridiculous it is. As the Bible describes it, there will be no partying in Hell, only extreme loneliness, blackness, and darkness forever.[339] The day of salvation will save you from this terrible existence throughout eternity.

Hell will be an awful place, separated from the presence of God, the rejected Lamb, the holy angels, and the redeemed. There will be no light, life, peace, joy, righteousness, or salvation. Only darkness and torment of conscience will be there for those who rejected and despised God's grace.

The critical thing to remember is that Jesus did not come to condemn the world. On the contrary, He came to save the world from this awful place of torment.[340]

John 3:17-19 For God did not send His Son into the world to condemn the world, but that the world through Him might be saved. He who believes in Him is not

---

[336] Matthew 13:42,50
[337] Luke 16:19-28
[338] Luke 16:24
[339] Jude 13
[340] The Foundations of Christian Doctrine - Kevin Conner

condemned, but he who does not believe is condemned already because he has not believed in the name of the only begotten Son of God. And this is the condemnation, that the light has come into the world, and men loved darkness rather than light because their deeds were evil.

2 Peter 3:9-11 The Lord is not slack concerning His promise, as some count slackness, but is longsuffering toward us, not willing that any should perish but that all should come to repentance.

A lot of people will end up in Hell. They come from every background, race, society, religion, and culture. Among their numbers will include those whom the Bible describes as:

- Those who do not know God – *2 Thessalonians 1:8*
- Those who don't obey the Gospel – *2 Thessalonians 1:8*
- Sinners and hypocrites - *Isaiah 33:14*
- Those who practice lawlessness – *Matthew 13:41*
- Cowardly, unbelieving, abominable, murders, sorcerers, sexually immoral, idolaters, and all liars – *Revelation 21:8*
- Adulterers, thieves, homosexuals, covetous people, drunkards, and extortioners – *1 Corinthians 6:9-10*

The Bible says the road to Hell is wide, and the road to Heaven is narrow. Which road are you traveling? *"Do not be deceived, God is not mocked; for whatever a man sows, that he will also reap."*[341]

Are We Secure in our Salvation?

You may be thinking, "I'm secure in my salvation. I can never lose it." If that's what you believe, this next section may be somewhat challenging. I would encourage you to read it and ponder it. Allow the Scriptures to speak for themselves without trying to interpret them through any school of thought. Our loyalty must be to God's Word, not schools of thought.

I do not believe a person goes through a continuous cycle of being saved and lost repeatedly. Therefore, I do not think because a person is in a backslidden condition, they have necessarily lost their salvation, but I do believe there is a point where you can become so deceived in your backsliding that you eventually disown Christ by no longer believing. At this point, you fulfill the Scriptures that speak of disowning Christ. The following passages reveal that Christ cannot disown you unless you first disown Him. Remember, Jesus cannot disown you unless He first owns you.

Matthew 10:33 (NIV) But whoever disowns me before others, I will disown before my Father in heaven.

---

[341] Galatians 6:7

2 Timothy 2:12 (NIV) If we endure, we will also reign with him, if we disown him, he will also disown us.

You may think you could never get to the point where you could disown Christ. The problem with that kind of thinking is once you begin the slippery slope of backsliding, you open yourself up to Satan's devices and deception to a greater degree. You have no idea where deception could lead you. Jesus speaks of a strong delusion coming upon the world before His second coming. He says, *"If possible, even the elect would be deceived."* Paul speaks of a great falling away before the coming of Christ—a time when many will disown Christ. A great deception is coming. To keep from being deceived, we will need both guardrails in place. Those whose hearts are cold towards the Lord through their backsliding wouldn't have a chance. The enemy is already walking around looking for those whom he can devour. A backslider is easy picking for him.

I tell my Bible students I'm afraid to backslide because I don't know what will happen once deep deception settles in. That's the fear of God—my guardrail for protection! I understand the severity of God as much as I understand the goodness of God. I know it's a fearful thing to fall into the hands of a living God. Do you?

Now that I've disarmed you let's continue to see what the Bible says concerning our eternal salvation and security. Without this guardrail in place, we are all in extreme danger.

There will be a Great Falling Away.

Paul speaks of a great falling away in 2 Thessalonians.[342] Those who fall away have defected from the truth of the Christian faith. Falling away implies a strong rebellion or revolt before the Second Coming of Christ. The point is that some people will fall into this category. They are the ones who disown Christ.

Is it Possible to Fall Away, Never to be Saved Again?

There is a point where the once-saved believers are utterly depraved in their minds and actions. The writer of the Book of Hebrews addresses this very issue in the following passage. However, the stipulations below reveal that only a mature believer can commit this sin.

Hebrews 6:4-9 For it is impossible for those who were once enlightened, and have tasted the heavenly gift, and have become partakers of the Holy Spirit and have tasted the good word of God and the powers of the age to come, if they <u>fall away</u>, to renew them again to repentance, since they crucify again for themselves the Son of God and put Him to an open shame.

---

[342] 2 Thessalonians 2:3

This passage clearly shows a point where a Christian has backslidden so far that they can't return. The Greek word for *"fall away"* is *"parapipto,"* which means to fall aside or to apostatize.[343]

These Christian believers were once:
- Enlightened - *John 1:6-12*
- Tasted of the Heavenly Gift - *John 3:16 & Romans 6:23*
- Made Partakers of the Holy Spirit - *Acts 19:2*
- Tasted of the Good Word of God - *Hebrews 5:12-14*
- Tasted of the Powers of the World to Come - *Acts 1:8*

This person has given up their birthright in the same way that Esau did. Giving up one's birthright is where backsliding leads to the extreme position of disowning Christ, as Paul warned Timothy.[344] John refers to disowning Christ as the sin that leads to death.[345] The writer of the Book of Hebrews refers to it as "willful sin" in a later chapter about the person who has trodden underfoot the Son of God and insulted the Holy Spirit. Jesus referred to it when He spoke of the individual who blasphemes the Holy Spirit and commits the unpardonable sin.

Mark 3:29 (NIV) But whoever blasphemes against the Holy Spirit will never be forgiven; they are guilty of an eternal sin.

The words *"fall away"* describe the person's willful and independent position. It means to walk alongside or out of the will of God with no intent of returning to God's way—total apostasy. There is an open renunciation of Jesus Christ and a gathering together of the enemies of Christ.

There Is a Point Where God Cuts off Those Who Disown Him

If God did not spare natural Israel when they committed apostasy, what makes us think He will save us if we fall away? We must continue in the goodness and severity of God. Otherwise, we, too, will be cut off.

Romans 11:21 For if God did not spare the natural branches, He may not spare you either.

The writer of the Book of Hebrews gives us a strong warning about drawing back unto perdition by letting us know that it is a fearful thing to fall into the hands of the living God. God takes no pleasure in those who draw back. We see this again in chapter ten.

Hebrews 10:31,38-39 It is a fearful thing to fall into the hands of the living God. [38] Now the just shall live by faith; but if anyone draws back, my soul has no pleasure in him." [39] But we are not of those who <u>draw back to perdition</u>, but of those who believe to the saving of the soul.

---

[343] Strong's Greek Dictionary Concordance #3895
[344] 2 Timothy 2:12
[345] 1 John 5:16

When the above passage speaks of those who *"draw back unto perdition"* or waste and destruction, it is possible, or it would not have been written to warn us. The word perdition indicates loss of well-being, not of being. The destruction then is everlasting without annihilation.

Hebrews 10:26-27 If we sin willfully after we have received the knowledge of the truth, there no longer remains a sacrifice of sins, but a certain fearful expectation of judgment, and fiery indignation which will devour the adversaries.

Some would like to say this refers to someone who continually rejects Jesus after being convicted many times. However, as we see in the following Scriptures, it's not so.

Hebrews 10:29 Of how much worse punishment, do you suppose, will be thought worthy who has trampled the Son of God underfoot, counted the blood of the covenant by which he was sanctified a common thing, and insulted the Spirit of grace? ³¹ It is a fearful thing to fall into the hands of the living God.

This person:

- **Was sanctified by the blood of Jesus**: To be sanctified means to be set apart from the world unto God.
- **Has trodden underfoot the Son of God:** To trample underfoot the person of Jesus and all that He is and has done is to count Him as refuse. Trodding underfoot the Son of God is an act of utter contempt for Christ.
- **Has counted the blood of Jesus as unholy:** To value the precious, sinless blood of Jesus as that of a pig or unclean thing.
- **Has done despite unto the Spirit of Grace:** He insults the Holy Spirit, who he had received by God's grace, by insulting all the work of the Spirit he had been a partaker of, such as salvation, baptism, healing, gifts, fruit, etc.

As we have seen, "falling away" consists of total renunciation or disowning of Christ and Christianity. However, we must remember that backsliding is where the process begins. Once people start to backslide, they open themselves up to more incredible deception from Satan. Our enemy is a devouring lion who goes after those weak in the faith. Don't be fooled! Satan will come after you with everything he has. As you begin the downward spiral of backsliding, his goal will be to get you to commit apostasy. That's why I'm afraid to backslide. I am well aware that I have fallen into the hands of a living God.

Remember that God will never disown you unless you disown Him first. According to the passage below, He equates disowning with blaspheming the Holy Spirit.

2 Timothy 2:12 (NIV) If we endure, we will also reign with Him. If we disown Him, He will also disown us.

Luke 12:9-10 But whoever disowns me before others will be disowned before the angels of God. ¹⁰ And everyone who speaks a word against the Son of Man will be forgiven, but anyone who blasphemes against the Holy Spirit will not be forgiven.

I don't believe anyone knows where this cut-off point is. We are not the judge, nor could we because we don't have all the facts in each case. Even if we did, we would not have the wisdom to analyze them. God is the righteous judge, and there is a point where God says, "No more—that's it!"

Judgment Awaits Those Who Have Blasphemed the Holy Spirit

The entire chapter of Peter's second epistle describes believers who go back and become apostates.

2 Peter 2:20-21 For if, after they have escaped the pollutions of the world through the knowledge of the Lord and Savior Jesus Christ, they are again entangled in them and overcome, the latter end is worse for them than the beginning. ²¹ For it would have been better for them not to have known the way of righteousness, than having known it, to turn from the holy commandment delivered to them.

These People Were Saved:

- The Lord had bought them—*Verse 1.*
- They had forsaken *(to leave down or behind, to abandon, to forsake)* the way—*Verse 15.*
- They had escaped the pollution *(uncleanness)* of the world.
- They are again entangled and overcome in the world.
- They had known the way of righteousness and turned from it.

We must seriously consider this passage. It says, *"It would have been better for them not to have known the way of righteousness."* How could it possibly be better not to have known the way of righteousness? Could it be because they have committed the unpardonable sin, and eternal judgment is what awaits them? There's no opportunity for them to turn back to the Lord. They're done!

Hebrews 10:26-27 If we sin willfully after we have received the knowledge of the truth, there no longer remains a sacrifice of sins, but a certain fearful expectation of judgment, and fiery indignation which will devour the adversaries.

2 Peter 3:17 You therefore, beloved, since you know these things beforehand, beware lest you also fall from your own steadfastness, being led away with the error of the wicked.

As seen from the testimony of Scripture, there is an agreement that it is possible to lose your salvation. I have been purposely laborious so that you can see how the Scriptures agree. As you take the Scripture warning to heart, you will have built a stronghold of righteousness as a solid guardrail to keep you safe and secure.

Be assured that you will be safe and secure as you stay close to the guardrail of God's goodness with a heart of thanksgiving. If not, the guardrail of the severity of God is there to stop you from your foolishness and falling into the abyss. As you take the time to build both of these guardrails by getting these Scriptures and principles embedded in your heart, you will be safe and secure throughout your journey in the Lord. As you carefully build your guardrails, you will experience eternal security!

Psalm 107:43 "Whoever is wise will observe these things, and they will understand the lovingkindness of the Lord."

Vision, Purpose, and Destiny Your Future

Chapter Thirteen

For I know the thoughts that I think toward you says the LORD, thoughts of peace and not of evil, to give you a future and a hope—Jeremiah 29:11

Knowing that we've been born again with a purpose is essential as born-again believers. As you grasp that God has invited you to be a part of His great plan and purpose on earth, an added excitement floods your spirit and soul as you realize God has given you destiny and purpose to fulfill.

2 Timothy 1:9, who has saved us and called us with a holy calling, not according to our works, but according to His own purpose and grace which was given to us in Christ Jesus before time began.

Before God conceived us in the womb, He had a plan and a purpose for our lives. Through the foreknowledge of God, He knows us from beginning to end. As a result, He has called and even molded us according to His divine purpose for our lives.[346]

To properly connect to our destiny and purpose, we must understand that God is always at work to bring us where we can discover and capture the destiny He has marked out for us. Understanding that we all have defining moments when God allows us to see things from His perspective will be significant. As we begin to view our lives through His lens, we begin to catch glimpses into our calling and destiny.

We were all created and designed by God with a unique calling and purpose to serve a God who comprehends our path and acquaints Himself with all of our ways.[347] He takes great delight in giving us a future filled with hope and anticipation of what He will do next. As we yield to the Holy Spirit, He outlines the details of our journey.

As we seek to capture the vision that reflects our passion and uniqueness, we soon discover we have a latent purpose within each of

---

[346] Please see, http://kenbirks.com/predestination.html
[347] Psalm 139:3

us. Our part is to discover the particular role God created us to play. It is a role uniquely designed according to our personality, gifting, innate abilities, and talents, as well as the many experiences, whether good or bad, we have picked up along the way.[348] Only as we willingly enter the role God designed for us can we fully discover all He has created us to be.

It has been said, *"The real test of a man is not when he plays the role he wants for himself, but when he plays the role destiny has for him."*[349]

When God created you, He had a definite purpose related to His purposes on the earth, as seen in the following Scripture.

Jeremiah 1:5 "Before I formed you in the womb I knew you; before you were born, I sanctified you; I ordained you a prophet to the nations."

We may not be called to be prophets to the nations, but just as God knew Jeremiah before forming him in the womb, He knew you and me. He had a role already ordained for Jeremiah, just as He does for us. In the same way that Jeremiah had a strong sense of the role God had planned for his life, David did as well, as seen in the following passage.

Psalm 139:16-18 Your eyes saw my substance, being yet unformed. ***And in Your book, they were all written, the days fashioned for me, when as yet there were none of them.*** *[17] How precious also are Your thoughts to me, O God! How great is the sum of them! [18] If I should count them, they would be more in number than the sand; when I awake, I am still with You.*

Ask yourself the following questions: "Am I living the role designed for me in particular, or am I a lost and wandering soul still searching for answers? Am I caught up in mundane, boring experiences that lead to nowhere in particular?"

You may have caught glimpses of His purpose at times but have never been able to capture them before they slip away. If so, it's time to lay hold of God's purpose and vision for you so that you will be in sync with His precious thoughts toward you.

It has been said, *"There is a goldmine hidden in every life. God never made a failure. Every man has success hidden away in his soul. No one else can find it but himself."*[350]

Discovering Hidden Destiny through Defining Moments

We all have an unknown future filled with purpose and vision, as the Scripture says, *"For you died, and your life is hidden with Christ in God."*[351] God is waiting for you to discover and seize what He hid. It's

---

[348] Romans 8:28
[349] Quote from *Vaclav Havel, President, Czech Republic*
[350] Quote from E.W. Kenyon
[351] Colossians 3:3

up to you to capture it. No one can do it for you. A life without purpose will cause you to chase endless rainbows, resulting in dissatisfaction, heartache, and disillusionment. With this comes a sense of failure, apathy, and emptiness, leading to a sense of worthlessness. No wonder many people today are strung out on meds to relieve their depression and anxiety. Some experience depression and anxiety because of chemical imbalances in their bodies, but many simply because of their lack of faith. They continually press the default button rather than pursue a life of faith and adventure in sync with God's purposes.

Have you ever had a fleeting thought that was gone before you could capture it and explore it in detail? It happens pretty frequently to me. If we want to grab it, we must immediately reel it by meditating and focusing on it. We experience something very similar with vision and purpose. Looking back over our lives, we can seize the defining or kairos moments that have shaped the person we are today.[352] In doing so, we notice threads that are woven through our circumstances. They can point toward our purpose and destiny in Christ as we tie them together. As we open our hearts to the movement of God in our lives, we can see and perceive how He providentially weaves the threads of our calling through our lives. He gives us the ability to distinguish them.

As I have been writing this book, I have shared some of the defining moments that have shaped my life. They have continually pointed me toward my purpose and vision. They have been a great help to me in interpreting the many incidents that have typified the relevant circumstances that have followed. In short, they have helped me understand how God has shaped me throughout my life. I have seen how God has created and designed me to function in the ministry and His calling for my life. Because I now understand how defining moments work, I quickly recognize and distinguish them as strong confirmations that God is still working in my life and moving me forward in purpose and destiny, which continually adds to my faith as I move from faith to faith.

One of the keys to moving forward in purpose and destiny is understanding that He who has begun a good work in you will perform it until the day of Christ.[353] When we observe that God is always at work in our lives, it gives us the confidence to move forward, knowing that everything He does relates to our purpose and destiny.

---

[352] From Wikipedia: **Kairos** is an ancient Greek word meaning the right or opportune moment (the supreme moment). The ancient Greeks had two words for time, chronos and kairos. While the former refers to chronological or sequential time, the latter signifies a time lapse, a moment of indeterminate time in which everything happens.

[353] Philippians 1:6

When considering your destiny and purpose in Christ, it's essential to remember that the Holy Spirit continually searches the heart of the Father concerning those things that affect your life. He is the great conductor who orchestrates the kairos moments of your life in such a way as to reveal to you through a glass darkly what your calling and purpose are.

Discover the Lessons of Your Past

As we accept by faith all of our past experiences, whether good or bad, as signposts pointing our way to the future, we can navigate more clearly in the present. Because God sees your life from the end as clearly as the past and present, He already knows the decisions you will make to determine your future. When we open our spiritual eyes to the defining moments of our history, we see them as the signposts they were intended to be. The invisible path of the future becomes more apparent as the pathways of our past become discernable by illuminating the defining moments of our history.

As people who live according to God's purposes, defining moments can be good or bad experiences. When we dedicate our lives to God's will, all things work according to His purpose.[354] Although it isn't God who caused the adverse events in your life, He can use them for His glory to help you discover your purpose and destiny amid the pain they may have caused you. So often, our pain combined with our passion helps define our destiny and purpose in Christ.

David's Example

When looking at the life of King David, it's easy to see how the kairos moments were all leading him in the same direction as he discovered his purpose and calling.

The account of David's great battle with the giant, Goliath, illustrates what it means to take a forcible charge of your destiny when you glimpse God's perspective and purpose at a defining moment.[355] It's also important to note that David had many defining moments leading up to one of the greatest kairos moments of his life.

When David first encountered the giant, his heart filled with indignation. "Who does he think he is that he defies the armies of the Lord?" David was looking at the big picture and seeing God's perspective and purpose, which resulted in a heart filled with faith as he took vigorous action. David was about to experience the most significant defining moment of his life. If he fails to respond correctly, he will miss an excellent opportunity to lay hold of his destiny. I wonder how often

---

[354] Romans 8:28
[355] 1 Samuel 17:26

we have altered our futures because of the right or wrong response at a critical juncture or an event we faced.

The Signposts of our Past Point to our Future

David responded with a heart of faith at this critical moment because he had already looked to his past and recognized the defining moments that led up to this great conquest. So when he went before King Saul to convince him he was up to the task, he began recounting his past experiences. By accessing his past, he understood better what God was doing in the present. They were clear signposts that ushered him into this moment.

1 Samuel 17:36 Your servant has killed both the lion and bear; and this uncircumcised Philistine will be like one of them, seeing he has defied the armies of the living God.

One of the defining moments that led up to this one was when the prophet Samuel anointed him to be the next king. I wonder how often God had already spoken to David's heart when he was alone with his flock of sheep, playing his harp and singing before the Lord? This was probably already in his heart when Samuel spoke to him concerning being the next king.

From then on, a series of defining moments would bring David into a deeper walk with God and add deeper dimensions to his faith. It was from faith to faith that he entered into his destiny. The same holds true for us as we journey towards our future.

Romans 1:17 For in it the righteousness of God is revealed from faith to faith; as it is written, "The just shall live by faith."

Forcible Action is Required

When we step out in faith and forcibly lay hold of what God has already apprehended for us, we solidify our belief and add to the measure of faith and vision already at work. David was able to seize his destiny by taking vigorous action.

1 Samuel 17:45-46 Then David said to the Philistine, "You come to me with a sword, a spear, and a javelin. But I come to you in the name of the LORD of hosts, the God of the armies of Israel, whom you have defied. ⁴⁶ This day the LORD will deliver you into my hand, and I will strike you and take your head from you. And this day I will give the carcasses of the camp of the Philistines to the birds of the air and the wild beasts of the earth, that all the earth may know that there is a God in Israel."

The events and lessons of David's past were not only God's tools to shape his young life but were signposts pointing toward his future. They gave young David a vision that captured the future from God's perspective. In the same way, as you look back over the timeline of your life, they will expose your defining moments, enabling you to see them as signposts as well. Looking back gives you the ability and confidence to live, grow, and minister intentionally, just as David did.

We all know how the story ends. David kills Goliath and becomes a great hero in Israel, only to have King Saul turn on him with a vengeance. He still had many defining moments to experience before he fulfilled Samuel's prophecy. However, by recognizing God's hand in his past, David could press forward during the many difficulties as he pursued his destiny and purpose.

Now that we understand its importance, let's look more specifically at what's needed to capture God's vision and purpose.

Observe, Reflect, and Consider Your Past

The key to unlocking our past is to observe, reflect, and consider it. After observing, reflecting, and discussing your history, the next step is to believe through developing a plan of action. Your planning will involve considering the kingdom of God first by praying, discussing, and finding the best course of action to glorify God. If your plan is going to succeed, there needs to be at least one person holding you accountable—someone to pray with and to keep up to date on how you're moving toward your destiny and purpose. Once a plan has been established and shared, the next step to take is to act. To believe is to act. Genuine faith will always produce in us some action. Thoughts and intentions that remain within the mind and are not acted upon, however fruitful, are not faith.[356]

As you look over your past, think about how God has already been at work in your life. You should be able to see His handiwork. Ephesians says, *"We are His workmanship, created in Christ Jesus for good works, which God prepared beforehand that we should walk in them."*

Henry Blackaby, the author of *Experiencing God*, says, *"When God gets ready for you to take a new step or direction in His activity it will always be in sequence with what He has already been doing.[357]"*

Getting a Vision is Foremost

Getting a vision is foremost in our walk with God as we journey toward our future. It helps and keeps us on track with what God desires to do in our lives. Without it, we will cast off all restraint and not fulfill the destiny He has marked out for us, as seen in the passage below.

Proverbs 29:18 (ESV) Where there is no prophetic vision, the people cast off restraint but blessed is he who keeps the law.

---

[356] This section was developed from Mike Breen's material on the Learning Circle and the "Focused Living Retreat Workbook" by Terry Walling, Gary Mayes and Steve Hoke.
[357] *Experiencing God* by Henry Blackaby.

Your Future – Vision, Purpose, and Destiny

It has been said, *"Vision is the ability to see God's preferable future by capturing in word pictures what God desires to accomplish through the unique contribution of our lives. It is God who designs it, but it is we who discover it."*[358]

An excellent way to help capture your vision is to use questions. They could include:

- Do I feel God has a purpose for my life?
- In what ways has God manifested His hand in my life?
- What brings me joy or satisfaction?
- What were some of my most painful experiences?
- What are my greatest strengths?
- Are there any harmful habits I would like to break?
- What would I do with my time if I did not have to work?
- What would I do with my money if it were unlimited?
- If my life ended now, would I have any regrets?

Answer each question as thoroughly and honestly as possible. Then, add other issues and responses if they come to mind.[359]

Melissa Young writes, *"Think about how you can use information from your past to shape the future. Our lives consist of different areas: home, marriage, family, school, ministry, spiritual, etc. Distill the information in each life category into one or two actionable statements. Write using first-person perspective and present tense. For example, under the spiritual category, you could write, "I am deepening my relationship with Christ through scripture study and prayer" or "I am experiencing the joy of drawing others to Christ through love." Write accurate statements based on your core values."*

As we have seen through the life of David, God can work on our behalf. Just as David received purpose and destiny, God has given each of us a divine destiny to fulfill, but it's up to us to discover and capture that which Christ has already apprehended for us. The kingdom of God is forcibly advancing, and mighty men and women are needed to seize it. Therefore, as you encounter each defining moment and discover your purpose and vision, determine whether you will respond forcibly to what God is leading you.

As Robin Williams said in the movie *Dead Poet's Society*, *"Carpe, carpe diem, seize the day, boys, make your lives extraordinary."*

---

[358] Quote from the "Focused Living Retreat Workbook" by Terry Walling, Gary Mayes and Steve Hoke

[359] This section from "Focused Living Retreat Workbook "by Terry Walling, Gary Mayes and Steve Hoke

Continue to Nurture and Keep Your Vision Fresh

Because we do not see clearly, we must incorporate the necessary ingredients to keep our vision alive and fresh in God.

Corinthians 13:12 Now we see in a mirror, dimly, but then face to face. Now I know in part, but then I shall know just as I also am known.

Relationships and communion with the Holy Spirit are essential to keep our vision alive and fresh in God. Once we understand how God desires to use us in connection to our purpose and vision, we must continue to nurture and strengthen it through prayer and communion with Him. Always remember that we see through a glass darkly through our spiritual eyes. There will always be adjustments, but the Holy Spirit will continually be with us to point us in the right direction. We must learn to trust in Him.

John 16:13-14 "However, when He, the Spirit of truth, has come, He will guide you into all truth; for He will not speak on His own authority, but whatever He hears He will speak; and He will tell you things to come. ^{14}"He will glorify Me, for He will take of what is Mine and declare it to you.

Keep your eyes on the big picture. But, unfortunately, it is very easy to lose sight of it when entrenched in the day-to-day challenges of life. The following article illustrates this very clearly:

In a "Leadership" magazine article, Lynn Anderson described what happens when people lose their vision.

A group of pilgrims landed on the shores of America about 350 years ago. They had come to settle in the new land with great vision and courage. In the first year, they established a town. In the second, they elected a town council. In the third, the government proposed building a road five miles westward into the wilderness. But in the fourth year, the people tried to impeach the town council because they thought such a road into the forest was a waste of public funds. Somehow, these forward-looking people had lost their vision. Once able to see across oceans, they could not look five miles into the wilderness.

We all require long-range and short-range vision. When we lose sight of the overall purpose and vision of what we are all about, we also lose sight of our immediate goals. The apostle Paul is an excellent example of this. He often stepped out in faith to pursue his calling because of his overall vision and understanding of what God wanted to do in his life. As he went forth, God would give him specific instructions that would bring short-term clarity to his overall vision and calling. We see this in the following passages.

Acts 15:36 "Let us go back and visit our brethren in every city where we have preached the word of the Lord, and see how they are doing."

Paul was merely responding to his burden and responsibility to the Lord, which was a part of his overall vision and purpose. Paul had a vision during this trip that gave him specific instructions on where to go.
Acts 16:6-10 And a vision appeared to Paul in the night. A man of Macedonia stood and pleaded with him, saying, "Come over to Macedonia and help us."

There should always be the overall vision and purpose that God has birthed into our hearts through His Word and Spirit. This image remains constant.

We need immediate vision and purpose to experience victories and a sense of accomplishment. They encourage us to keep moving towards our destiny so that we can say at the end of our lives, as Paul said, *"I have fought the good fight, I have finished the race, I have kept the faith."*[360]

Satan Will Try to Dim Our Vision

Our adversary wants to keep us from doing God's will. He knows that if he can blind or dim our vision of God, he can cause us to be ineffective in God.

2 Corinthians 4:3-4 But even if our gospel is veiled, it is veiled to those who are perishing, whose minds the god of this age blinded, who do not believe, lest the light of the gospel of the glory of Christ, who is the image of, God should shine on them.

As you go forward with vision and purpose, God is faithful in moving you toward your ultimate destiny as you continually lean upon Him for understanding.[361]

God is faithful. He cannot deny Himself and will bring to naught the enemy's schemes toward you. It's a matter of trusting God with a heart of expectation as He fills us with wisdom and revelation in His knowledge. The Holy Spirit continually opens the eyes of our understanding to all that He has for us so that we remain enlightened in the hope of our calling. As we are faithful to do this, He will show us the exceeding greatness of His power as we believe according to the working of His mighty power.[362]

Always keep in mind God is always at work! Our call is not to invent but to align ourselves with God's purposes! Alignment requires absolute surrender.[363]

---

[360] 2 Timothy 4:7
[361] Proverbs 3:5-6
[362] Ephesians 1:17-19
[363] Quote from "Focused Living Retreat Workbook" by Terry Walling, Gary Mayes and Steve Hoke

May God bless you richly as you press toward the goal for the prize of the upward call of God in Christ Jesus by laying hold and seizing that which He has already granted to you![364]

Your future awaits you!

---

[364] Philippians 3:12-14

Staying the Course

Chapter 14

For we have become partakers of Christ if we hold the beginning of our confidence steadfast to the end—Hebrews 3:14

The journey each of us is on is not a sprint. It's a lifetime race filled with many obstacles, traps, and unexpected twists and turns with the potential to throw us off course. As we rely on the Holy Spirit to continually guide us, we will stay the course with our confidence intact to the end. As we are faithful to rely on God's sufficiency, He faithfully guides us through every obstacle to keep us safe and secure as we move onward.

When considering the challenge of staying on course, we must be as enthusiastic and full of zeal today as when we first encountered Jesus. Our first love experience has a way of waning, so Paul urged us never to *be lacking in zeal or diligence but to be fervent in the spirit, serving the Lord.*[365] Therefore, we must continually press forward while stirring up our passion.

We Must Continually Stir up our First Love

Zeal and fervency are characteristics we must constantly stir up within us because of the many things that can potentially steal them. As we give ourselves to those things that are a part of who God created us to be, we maintain our zeal. As our passion ignites, natural zeal and fervency flood our souls with joy. In turn, the joy of the Lord strengthens and encourages us.[366]

I have been a Christian for over 40 years and have witnessed many who have not stayed the course. Watching those who have started well and then see them fizzle like shooting stars is heartbreaking.

Some have served God faithfully for many years but don't seem to do well in their later years. They begin to get bored, having heard the same messages repeatedly in one form or another, resulting in a loss of interest,

---

[365] Romans 12:11
[366] Nehemiah 8:10

vision, and purpose, which leads to forsaking the assembling of themselves together.[367] Before long, they're no longer involved and settle into a complacency that gives way to unbelief. We all deal with complacency as we grow and mature in the Lord. It's a battle!

We Must Not Grow Weary in Well-Doing

Some people lose interest because they get weary. The expected results from ministry opportunities didn't reap the results anticipated, which caused them to lose heart. We live in a culture where we're all accustomed to the instantaneous. Perseverance becomes unattractive, which causes us to wane in our desire and motivation to stay the course. To stay the course, we cannot afford to give into the whims of our culture. We must learn to persevere. It's a primary attribute that needs to be in our lives.

We Must Nurture and Protect our Vision and Purpose

To stay the course, we must nurture and protect the vision and purpose we receive by staying current and involved with what God desires to do in our lives. Then, knowing our best days are still ahead, we can keep our hearts focused. As we do, there will always be enough excitement and encouragement to keep us moving forward and staying the course. It's when we begin to say, "I've put my time in; I'm just going to rest and take it easy," that we lose sight of our vision and purpose.

Endeavor to Stay Fully Committed

No matter what season of life we are in, we must continue to serve God wholeheartedly. As we grow and mature, what we do and how we serve Him may change somewhat, but He continues to guide and show us new ways in which His grace and anointing are leading and working in us. The vehicle God uses to release our gifts and ministries may change, but His calling and gifting do not change.

Salvation involves believing with all of our hearts.[368] God is not interested in a piece of our hearts. He wants the whole thing. To be fully committed with all of our hearts means we are 100 percent dedicated to the purposes of God. It entails seeking to do what the Lord calls us while rooting out anything harmful or destructive. We must ruthlessly tear down strongholds and idols that prevent us from moving forward. God is looking for people totally committed with undivided hearts to His prophetic purposes. David recognized this as he prayed in *Psalm 86:11*, *"Give me an undivided heart."*

---

[367] Hebrews 10:25
[368] Acts 8:37

2 Chronicles 16:9 "For the eyes of the Lord run to and fro throughout the whole earth, to show Himself strong on behalf of those whose heart is loyal."

Satan and the world will do everything possible to keep us from wholeheartedly serving God. We cannot afford to allow our love to grow cold amid all the enemy and the world throw at us. By staying fully committed, we will stay the course without getting detoured or burning out like shooting stars.

Things that Cause Half-hearted Responses

Unrepented sin causes our love to grow cold. As we continually walk in a state of repentance before the Lord, we receive times of refreshing from His presence. With this comes the motivation to enter boldly into God's presence to receive the strength and encouragement to press forward as He continually refreshes us.

Acts 3:19 Repent therefore and be converted, that your sins may be blotted out so that times of refreshing may come from the presence of the Lord.

Broken relationships in the body cause spiritual blindness, which dims our vision and results in half-heartedness. For example, when we allow offenses from a brother or sister to turn to bitterness rather than dealing with them and forgiving one another, we open ourselves up to the devil's devices. As a result, we become blinded to the truth and lose our way.

John 2:9-11 He who says he is in the light and hates his brother is in darkness until now. But he who hates his brother is in darkness and walks in darkness, and does not know where he is going because the darkness has blinded his eyes.

I have seen many people over the years give up on the church because of an offense or merely because they didn't agree with something that was taking place. When you leave your place of nurturing and ministry, it's tough to start over. Some do, but others drift until they're no longer in fellowship. Their hearts begin to grow cold as they compromise in areas.

An unhealthy focus on worldly things causes loss of vision and the hardness of the heart. We see this in the life of Lot. His desire for earthly and temporal things caused him to lose his vision of God by becoming very callus. When the angels of the Lord came to destroy Sodom and Gomorrah, Lot was rescued, but his testimony was so tarnished that his sons-in-law could not take him seriously. He's a type of those who are saved by fire, whose works are burned. In the process, he was rescued, even though he lost everything.[369] The lesson is that we must willingly

---

[369] Genesis 13 & 19

turn our eyes away from looking at useless things. When we do, we are revived and can stay the course, as seen in the following Scripture.

Psalm 119:37 Turn my eyes from looking at worthless things and revive me in Your way.

Many things often distract us from what God desires to do in our lives. We are in a constant battle to stay focused. Our world today is filled with sensory overload. It is hard to keep focused with so many enticing distractions. It's not that they're sinful, but if there's an unhealthy attraction, they become snares and steal our hearts from being wholehearted in our approach to God. We deal with television, Facebook, the internet, video games, entertainment, sports, movies, hobbies, and many other things that can become useless. If there is an unhealthy attraction to them that steals our time and energy from the purposes of God, they become dumb idols to us.

God is a jealous God and is very envious of the things that stand in the way of His purpose in our lives. He considers it spiritual adultery when we get caught up in worthless worldly things.[370]

1 John 3:15-15 Do not love the world or the things in the world. If anyone loves the world, the love of the Father is not in him.

Too much time focusing on difficulties causes blindness and hardness of the heart. It's not enough that our natural inclination is to focus on our problems. Still, we have an enemy whose objectives are to get us to concentrate on the difficulties that lie ahead rather than the promises of God's Word. As a result, we become half-hearted and lose our way.

The book of Numbers gives us the account of the spies Moses sent to spy out the land. They returned with an evil report because they focused too much on the difficulties before them. They had no heart to stay the course. Out of the twelve, only Joshua and Caleb stayed focused on God's ability to go before them on the path ahead. They tried to persuade the people of God to believe in God and His promises but could not convince Israel to do the right thing. As a result, Israel did not stay the course. Their focus and attention remained on the spies who gave an evil report—a report based on the difficulties rather than what God was able to do. Their vision dimmed, and they failed to accomplish what God had set before them. As a result, they spent 40 years wandering in the desert with a wilderness complex. All those who came out of Egypt died in the desert. Only their descendants went into the Promised Land.

---

[370] James 4:4-5

Do you have a wilderness complex that is too focused on the difficulties ahead rather than the promises of God? If so, believe what God has promised you and what He has said concerning who you are in Christ. The road ahead is filled with many beautiful promises and blessings as you are faithful to stay the course.

I pray that we will all continually examine our hearts to ensure that we are not growing cold or stale in the things of God. A great cloud of witnesses surrounds us as they cheer us on, so *let us run with endurance the race that is set before us, looking unto Jesus, the author and finisher of our faith.*[371]

As it says in the Book Psalms, *"You're blessed when you stay on course, walking steadily on the road revealed by God. You're blessed when you follow his directions, doing your best to find him."* [372]

---

[371] Hebrews 12:1-2
[372] Psalm 119:1-2 (MSG)

New Jerusalem Awaits Our Arrival

Chapter Fifteen

For here, we have no continuing city, but we seek the one to come. Therefore, by Him let us continually offer the sacrifice of praise to God, that its the fruit of our lips, giving thanks to His name—Hebrews 13:14-15

Just as Abraham obeyed God and went forth to the place where he was to receive an inheritance while waiting for the city whose builder and maker is God, so are we as we journey forward in this world while waiting for the same city.[373] Hebrews 11 speaks of the patriarchs of our faith and how they all died, not having received the promises but having seen them afar off.[374] They were all pilgrims, just as we are as we await the new heavenly city whose builder and maker is God.

Revelation 21:2 Then I, John, saw the holy city, New Jerusalem, coming down out of heaven from God, prepared as a bride adorned for her husband.

God's glory will fill Jerusalem's new city with a light like a most precious stone, a jasper stone, and clear as crystal.[375] It will have a great and high wall with twelve gates and twelve angels at the gates, representing the twelve tribes of Israel.[376] The city's wall will have twelve foundations representing the twelve apostles of the Lamb.[377] The construction of the wall will be like Jasper, and the city will be made of pure gold, like transparent glass, with streets paved with pure gold, like transparent glass.[378] There will be no need for the sun or the moon, as the glory of God will illuminate it. The Lamb is light. There will be no night.[379]

---

[373] Hebrews 11:8-10
[374] Hebrews 11:13
[375] Revelation 21:11
[376] Revelation 21:12
[377] Revelation 21:14
[378] Revelation 21:18
[379] Revelation 21:23

The above description of New Jerusalem gives us a glimpse into the beauty and majesty that awaits us as we prepare to enter a kingdom realm far exceeding anything we could imagine or dream. The vision of New Jerusalem gives us an understanding of what the apostle Paul said after he entered the third realm of heaven via a vision. He said, *"For to me, to live is Christ, and to die is gain. For I am hard-pressed between the two, having the desire to depart and be with Christ, which is far better."*[380]

The more we understand about heaven and all that it offers us, the more excited we become as we await that day. As I get older and witness how fast a decade passes, it becomes more of a reality as I realize we are like a vapor that quickly disappears.

As we observe the generation before us passing away like the sands of time, it, too, becomes a witness to the brevity of life here on earth. Just recently, my father and mother passed away. My brother, Jerry, was with my father in his final days and had the following story about his anticipation of dying and going to heaven. He was 95 and very ready to go.

~

My Father's Gurney Ride to Heaven—Well, Almost
By Jerry Birks – July 2011

Yesterday, my father took another ride to the ER with breathing problems—pneumonia, congestive heart failure, being 95, and quite a few other pains were the reason.

My father has been waiting for his life to end to eliminate the misery of "being old." He couldn't wait to receive his new heavenly body. He yearns for this to the point of obsession. I don't blame him; his body is completely worn out, and his legs are amputated due to diabetes. He still has a reasonably clear mind most of the time, although there are moments. The trip to the ER was one of those moments when the desire to be out with the old and in with the new was overwhelming.

He goes to the ER with doctors, nurses, and aids coming and going. When he finally gets the doctor's attention, he asks the doctor to end his life, or as the doctor tells me, to give him the death shot. Dad is serious, and the doctor is gentle with his explanation. With Dad's hearing 80 percent gone, he understands little of what is said. As the nurse puts the IV in, my dad believes this is the death drug. He asks the doctor how long it will take to go home. Of course, "home" to my father is Heaven.

---

[380] Philippians 1:21, 23

However, the doctor thinks, "How long will it take him to return to his apartment?" So he says, "About two hours."

Dad isn't feeling much of anything as time passes, as they give him morphine. Meanwhile, he waits patiently to leave this life and enter heaven. Doctors, nurses, and aids are still coming and going. Finally, a gurney arrives with the ambulance attendants to take him back to the apartment shortly. Well, Dad is now thinking to himself, "This just isn't quite right. Why are they taking me to heaven on a gurney?"

He says nothing now but wonders, "What's in store?"

I arrived at the apartment just as the ambulance pulled away, only to discover that Dad was ticked.

He immediately tells me, "There's been a huge mistake, and I need to get these people straightened out. This is not how it's supposed to be. You do not take people to heaven on a gurney and then take them back to this 'hole of misery.'" (He's actually been living in an assisted living home that is the best in town).

He then commands me, "Go straighten that doctor out and tell him they don't know how to send people home (heaven), and they had better start getting their act together."

I spent the next couple of hours explaining to Dad what had happened and was sorry for the misunderstanding.

I had to tell him, "Dad, they didn't give you the death drug."

The defeat on his face was overwhelming. My heart broke for this man I love so much. We had a long talk, and he decided to stop all his medications, including insulin. We'd had this conversation before, but this time, it was different, and he made his peace.

We brought the head staff in and did all the paperwork to send to the doctor to get Hospice care for the end-of-life requirements.

The story of my Dad's gurney ride to heaven is not sad as I have not seen such a light of joy in my Dad's eyes for years. However, when we met with Hospice care and social services, they questioned him as to whether he was sure or not.

He shouted for joy and said, "I can't wait!"

He lit up like the Fourth of July fireworks were exploding within him. The Hospice workers were amazed! They'd never seen anyone so ready for the end of their life to come.

They didn't know that the end of this life would be the beginning of eternity with the God my father loves so much.

My daughter just left a little bit ago after visiting with my dad and seeing him so happy and joyful. She said, "Wow! I've never seen Grandpa so excited!"

Though I've had to leave a few times while writing this, it is from tears of joy for the father I love so much.

Within a few days after being under hospice care, my father's yearning and prayers were finally answered. He went to be with the Lord Jesus, whom he had loved since childhood.

~

Our Journey on Earth will Come to an End.

There's a day coming when our journey here on earth will be over, just as it was for my father and countless others. We will no longer be pilgrims traveling through this world with our sights set on the invisible realms of the kingdom but will experience the beauty and glory of all that eternity with God, our Father, has to offer us.

Whether we are among those who will be alive and remain at the Second Coming or among those who are the dead in Christ, who rise first, we will all be united with Christ throughout eternity.[381] We shall be changed into our incorruptible celestial bodies in the twinkling of an eye at the last trumpet.[382]

Meeting Jesus at our death or His Second Coming is the hope and culmination of all this journey on earth represents. We will then enter a journey that will last throughout eternity—a place where we will never experience pain, sorrow, or suffering. Death and injustice will have no part of heaven, either. Heaven will be much more than all this, but these things are enough for me to desire, and look forward to it with great anticipation. But wait, there's much more!

Heaven Will be Beyond our Wildest Dreams

Eternity in Heaven will have more to offer us than we can imagine. Our eternal home in Heaven will be beyond our wildest expectations and dreams. We will discover new dimensions of God's glory and beauty throughout all eternity with our new celestial bodies that will never grow old or tired. Sounds pretty good to me! I don't know about you, but I'm tired of all the pain, turmoil, wars, injustice, politics, and the evil workings of man. I'm ready for the permanent change that will bring everlasting delight to my soul.

---

[381] 1 Thessalonians 4:15-17
[382] 1 Corinthians 15:51-53

2 Corinthians 2:9-10 But as it is written: "Eye has not seen, nor ear heard, nor have entered into the heart of man the things which God has prepared for those who love Him." ¹⁰ But God has revealed them to us through His Spirit. For the Spirit searches all things, yes, the deep things of God.

Try to imagine the Garden of Eden. Think of the most beautiful and scenic places on earth or some beautiful music or art. What about the moments you experienced an overwhelming sense of God's presence that flooded your soul with peace and assurance—what did you experience? Meditating on these things gives you a foretaste of heaven's beauty and glory. As the above Scripture says, *"Eye has not seen, nor ear heard, nor have entered into the heart of man the things which God has prepared for those who love Him."* Let your imagination run wild and begin to meditate on the beauty of the Lord, and you will not be able to scratch the surface of all that God has prepared for those who love Him and endure to the end.

Our Place in Heaven is Created According to our Desires

Jesus is now in heaven, preparing a place for us to dwell throughout all eternity. It will be a special place created just for you. It will be perfect in every way. You will be astounded at the beauty and magnificence of what He is preparing for you. We see this in the following passage.

John 14:1-3 "Let not your heart be troubled; you believe in God, believe also in Me. ² "In My Father's house are many mansions; if it were not so, I would have told you. I go to prepare a place for you. ³ "And if I go and prepare a place for you, I will come again and receive you to Myself; that where I am, there you may be also."

The above Scripture is one of my favorites because it gives me so much hope and excitement as I look toward eternity. Just think, the greatest architect and carpenter ever on earth and in heaven is building your dream home. Think about some of the most beautiful homes you have ever seen and the talent that went into designing and making them. They are nothing in comparison to what Jesus is preparing for those who endure to the end. All the most extraordinary talents ever in designing and building homes came from Him. He is the most talented architect ever, and He is now preparing a place for you—your eternal home where you will reside throughout all eternity. We see in the following passage that Jesus is the creator of everything in heaven and earth, which includes the special place He is preparing for you and me.

Colossians 1:15-16 He is the image of the invisible God, the firstborn over all creation. ¹⁶ For by Him all things were created that are in heaven and that are on earth, visible and invisible, whether thrones or dominions or principalities or powers. All things were created through Him and for Him.

God is acquainted with all of our ways. He wants nothing more than to give us the desires of our hearts. God knows us better than we know ourselves. He is well aware of our desires, even our unaware ones.

Psalm 139:3 You comprehend my path and my lying down and are acquainted with all my ways.

Psalm 37:4 Delight yourself also in the LORD, and He shall give you the desires of your heart.

How many of us have been somewhere, maybe in someone else's home, and said, "Wow! This place is totally me. It has my name written all over it. When we arrive at our eternal dwelling, we will probably say something like, "How did You know? I mean, this is beyond my wildest dreams and desires!"

You see, God knows everything there is to know about us, even things we don't quite understand or have grasped about ourselves. The beautiful thing is that when we see and experience it, we will recognize our desires and unspoken ones as fulfilled.

Eternal life in heaven will be awesome and beautiful beyond our wildest imaginations. We will have the opportunity to make incredible discoveries about who we are and our desires, which is why the Psalmist says with such assurance, *"Precious in the sight of the LORD is the death of His saints."*[383]

Understanding and seeing all that awaits us in eternity and how short our life here on Earth is helps us navigate our journey on Earth. As we invest our time, energy, and talents, we need to focus on God's purposes rather than worldly things and desires. The dividends we will receive in heaven will far outweigh anything we could ever receive in this life. What we sow, we shall also reap in this life and in the life to come.

May God bless you as you continue to navigate the invisible path of authentic Christianity that leads to your eternal home and destiny in Christ! It has been a joy to share "The Journey" with you. Thank you for taking the time to read it. You'll be blessed. May the invisible become visible to you as He continually opens the eyes of your understanding.

---

[383] Psalm 116:15

Bible Study Questions

For Personal Study or Small Group Study

If you want to download these studies as one printable document, please visit the link below.

booksbyken.com/downloads/journey-bible-studies

Exploring the Beauty and Majesty of God
Chapter One Study Questions

One of life's greatest pursuits is discovering who God is in all of His glory and majesty. It enables us to reach a deeper understanding and revelation that enhances our relationship with Him by bringing us deeper intimacy.

What had the most significant impact on you in this chapter?

_____
_____
_____

Psalm 145:3 (NLT) Great is the LORD! He is most worthy of praise! His greatness is beyond discovery.

How has getting to know Who God is, by coming into a deeper understanding and revelation of His true nature, causing you greater intimacy with Him?

_____
_____
_____
_____

How did your view of authority figures as a child affect how you viewed God?

_____
_____
_____

In what way did you view God during your formative years?

- [ ] Loving, warm and fuzzy
- [ ] Mean and Cruel
- [ ] Distant, uncaring, and uninvolved
- [ ] Drill Sergeant – unreasonable demands
- [ ] Abusive, pushy, inconsiderate
- [ ] Must measure up
- [ ] Critical, not believing in you

Jeremiah 29:11-13 For I know the thoughts that I think toward you, says the LORD, thoughts of peace and not of evil, to give you a future and a hope. [12] Then you will call upon Me and go and pray to Me, and I will listen to you. [13] And you will seek Me and find Me when you search for Me with all your heart.

How has having a Biblical view of God caused you to seek Him more?

Chapter One Study Questions

_____
_____
_____

The kingdom life we experience as a result of agreeing with what God has revealed about Himself in the Scriptures has the power to transform our lives. A new level of freedom and deliverance comes from each paradigm shift God takes us through.

Ephesians 1:19 and what is the exceeding greatness of His power toward us who believe, according to the working of His mighty power.

How has having a correct Biblical view of God helped you to become more Christ-like?

_____
_____
_____

Which of God's transcendent attributes do you value the most?

[ ] God is Self-Existent   [ ] God is Spirit
[ ] God is One   [ ] God is Omnipotent (All-Powerful)
[ ] God is Eternal   [ ] God is Omnipresent (All-Present)
[ ] God is Immutable   [ ] God is Omniscient (All-Knowing)

Why do you value this attribute?

_____
_____
_____
_____

A New Beginning – The Journey Begins
Chapter Two Study Questions

The Bible refers to our common salvation experience as a great salvation that Old Testament prophets, righteous men, and even angels desired to look into but could not experience. We now have the privilege of experiencing being drawn into the very heart of God in a way they could never do.

Matthew 13:16-17 Blessed are your eyes for they see, and your ears for they hear; ^{17}for assuredly, I say to you that many prophets and righteous men desired to see what you see and to hear what you hear and did not hear it.

1 Peter 1:12 To them it was revealed that not to themselves, but to us they were ministering the things which now have been reported to you through those who have preached the gospel to you by the Holy Spirit sent from heaven—things which angels desire to look into.

When you consider that the Old Testament prophets, patriarchs, and even angels could not experience what we have in Christ, how does that make you feel?

_____
_____
_____

In salvation, God has promised to give us everything that pertains to life and godliness.

2 Peter 1:3 As His divine power has given to us all things that pertain to life and godliness, through the knowledge of Him who called us by glory and virtue.

What does the promise of being given all things pertaining to life mean to you? Has this been true for you? If not, why do you think it hasn't?

_____
_____
_____

Before we were saved, our minds were trained to respond according to our carnality and natural reasoning. This means we can no longer lean upon our own understanding.

Proverbs 3:5-6 Trust in the Lord with all your heart, and lean not on your own understanding. ^{6} In all your ways acknowledge Him, and He shall direct your paths.

In what ways do you no longer lean upon your own understanding? How do you acknowledge God in all of your ways?

Chapter Two Study Questions

_____
_____

What was it that initially drew you to Christ? What need in your life drew you unto Him?

_____
_____

One of the most amazing facts concerning Christ and the atonement He made for our sins is that He became sin for us. Jesus, who was totally without sin, was filled with sin as He hung on the cross and cried to the Father in agony, *"Why have You forsaken Me?"*

2 Corinthians 5:21 For He made Him who knew no sin to be sin for us, that we might become the righteousness of God in Him.

How does it make you feel, knowing it was your sins that put Christ on the cross?

_____
_____

Our sins and past transgressions are totally forgiven. As far as the East is from the West, the past is wiped clean with the weight of sin and guilt removed from our lives.

Hebrews 10:17 Their sins and their lawless deeds I remember no more.

How does it make you feel knowing God no longer remembers your sins?

_____
_____

Repentance: The Path Less Traveled
Chapter Three Study Questions

As wonderful and adventurous as this path may be, many will never find it. It is a hidden path that can only be found or seen by those whose eyes are enlightened. Therefore, we must pick up the cross at the entrance so that our spiritual eyes are enlightened to all that exists on the path.

Jesus said, "he who does not take up his cross and follow after Me is not worthy of Me. He who finds his life will lose it, and he who loses his life for My sake will find it.[384]"

The only way to discover the path less traveled is by coming to Jesus with child-like faith and adhering to His words.

Matthew 18:2-3 Then Jesus called a little child to Him, set him in the midst of them, and said, "Assuredly, I say to you, unless you are converted and become as little children, you will by no means enter the kingdom of heaven.

What does becoming converted and childlike in your faith mean for you? Or how does coming to Christ as an innocent child prepare you to learn from Him?

_____

_____

_____

In what way did you express child-like faith in coming to Christ? Or how did it manifest itself?

_____

_____

Colossians 2:8 Beware lest anyone cheat you through philosophy and empty deceit, according to the tradition of men, according to the basic principles of the world, and not according to Christ.

What are some ways Christians today are being seduced by a Hollywood version of Christianity or a watered-down version of the gospel?

_____

_____

_____

---

[384] Matthew 10:38-39

Chapter Three Study Questions

Matthew 16:24 Then Jesus said to His disciples, "If anyone desires to come after Me, let him deny himself, and take up his cross and follow Me.

What does it mean to surrender to the cross of Christ? And how does this play out in your life?

_____
_____
_____

2 Corinthians 6:17 Therefore come out from among them and be separate, says the Lord. Do not touch what is unclean, and I will receive you, and you shall be My sons and daughters, says the Lord Almighty.

Why is separating ourselves from all that is ungodly and our worldly friends important when we are newly converted?

_____
_____
_____

1 John 2:29 If you know that He is righteous, you know that everyone who practices righteousness is born of Him.

What does it mean to practice righteousness?

_____
_____
_____

What is the difference between one who practices righteousness and occasionally falls vs. the one who does not practice righteousness?

_____
_____
_____

Getting an Identity Makeover
Chapter Four Study Questions

In coming to Christ, we are challenged to put on the new man created after Christ, which allows us to have a complete identity makeover. We now have an identity birthed from heaven's beauty and glory rather than hell's depravity.

2 Corinthians 5:17 Therefore, if anyone is in Christ, he is a new creation; old things have passed away; behold, all things have passed away; behold, all things have become new.

What had the most significant impact on you in this chapter?

_____
_____
_____

Matthew 10:39 He who finds his life will lose it, and he who loses his life for My sake will find it.

What does this Scripture have to do with your new identity in Christ?

_____
_____
_____

The essence of who we are is an accumulation of our thought life. During our formative years, these thoughts and attitudes began to shape and form our identity.

Proverbs 23:7 For as he thinks in his heart, so is he.

What were some ways your old identity was shaped through how you thought about things?

_____
_____
_____

True deliverance comes as we embrace the new nature Christ has ordained for us. The anointing that comes with the new nature breaks the yoke of sinful addictions and strongholds in our lives.

Ephesians 4:23-24 And be renewed in the spirit of your mind, and that you put on the new man which was created according to God, in true righteousness and holiness.

Chapter Four Study Questions

How have you experienced the new nature breaking the bondages of sin in your life? If so, how is this true for you?

_____
_____
_____

Francis Frangipane writes, *"Many of our opinions about life are ours only because we know of no other way to think. Yet, we protect and defend our ideas and justify our opinions as though they were born in the wombs of our own creativity.*

Do you have opinions and ideas you are protecting and justifying because you know no other way to think? If so, what are they?

_____
_____
_____

In baptism, we totally identify with Jesus Christ and all He has accomplished for us.

Romans 6:6 knowing this, that our old man was crucified with Him, that the body of sin might be done away with, that we should no longer be slaves of sin.

How does water baptism prepare us for our new identity?

_____
_____
_____

Romans 6:11 Likewise you also, reckon yourselves to be dead indeed to sin,

What does it mean to consider yourself dead to sin?

_____
_____
_____

Navigational Tools: Word and Spirit
Chapter Five Study Questions

What did you find most interesting about this chapter?

_____
_____
_____

Proverbs 11:1 (KJV) A false balance is an abomination to the LORD: but a just weight is His delight.

With an understanding that it is essential to be equally balanced with the influence of the Word of God and the Holy Spirit, would you say that you are more Word or Holy Spirit-oriented? How does it play out in your life? What do you need to do to make sure they are balanced?

_____
_____
_____
_____

Psalm 119:105 Your word is a lamp to my feet and a light to my path.

Psalm 119:133 Direct my steps by Your word, and let no iniquity have dominion over me.

How is the word of God a lamp unto our feet and light to our paths? Give an example of how this is true in your life.

_____
_____
_____

How would you rate your knowledge of the Bible? Excellent, fair, or poor? Why?

_____
_____

John 16:12-13 I still have many things to say to you, but you cannot bear them now. [13] However, when He, the Spirit of truth, has come, He will guide you into all truth; for He will not speak on His own authority, but whatever He hears He will speak; and He will tell you things to come.

Chapter Five Study Questions

What are some of the ways the Holy Spirit leads us?

_____
_____
_____

Amos 3:7 Surely the Lord God does nothing unless He reveals His secret to His servants the prophets.

1 Corinthians 14:3 But he who prophesies speaks edification and exhortation and comfort to men.

In what manner has God spoken to you the most? Dreams, visions, prophecy, audible voice, still small voice, or spiritual impressions? Give an example of how one of the above has impacted your life.

_____
_____
_____
_____

_____

With an understanding that we need to be appropriately balanced in our relationship with the Holy Spirit and our relationship with the Word, why and how does deception occur when we rely too much on one without the other?

_____
_____
_____
_____

Who is responsible for ensuring the Word and the Spirit partner to guide us? Why is that?

_____
_____
_____
_____

Seven Essentials Needed for the Journey
Chapter Six Study Questions

The Christian experience is a lifetime event that will take you through many twists and turns filled with joys and sorrows, heartaches and disappointments, trials and tribulations, victories and defeats, and from moments of despair to moments of great jubilation.

The longer we travel, the more we realize we must pick up a few necessities to prepare us for what's ahead. Acquiring the essentials along the way will make the journey more rewarding and less stressful when we begin to experience some of the hardships and difficulties.

What did you find most interesting about this chapter?

_____
_____
_____

2 Peter 1:3 As His divine power has given to us all things that pertain to life and godliness, through the knowledge of Him who called us by glory and virtue.

The Seven Essentials: Baptism of the Holy Spirit, Prayer, Faith, Hope, Love, Fruit of the Spirit, Practice of Giving. Of the seven, which do you value the most? Why?

_____
_____
_____

Have you ever been caught off guard or blindsided by something that happened to you? How did you handle it?

_____
_____
_____

Acts 1:8 But you shall receive power when the Holy Spirit has come upon you, and you shall be witnesses to Me in Jerusalem, and in all Judea and Samaria, and to the end of the earth.

Why is the baptism of the Holy Spirit so necessary?

_____
_____
_____

Chapter Six Study Questions

Isaiah 40:31 But those who wait on the Lord shall renew their strength; they shall mount up with wings like eagles, they shall run and not be weary. They shall walk and not faint.

What is your definition of prayer, and why is it important to you?

_____

_____

1 Corinthians 13:13 And now abide faith, hope, love, these three; but the greatest of these is love.

Why do you think faith, hope, and love are linked together? Which one do you value the most? Why

_____

_____

Psalm 17:7-9 (NIV) Show me the wonders of your great love, you who save by your right hand those who take refuge in you from their foes. Keep me as the apple of your eye; hide me in the shadow of your wings from those who are out to destroy me, from my mortal enemies who surround me.

Why is it essential that we understand God's great love toward us?

_____

_____

2 Peter 1:5-10 But also for this very reason, giving all diligence, add to your faith virtue, to virtue knowledge, ⁶ to knowledge self-control, to self-control perseverance, to perseverance godliness, ⁷ to godliness brotherly kindness, and to brotherly kindness love. ⁸ For if these things are yours and abound, you will be neither barren nor unfruitful in the knowledge of our Lord Jesus Christ. For he who lacks these things is shortsighted, even to blindness, and has forgotten that he was cleansed from his old sins.

Why is it essential to diligently add the fruit of the Spirit to our faith? Which one do you find the most difficult?

_____

_____

_____

Why is *giving* essential to the faith? What lessons do we learn from the parable of the Talents?

_____

_____

_____

Finding Purpose in Trials – Into the Wilderness
Chapter Seven Study Questions

Our journey will eventually lead us to wilderness periods at various times, just as it did for Jesus and countless others who have gone before us. The more prepared we are, the better equipped we are to handle these seasons. The key is to have God's Word hidden in our hearts so that we do not sin against God as the Israelites did.

What had the most significant impact on you in this chapter?

_____
_____
_____
_____

Deuteronomy 8:2-3 And you shall remember that the Lord your God led you all the way these forty years in the wilderness, to humble you and test you, to know what was in your heart, whether you would keep His commandments or not. ³ So He humbled you, allowed you to hunger, and fed you with manna which you did not know nor did your fathers know, that He might make you know that man shall not live by bread alone, but man lives by every word that proceeds from the mouth of the Lord.

Do you find it challenging to go through the wilderness or dry seasons? What is it that sustains you during these times?

_____
_____

Following your first love experience with the Lord, how did you deal with things when the newness began to wear off?

_____
_____

Galatians 3:3-4 Are you so foolish? Having begun in the Spirit, are you now being made perfect by the flesh? Have you suffered so many things in vain—if indeed it was in vain?

Have you ever been stuck in forms of legalism? What transpired in your life to get you back on track?

Looking at the diagram, where do you see yourself on it?

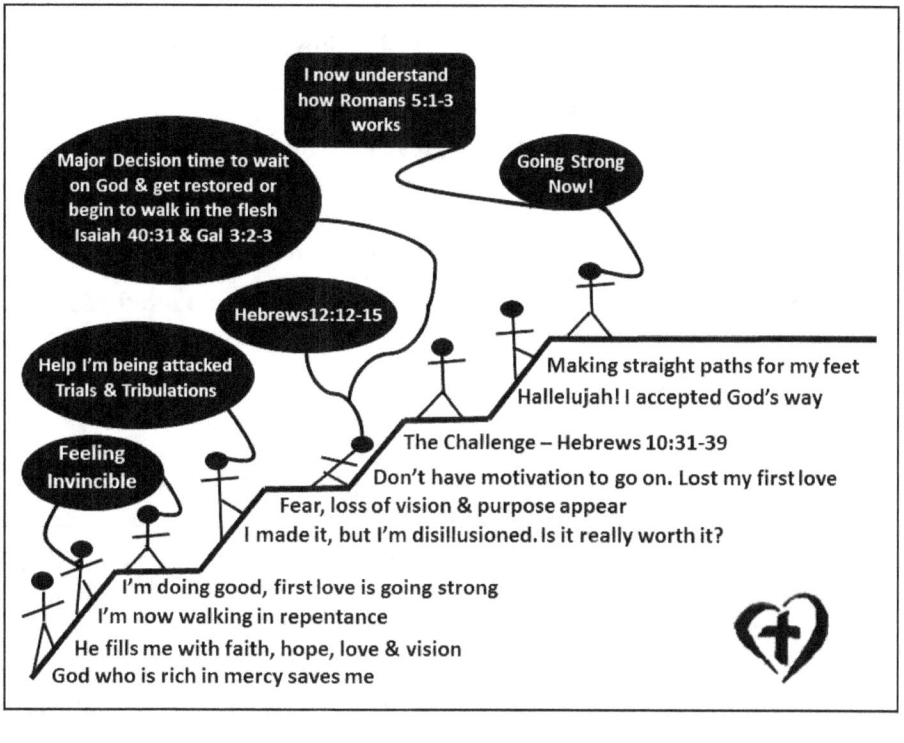

Have you experienced significant disillusionment or disappointment in your walk with the Lord? How do you get over it?

Hebrews 12:12-13 Therefore strengthen the hands which hang down, and the feeble knees,[13] and make straight paths for your feet, so that what is lame may not be dislocated, but rather be healed.

Have you ever been so severely wounded that you became immobilized from moving forward in the faith? If so, how did you eventually begin to move forward again?

Breaking Free From Your Past
Chapter Eight Study Questions

When we first came to Christ, the joy and anticipation that often results from our first love experience in Christ had a way of overshadowing the wounds of our past. As we experience hardship, they have a way of resurfacing and compounding the present difficulties. As these wounds resurface, Satan has opportune moments to move in and wreak havoc. Because his purpose is to steal, kill, and destroy the work of God in us, it's of the utmost importance that we apply God's healing ability. [385]

What spiritual truth in this chapter significantly impacted you, and how did it affect you?

_____
_____
_____
_____

Luke 4:18 "The Spirit of the Lord is upon Me because He has anointed Me to preach the gospel to the poor; He has sent Me to heal the brokenhearted, to proclaim liberty to the captives and recovery of sight to the blind, to set at liberty those who are oppressed;

What kind of emotional wounds began to surface after the newness of your relationship with the Lord began to wane?

_____
_____
_____
_____

Psalm 109.22 For I am poor and needy, and my heart is wounded within me.

Just as David was wounded from his past, most of us have also been. Where are you at in dealing with the wounds of your past?

- [ ] I am walking in healing by openly acknowledging them and moving on in the process.
- [ ] I have accepted them and am dealing with life the best I can, but I am not functioning at full throttle.
- [ ] I can barely function because of the severity of the wound.

---

[385] John 10:10

Chapter Eight Study Questions

How have your wounds shaped the person you are today?

_____

_____

Which of the following did you incur as a result of your wounds?

Inability to respond well to trials	Low self-esteem	Lack of trust in others
Hurting others	Lonely or withdrawn	Misconceptions of God
Anger, bitterness, hate	Eating disorders	Lethargic about life
Repeat offense	Drug & alcohol abuse	Despair and depression
Shame, guilt, condemnation	Afraid to show love	Suicidal tendencies

In the space below, write out the areas resulting from your wounds. Have any of these areas become strongholds? If so, which ones?

_____

_____

Do you believe God wants to heal you completely from the wounds of your past? If so, which of the following do you need to do to come into agreement with what God wants to do in your life?

[ ] Believe healing is God's will.   [ ] Forgive and let go.
[ ] Come out of denial.   [ ] Confess to another person.

Some wounds are so deeply rooted they become strongholds. They take a little more work to overcome, so we are encouraged to work out our salvation with fear and trembling.[386] However, if we are to be conformed to the image of Christ, we must be willing to tackle these strongholds. To do so, we must become violent about taking the kingdom by force so that the kingdom of God reigns in those areas rather than the kingdom of darkness.[387]

Paul said, *"To this end I also labor, striving according to His working which works in me mightily."* Aggressive, focused behavior with intent involves bringing every thought into the captivity of the obedience of Christ. *(Colossians 1:29 and 2 Corinthians 10:4-6)*

What kind of aggressive behavior must you take to break the strongholds in your life? *Refer to page 102 for common strongholds.*

_____

_____

---

[386] Philippians 2:12
[387] Matthew 11:12

Immersed Into the Body of Christ
Chapter Nine Study Questions

When we were born again, we were saved and called with a holy calling, not according to our works, but according to God's purpose and grace that was given to us in Christ Jesus before time began. As we allow God to set or place us in the body of Christ, we become a part of His purpose to function in the area He has designated. So God sets the solitary in families as it says, *"God has set the members, each one of them, in the body just as He pleased."* [388]

What did you find most interesting about this chapter?

_____

_____

What does it mean to you to be set in the body as it has pleased God?

_____

_____

_____

1 Corinthians 12:12-13 For as the body is one and has many members, but all the members of that one body, being many, are one body, so also is Christ. For by one Spirit, we were all baptized into one body—whether Jews or Greeks, whether slaves or free—and have all been made to drink into one Spirit.

What does the term *"Baptized into one body"* mean to you? How is it played out in your life?

_____

_____

_____

Ephesians 4:16 from whom the whole body, joined and knit together by what every joint supplies, according to the effective working by which every part does its share, causes growth of the body for the edifying of itself in love.

What does it mean to you to find your place at the Father's table?

_____

_____

_____

---

[388] Psalm 68:6, 1 Corinthians 12:18

Chapter Nine Study Questions

_____
_____
_____

1 Corinthians 12:21 And the eye cannot say to the hand, "I have no need of you"; nor again the head to the feet, "I have no need of you."

Why does it take a revelation and understanding of how we fit into the body of Christ to achieve the full potential of who we are in Christ?

_____
_____
_____

John 12:23-24 But Jesus answered them, saying, "The hour has come that the Son of Man should be glorified. "Most assuredly, I say to you unless a grain of wheat falls into the ground and dies, it remains alone; but if it dies, it produces much grain."

Why did the divine seed of God have to be planted in the earth? What does that mean for you?

_____
_____
_____

Romans 12:5 So in Christ we who are many members form one body, and each member belongs to all the others (NIV).

Jesus bought and paid for us with His blood, which means we now belong to Him and one another in the body. Therefore, we cannot say, "I don't need other body members."

What does it mean to you to belong to the other body members? How does it affect your life and how you live it?

_____
_____
_____
_____
_____

Spiritual Gifts and the Body of Christ
Chapter Ten Study Questions

Jesus was the complete expression of the body of Christ with the full measure of God's Spirit working in and through Him during His time on earth. He expressed God's image in character, power, and authority. He had all of the gifts of the Spirit working in Him, with the fruit of the Spirit fully developed in His life.

The gifts of the Spirit are an integral part of our spiritual growth and function within the body of Christ. Paul said concerning spiritual gifts, *"I don't want you to be ignorant nor come short in any gift while eagerly waiting for the second coming of Christ."*[389] It is God's will and purpose to discover what our particular gift or gifts are.

Ephesians 4:7-8 But to each one of us grace was given according to the measure of Christ's gift. ⁸ Therefore, He says: "When He ascended on high, He led captivity captive, and gave gifts to men.

Why are the gifts of the Spirit valuable to the church?

_____

_____

Why is it necessary to develop the gifts we have been given?

_____

_____

1 Corinthians 12:7-10 But the manifestation of the Spirit is given to each one for the profit of all. ⁸for to one is given the word of wisdom through the Spirit, to another the word of knowledge through the same Spirit, ⁹to another faith by the same Spirit, to another gifts of healings by the same Spirit, ¹⁰to another the working of miracles, to another prophecy, to another discerning of spirits, to another different kinds of tongues, to another the interpretation of tongues. ¹¹ But one and the same Spirit works all these things, distributing to each one individually as He wills.

What is your experience with the gifts of the Spirit? Which ones have you observed in action?

_____

_____

_____

Do you know what your spiritual gift is? If so, what is it? Have you been used in it?

---

[389] 1 Corinthians 1:7, 12:1

Chapter Eleven Study Questions

_____

_____

_____

How is the word of wisdom different from the word of knowledge?

_____

_____

What is the difference between the gift of tongues and the tongues one receives due to the baptism of the Holy Spirit?[390]

_____

_____

_____

How does having an attitude of expectation work with receiving the gifts of the Spirit?[391]

_____

_____

_____

Why is it important to practice and stir up the gifts you have been given?[392]

_____

_____

What can happen when a Christian chooses not to pursue spiritual gifts?

_____

_____

_____

_____

_____

---

[390] 1 Corinthians 12:30, 14:3-5
[391] Hebrews 11:6
[392] Romans 12:6-8, Ephesians 4:16

Discipleship and Ministry
Chapter Eleven Study Questions

Becoming a true disciple of Jesus involves understanding that discipleship is at the core of all we do as Christians. Everything, Including evangelism, ministry, and serving, flows out of our calling as disciples of Jesus. We are all called to be disciples—there are no exceptions. If we get this wrong, it will affect everything we do. Discipleship is the foundation we must build on, as no foundation is established other than the Lordship of Christ. Therefore, we are to take heed of how we build.[393]

What was the most important truth you learned about discipleship from this chapter?

_____
_____
_____

Jesus told his disciples, *"If anyone would come after me, he must deny himself, take up his cross, and follow me."*[394]

What does it mean to you to take up your cross and follow Jesus?

_____
_____
_____

Jesus said, "A *disciple is not above his teacher, but everyone who is perfectly trained shall be like his teacher."*[395]

When you read the above statement by Jesus, what comes to your mind? What does it mean to you?

_____
_____
_____

Jesus also said, *"Any of you who does not give up everything he has cannot be my disciple."*

---

[393] 1 Corinthians 3:9-15
[394] Matthew 16:24
[395] Luke 6:40

Chapter Eleven Study Questions

What does it mean to give up everything you have? How did that play out in your life?

_____
_____
_____

Luke 14:28-30 For which of you, intending to build a tower, does not sit down first and count the cost, whether he has enough to finish it—²⁹lest, after he has laid the foundation, and is not able to finish, all who see it began to mock him, ³⁰saying, "This man began to build and was not able to finish?"

Have you ever sat down and counted the cost of what it means to be a disciple of Jesus? If so, what was the price? If not, take the time now to write down some things that would cost you to become a dedicated disciple of Jesus.

_____
_____
_____
_____
_____
_____
_____

How does becoming a dedicated disciple give birth to ministry?

_____
_____
_____
_____
_____
_____
_____

The Need for Guardrails
Chapter Twelve Study Questions

As we continue our journey with Christ, we need spiritual guardrails in place for our security and protection. There will be innumerable occasions along the way where we will need them to keep us on track with God and His purpose for our lives.

What was the primary truth you learned in this chapter?

_____

_____

Two major guardrails in the Christian experience are designed to keep us on the straight and narrow so that we don't lose sight of our eternal destiny and purpose. They are God's goodness and severity, as we saw in the opening Scripture.

Romans 11:21-22 For if God did not spare the natural branches, He may not spare you either. Therefore consider the goodness and severity of God: on those who fell, severity; but toward you, goodness, if you continue in His goodness. Otherwise, you will also be cut off.

Do you relate more to God's goodness or His severity? Why?

_____

_____

We experience the goodness of God in many ways. It comes from being redeemed from the hand of the enemy, deliverance in times of trouble, being led by the Spirit, satisfying our hungry souls, being comforted during times of distress, deliverance from our destructive ways, blessings beyond measure, successful seasons, and much more.[396] God desires to pour His goodness into us in ways beyond our imagination. He has given to us all things that pertain to life and godliness.

Psalm 34:8 "Taste and see that the LORD is good; blessed is the one who takes refuge in him."

In what ways do you experience the goodness of God washing over you?

_____

_____

_____

---

[396] Psalm 107

Chapter Twelve Study Questions

_____
_____

Do you think about the concept of Hell very often? What are your thoughts about it? Does it produce the fear of God in you?

Jesus spoke of the severity of God when He said, *"Do not fear those who kill the body but cannot kill the soul. But rather fear Him who can destroy both the soul and body in Hell."*[397] Solomon said, *"The fear of the Lord is the beginning of wisdom, and the knowledge of the Holy One is understanding."*[398]

_____
_____
_____
_____

Jesus' story of the *"Rich Man and Lazarus"* illustrates the intensity of the pain that will exist in Hell. The rich man tormented in the flame did not wish this place of torment upon anyone.[399] At one point, he cried out, saying, *"Father Abraham, have mercy on me, and send Lazarus that he may dip the tip of his finger in water and cool my tongue, for I am tormented in this flame."*[400]

Why do you think Jesus shared this story with His disciples? What can we learn from it?

_____
_____
_____

Have you ever fallen into a backslidden condition? What was it like? Did you sense you were falling into more profound deception?

_____
_____
_____
_____

---

[397] Matthew 10:28
[398] Proverbs 9:10
[399] Luke 16:19-28
[400] Luke 16:24

Your Future—Vision, Purpose, and Destiny
Chapter Thirteen Study Questions

As born-again believers in Christ, it is of the utmost importance to know we've been born again with a purpose. As you begin to grasp that God has invited you to be a part of His great plan and purpose for the earth, an added excitement floods your spirit and soul as you realize God has given you destiny and purpose to fulfill.

2 Timothy 1:9 who has saved us and called us with a holy calling, not according to our works, but according to His own purpose and grace which was given to us in Christ Jesus before time began.

After reading this chapter, do you feel you are in touch with your destiny? Do you have a sense as to what your purpose and vision in life are? If so, briefly describe what you believe it to be.

_____
_____
_____
_____

It has been said, *"The real test of a man is not when he plays the role he wants for himself, but when he plays the role destiny has for him."*[401]

Is this true in your life? If not, what do you need to do to begin to play the role destiny has for you?

_____
_____
_____
_____

In this chapter, there was much to say about defining moments and how they are signposts that point toward our destiny. Jot down at least two significant defining moments in your past that are signposts to what God is presently doing in your life.

_____
_____
_____
_____

---

[401] Quote from *Vaclav Havel, President, Czech Republic*

Chapter 13 Study Questions

_____
_____

One of David's most significant defining moments was being confronted with the giant Goliath. David had to take forcible action to seize his destiny.

What kind of forcible action does God require of you to seize your destiny?

_____
_____
_____
_____

An excellent way to help capture your vision is to answer questions such as these:

Do I feel God has a purpose for my life? _____

In what ways has God's hand been manifested in my life? _____
_____

What brings me joy or satisfaction? _____
_____

What were some of my most painful experiences? _____
_____

What are my greatest strengths? _____
_____

Are there any harmful habits I would like to break? _____
_____

What would I do with my time if I did not have to work? _____
_____

What would I do with my money if it were unlimited? _____
_____

If my life ended now, would I have any regrets? _____

Answer each question as thoroughly and honestly as possible.

Add other issues and responses if they come to mind.

Chapter 13 Study Questions

_____
_____
_____

Think about how you can use information from your past to shape the future. Our lives consist of different categories: work, home, marriage, family, school, ministry, spirituality, etc. Distill the information in each life category into one or two actionable statements. Write using first-person perspective and present tense. For example, under the spiritual category, you could write, "I am deepening my relationship with Christ through scripture study and prayer" or "I am experiencing the joy of drawing others to Christ through love."

Write accurate statements based on your core values.

Spiritual Life:
_____
_____
_____

Work:
_____
_____
_____

Home:
_____
_____
_____

Marriage:
_____
_____
_____

Chapter 13 Study Questions

Family:

_____

_____

_____

Ministry:_____

_____

_____

_____

_____

Other Areas:

_____

_____

_____

_____

_____

_____

_____

_____

_____

_____

_____

_____

_____

Staying the Course
Chapter Fourteen Study Questions

When considering the challenge of staying on course, we must be as enthusiastic and full of zeal today as when we first encountered Jesus. Of course, our first love experience doesn't last forever, so Paul urged us never to *be lacking in zeal or diligence but to be fervent in the spirit, serving the Lord.*[402]

Thinking back over your walk with the Lord, were there times you lacked zeal and enthusiasm? What were some of the things that caused your love to grow cold?

_____

_____

How did you regain your zeal and diligence?

_____

_____

Galatians 6:9 And let us not be weary in well doing: for in due season we shall reap, if we faint not.

Have you ever grown weary in well-doing? How did you refresh and strengthen yourself in the Lord?

_____

_____

2 Chronicles 16:9 For the eyes of the Lord run to and fro throughout the whole earth, to show Himself strong on behalf of those whose heart is loyal to Him. In this you have done foolishly; therefore, from now on, you shall have wars."

What does it mean to you to have a fully committed heart and be loyal to the Lord?

_____

_____

How does having a heart fully committed and loyal to the Lord help you to stay the course?

---

[402] Romans 12:11

Chapter Fourteen Study Questions

_____
_____
_____

Which of the following do you battle with the most?

[ ] Unrepented Sin – *Acts 3:19*
[ ] Broken Relationships – *1 John 2:9-11*
[ ] An unhealthy focus on worldly things – *Psalm 119:37*
[ ] Too much time focusing on difficulties – *Numbers 13:31-33*

How have you overcome the area that causes you the most grief?

If you have not overcome it, how can you overcome it?

_____
_____
_____

The road ahead is filled with many wonderful promises and blessings as you are faithful to stay the course. I pray that you will continually examine your heart to ensure that you are not growing cold in the things of God. A great cloud of witnesses surrounds us. As they cheer us on, let us run with endurance the race *set before us, looking unto Jesus, the author and finisher of our faith.*[403]

As it also says in the Book of Hebrews, *"Therefore do not cast away your confidence, which has a great reward. For you need endurance, so that after you have done the will of God, you may receive the promise."*

Psalm 119:1-2 (MSG) You're blessed when you stay on course, walking steadily on the road revealed by God. You're blessed when you follow his directions, doing your best to find them.

---

[403] Hebrews 12:1-2

New Jerusalem Awaits Your Arrival
Chapter Fifteen Study Questions

As Abraham obeyed God and went to where he was to receive an inheritance while dwelling in tents, he waited for the city whose builder and maker is God.[404] Hebrews 11 speaks of the patriarchs of our faith and how they all died, not having received the promises but having seen them afar off.[405] They were all pilgrims, just as you and I are as we await the new heavenly city whose builder and maker is God.

Revelation 21:2 Then I, John, saw the holy city, New Jerusalem, coming down out of heaven from God, prepared as a bride adorned for her husband.

Do you have fear or anticipation of your place in eternity? Why?

_____
_____
_____

How did the story *"My Father's Gurney Ride to Heaven"* affect you?

_____
_____
_____

Jesus is now in heaven, preparing a place for us to dwell throughout all eternity. It will be a special place created just for you. It will be perfect in every way. You will be astounded at the beauty and magnificence of what He is preparing for you. We see this in the following passage.

John 14:1-3 "Let not your heart be troubled; you believe in God, believe also in Me. ² "In My Father's house are many mansions; if it were not so, I would have told you. I go to prepare a place for you. ³ "And if I go and prepare a place for you, I will come again and receive you to Myself; that where I am, there you may be also."

Briefly describe what you would like your place in eternity to look like. Don't be afraid to let your imagination run wild.

_____
_____
_____
_____

---

[404] Hebrews 11:8-10
[405] Hebrews 11:13

About Kenneth L Birks

Ken Birks is an ordained Pastor/Teacher in the Body of Christ. He functioned as an elder, staff pastor, and Bible teacher at The Rock of Roseville in California for the past 20 years. He is semi-retired with a writing ministry and serves as a wedding officiant in the Sacramento region. Before this, Ken was the Senior Pastor of Golden Valley Christian Center, a Spirit-filled, non-denominational church in Roseville, for twelve years.

Ken attended and graduated from the Charismatic Bible College of Anchorage. He entered the relationship with Apostle Dick Benjamin, the Sr. Pastor of Abbott Loop Christian Center (ALCC) in Anchorage, Alaska.

Aside from The Lord Jesus Christ, the core of Ken's spiritual being and the person he's become directly results from the influence and teaching he received from Dick Benjamin for more than 25 years." Other influences have been Bob Mumford from Life Changers and, in the past 18 years, Pastor Francis Anfuso of The Rock of Roseville.

Ken has been married to Lydia for 44 years plus. They have two adult children and consider them their highest calling, along with the many teens and children they have been foster or surrogate parents to over the past 25 years.

Ken also has an internet ministry called "Sowing Seeds of Faith" at kenbirks.com. Sowing Seeds of Faith reaches over 4,500 unique visitors a month with free Bible studies, devotional poetry, sermon outlines, audio, video messages, podcasts, and other Bible study materials to help equip saints for the work of the ministry.

Devotional Books

The Rise of the Anointed Ones

Ken Birks has written a masterpiece of superb continuity. Each devotional stands on its own, but together, they propel you into a rewarding journey of experiencing God's presence in tumultuous times. The majestic flow from theme to theme contains powerful prophetic revelation as God calls His end-time warriors to arise. The poems that follow each devotional are Davidic and musical. This book is like a voice in the wilderness calling God's beloved away from all that distracts to Him who is jealous for His bride.

Treasures From Above

These devotionals enhance your relationship with the Lord Jesus Christ in all aspects of your walk. Each devotional is intended to draw you into a deeper relationship with the Lord and inspire you to be all you can be in Christ as you embrace the wonderful promises of God to help you receive all that pertains to the life God has given you. The aspect that separates this book from other devotionals is that each devotional ends with a biblically inspired poem that encapsulates the essence of the devotional.

Treasures of the Heart
Prose and Poetry Refreshing the Soul

As you read through this book's devotional prose and poetry, you will find a beautiful blend of timeless truths fitly applied to today's culture and challenges that fill your heart with treasures from above. The majestic flow from one poem to the next contains powerful prophetic wisdom and revelation that will fill your hearts and minds with the beautiful treasures God intends you to enjoy.

Books and Workbooks

By Kenneth L. Birks

Prophetic Purposes and the Zeal of the Lord

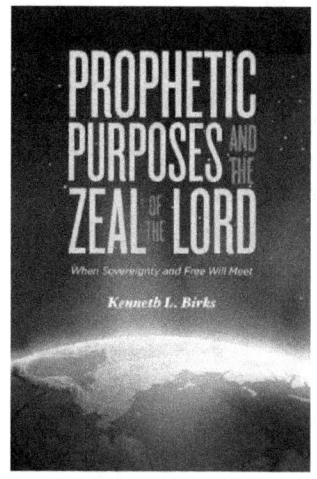

Do you believe worldwide revival is possible? Try to imagine what it will be like when the Church rises in the glory spoken of by Isaiah, the prophet. Just as God, in His sovereignty, brought forth the Messiah according to Daniel's prophecy, He will bring forth the prophetic purpose of a worldwide revival according to His timing. God's people, whom He planted in every city, village, town, and countryside throughout the world, will stand up as the vast army, just as Ezekiel prophesied. His prophetic purpose will be fulfilled. As God breathes on the dry bones prophesied by the prophet Ezekiel, His glory will fill all in all, just as Paul prophesied to the Ephesians. This book explores and instructs how to be ready for this prophecy and others that God will fulfill before the coming of Christ to set up His eternal kingdom on earth as it is in heaven.

The Adventures of Space and Hobo

The Adventures of Space and Hobo tells the story of Ken's nomadic life after Vietnam. The book explores the on-the-ground confusion and chaos of the Vietnam War and its effects on a generation and those who served. Named "Space" by a new friend, Hobo, Ken, and his traveling companion hit the road to partake of all the possibilities of that generation in search of adventure and uncharted experiences. The story takes us step by step along the path of awakening a lost soul on his way to understanding himself, his path, and the meaning of his life.

Books and Workbooks

By Kenneth L. Birks

Biblical Perspectives Course

This course features lessons designed to give you a solid Biblical foundation in the elementary truths of God's Word. The studies have three things in mind—building a doctrinal foundation, developing godly character, and helping you discover and find God's destiny and purpose for your life.

Please see the following website for more information and Lesson Titles:

kenbirks.com/perspectives-both/

More Biblical Perspectives Course

This course features lessons focused on three major areas of our Christian growth: Doctrine, character, and destiny.

These lessons will give you the Biblical understanding to strengthen your Christian foundation and take you on a deeper walk with God.

Please see the following website for more information and lesson titles:

kenbirks.com/perspectives-both/

Reviews and References

I have just read a book entitled *"The Journey"* written by Kenneth L. Birks. I have known my friend, Ken Birks, for 38 years. He is a man of absolute integrity. He is a diligent student of the Bible. He is a Holy Spirit-filled teacher. This book contains many scriptures referred to and identified at the bottom of the pages. In short, this book is based on the Bible. I believe Ken is also an example of his writing in this book. I recommend this book to individuals, small group leaders, pastors, churches, Bible schools, and seminaries. *"The Journey"* will help make disciples out of believers. —*Richard C. Benjamin Sr., Apostle/Pastor/retired*

~

I have seen many Christians enter the Kingdom of God without knowing what to do next. They accept Jesus Christ as their Lord and Savior, attend church, and even start hanging around with other believers. They know something has happened and changed with them but are unsure what to do. There comes a point when they may say. "Now what?" In Ken's book, I see a path laid out with an understanding that unfolds and explains their feelings. They can now grasp new ideas because they are filled with God's Word and know what to do next.

I have always believed that the life God lays out for us is a journey—a path to follow and an adventure where Jesus is in the lead. This book shows the Invisible Journey and how it opens up before us.

God has blessed Ken with the ability to teach from His Word substantially, giving us something to hold onto that puts the power in God's hand. With ease, Ken takes the reader on that journey, sharing his life in transparency and humility while giving God all the glory. He encourages us to partner with God to work out our salvation in awe of who God is.

This book is an amazing disciplining tool for the new believer and those of us who have been in the kingdom for a while but desire to be brought back to our first love—a time when everything was fresh and new.

I love that there are questions at the end to go through as a study with others. I know God calls us to make disciples of people, and I believe this book will be a powerful instrument to accomplish that purpose. Thank you, Ken, for being obedient to God to use your gifts to empower the body of Christ. —*Eileen Coia*

Jim Feeney, Ph.D., Former Sr. Pastor and "Owner and Webmaster at Pentecostal Bible Studies and Free Pentecostal Sermon Central"

I've known Pastor Ken Birks for several decades. He and I have worked in various ministerial capacities in the same family of churches. Ken is held in very high esteem among our many pastoral colleagues. He is a minister with a strong grasp of the Word of God, a broad variety of administrative skills, a heart for souls, a proven experiential familiarity with the gifts of the Holy Spirit, and an unwavering commitment to the work of the Lord. His wife, Lydia, is likewise a dedicated servant of God. The two of them have been an exemplary couple in the Lord's work, and I have been honored to know them and see the lasting fruits of their labors since the 1970s.

John Dubler, Retired Senior Pastor Chapel

Ken Birks is an extremely effective teacher of the Scriptures. He combines a healthy respect for the Word with enthusiasm and personal experiences that match his teaching. I strongly recommend him and his teaching. Ken is a man of unimpeachable integrity, and his longevity in the Body of Christ as a pastor gives credence to the message of hope and encouragement that he brings to all.

It is an excellent description of the Christian journey as well as a description of his particular journey. —*Mary London*

~

The Journey by author and Pastor Ken Birks is undoubtedly an inspired guide to "discovering the invisible path." This book is a practical writing that sheds light on the Christian path from the experience of someone (Ken) walking The Journey he has written about. It is a constructive scriptural explanation for everyday Christian guidance in an easily understandable format. It could also serve as a source for Bible study groups in that it already includes the bible study questions. Easy to read, well organized, and filled with the timeless truth of scripture to keep climbing the heavenly path! —*Steve-JG*

~

It is a Good book with a wealth of thoughtful teaching. —*Darryl Trimble*

Connect with Ken Birks Online

Social Media
X (Formerly Twitter) @klbirks
Facebook: facebook.com/seedsfaith—A daily devotional site
Linkedin: http://www.linkedin.com/in/kenbirks
Instagram: kenlbirks

Websites:
straitarrow.net – Bible Teaching Seminars, Books, Bible Studies, Sermon Outlines. Devotionals, Poetry, and Other Resources
kenbirks.com – Sowing Seeds of Faith – Sermons & Bible Studies
booksbyken.com – Ken's Bookstore
spaceandhobo.booksbyken.com – Details on Ken's first book, which is his autobiography

Email:
klbirks@gmail.com

Comments:
I welcome your comments. Please write a review on Amazon.

You may also leave your comments on the Facebook page for this book located at: https://www.facebook.com/klbirksbook

If you purchased this book from Amazon.com, please leave a review there.

www.ingramcontent.com/pod-product-compliance
Lightning Source LLC
Chambersburg PA
CBHW071729080526
44588CB00013B/1961